The Right Blood

The Right Blood

America's Aristocrats in Thoroughbred Racing

CAROLE
CASE

RUTGERS UNIVERSITY PRESS
New Brunswick, New Jersey, and London

Library of Congress Cataloging-in-Publication Data
Case, Carole, 1942–
The right blood : America's aristocrats in thoroughbred racing / Carole Case
p. cm.
Includes bibliographical references.
ISBN 0-8135-2840-2 (cloth : alk. paper)
1. Horsemen and horsewomen—United States—Biography.   2. Horse
racing—Social aspects—United States.   3. Jockey Club (New York,
N.Y.)   4. United States—Social life and customs.   I. Title.

SF336.A2 C37   2000
798.4'0092'273—dc21
[B]   00-025356

British Cataloging-in-Publication data for this book is available from the
British Library

Manufactured in the United States of America

To Pete Splendore

Contents

Tables

Preface and Acknowledgments

My primary sources for this work were Jockey Club members and others close to the Club. While wealthy individuals often guard their privacy jealously, some Club members (most of whom are well off) were quite open to talking to me. I first contacted them almost by chance: At the races at Gulfstream Park in Miami, a family friend and enthusiastic racetrack fan introduced me to a jockey agent, who told me to phone a Club member he knew and to use his name as a contact.

Many of the members I later spoke to as a result of that first phone call talked with ease and at length about their childhood experiences with horses. They were less open and discursive about the Club. Some wanted to discuss issues of general concern in racing. Others told "stories" about members. A few mentioned disagreements among members of the Club. Still fewer warned me about what to avoid, what to expect, whom to trust, what was important, and what the rules were. I gave the Club members I talked to opportunity to review my notes from our discussions. Further, I have been inclined to use what individuals told me when what they said was corroborated and when its intent was to inform more than to criticize.

All the members with whom I spoke could be described as

intense and highly energetic, although they were also congenial, gracious, and approachable. Several were very generous with their time and far more than polite. As a rule, "old-money" members (those whose families had been wealthy for at least three generations) had more experience with racing, were more difficult to access, were slightly more gracious, and referred to the Club as "we." By contrast, "new-money" members (self-made persons whose wealth is relatively recent) were more often professionals and slightly more inclined to criticize the policies of the Club.

Along with these interviews, my primary sources (the next best thing to the horse's mouth itself), included official Jockey Club documents. I also relied on the historical accounts that I judged most accurate and objective. I approached the biographical sources I consulted with caution and corroborated their accounts where I could. For background, I found early historical works on industrial elites most informative, especially Gustavus Myers's *History of the Great American Fortunes* and *The Ending of Hereditary American Fortunes*, Matthew Josephson's *The Robber Barons,* and Ferdinand Lundberg's *America's 60 Families*. Volumes of particular note that dealt with the families of Jockey Club members or with the Club itself were Frederic Jaher's *The Rich, the Well Born, and the Powerful* and *The Urban Establishment*, Stephen Birmingham's *The Right People* and *America's Secret Aristocracy,* Bernard Livingston's *Their Turf,* and Edward Bowen's *The Jockey Club's Illustrated History of Thoroughbred Racing in America*—a book commissioned by the Club in honor of its centennial.

Thanks are due first to the members of the Jockey Club and to others familiar with the Club who were willing to share with me their experiences and observations regarding thoroughbred racing. Without their help, this book would not have been possible. I hope they will find their informative and interesting interviews put to good use.

A number of other individuals also provided important leads and information. Of note are Tom Davide, former executive secretary of the New York Racing and Wagering Board, Calvin Rainey, former executive director of the Jockey Club, and Dennis Brida, former president of the New York Thoroughbred Horsemen's Association. Others who were helpful include: Field Horne, curator, and Tom Gilcoyne, volunteer, National Museum of Racing and Hall of

Fame; Cathy Schenck, librarian, and Phyllis Rogers, library assistant, Keeneland Association; Patty Lankford, former librarian, and Diane I. Viert, staff, *The Blood-Horse*; Debra Randorf, reference librarian, the New-York Historical Society; Carla Tobias, librarian archivist, Monmouth County Historical Association; Nancy C. Kelly, executive director, the Jockey Club Foundation; David Levesque, archivist, St. Paul's School; Peter Winants, director, National Sporting Library; Julie Ludwig and William R. Massa, Jr., Manuscripts and Archives, Yale University Library; Kathleen Smith, reference archivist, the Jean and Alexander Heard Library, Vanderbilt University; Debra Ginsburg, staff writer, *The Thoroughbred of California*; Meg Ventrudo, director of exhibits and education, Museum of American Financial History; and Jane Goldstein, director of communications, Santa Anita Park.

Colleagues and friends provided important help. I want to thank William Domhoff of the University of California, Santa Cruz, for referring me to relevant materials and critiquing early papers in a detailed fashion; William Epstein of the University of Nevada, Las Vegas, for his critical reading of the manuscript; sociologist Henry Steadman, who also races thoroughbreds and has his silks registered with the Jockey Club, for his careful review of the work; John Galliher of the University of Missouri, Columbia, for advice regarding the use of interview material; and at the City College of New York, Lilly Hoffman for giving me the idea of "totemism" as possibly applicable to these individuals, Lawrence Fleischer for the legal abstracts of the cases that Howard Jacobson brought against the New York Racing Association; and Marshall Berman, for raising questions about some of my assumptions. At the University of Nevada, Las Vegas, June Darrow and Cinda Dillahunt provided clerical assistance and archival research, respectively, and the university itself awarded me two grants to cover travel and other expenses connected to interviewing.

Other friends are due tremendous credit. Bill and Jan Hoefelt, who have firsthand experience with the industrial elite of Western Pennsylvania, shared their personal insights. Bernard Herold, head of his own investment firm and member of the New York Stock Exchange, arranged for me to visit the floor of the exchange and provided material on its history. Leonard Gilbert provided relevant historical information from his personal library. It was family friend Pete Splendore who provided me entree to the Club itself. He introduced me to his friends and inveterate track regulars, who introduced me to jockey agent Lenny Goodman, who personally knew a Club member.

Without my family, the book would never have been completed. My daughter Christine Kray, a postdoctoral anthropologist at Dartmouth College, listened patiently and suggested relevant materials on totemism. Little would have been possible without the constant encouragement, support, and advice of my husband, Ron Farrell.

The Right Blood

INTRODUCTION
The Jockey Club

This is a story about money and power, and about a particular group of rich and powerful Americans—the men (and a very few women) of the Jockey Club. With its founding in New York City at the turn of the twentieth century, the Club took the reins of thoroughbred racing in the United States, and it has never entirely let them go.

For more than a century, then, the Jockey Club has dominated horseracing in this country. Club members have registered the horses, owned the tracks, developed and applied the rules that regulate racing, and bred and raced some of the sport's most successful horses. In the process, they have shaped the sport to their view of the world. This view holds that the worth of human beings—and also of horses—lies in the bloodline. That line of thinking is, of course, debatable. It has been debated for eons. But every new generation adds its own twist.

The founders of the Jockey Club—who aspired to being regarded as well bred—were moguls and the descendants of moguls who had made millions in mining, transportation, and finance. Their family names were Vanderbilt, Belmont, and Whitney, and their forebears' success was both criticized and admired. Their critics called them robber barons. Admirers saw their success as an indicator of "the survival of the fittest," that basic tenet of social

Darwinism that in the 1880s had arrested the attention of many Americans.

At the dawn of the twenty-first century, America's rich and powerful still have the power to fascinate—even when those rich and powerful have made their fortunes at the expense of the general public. Today's computer moguls, more wealthy by any measure than the robber barons, are equally revered and criticized.

And today, again, the search accelerates for biological and genetic explanations for human behavior.[1] It is as if the wheel has turned, and once more many of us are eager to believe that the "fit" are born that way. Our yearnings are mostly satisfied by movie adaptations of turn-of-the-century Henry James novels about Gilded Age Bostonians and New Yorkers, but some of us, more than nostalgic for the life-styles of the rich and famous of times past, try to recreate them. We may mortgage our homes to send our children to prep school, move to the country to join pony clubs and take dressage classes, and dress as if we were on our way to play polo. One man who has capitalized on the life-style of old money named his fashion line Polo and made himself a millionaire— Bronx-born, former member of the working class Ralph Lauren.

Contemporary members of the Jockey Club continue to benefit from their association with thoroughbreds and from the status it confers on them. These wealthy and well-positioned corporate and financial moguls still breed and race fine horses. Over the century, horse racing has become a major industry, and the courts have transferred the Jockey Club's exclusive licensing prerogatives to state regulators in New York. Yet Club members' involvement with thoroughbreds, animals of superior blood (a hypothesis the Jockey Club itself has persuaded many to accept), still contributes to their social standing and gives vitality to their way of life. This is probably as true today as it was during the Gilded Age when the Club began.

What prompted the founding of the Jockey Club just then, in the second half of Victoria's reign in England? After the Civil War, a small group of American men, mostly in the Northeast—call them robber barons or canny entrepreneurs—came to control the nation's business. These nouveau riche then became preoccupied with legitimacy and the trappings of old-world aristocrats—especially the British. They married up, built grand mansions, sailed yachts, and bought fine horses. They took up the fox hunting and coach racing of the British upper class, whom they emulated, and the ultimate sport of kings—thoroughbred racing.

A few of these new-money aristocrats in 1894 began to organize the informal races that added zest to their leisure into a major spectator sport. They wrote the rules for horse racing, developed sanctions and procedures for penalizing violators, licensed officials and employees, set the dates for races, and controlled the registry of the horses. Many of them also exploited the poor to work their horses, ingratiated and co-opted some who posed a threat to their interests, and excluded and disregarded those of different backgrounds—all in the name of improving the breed and promoting the sport. These men called themselves the Jockey Club, as horsemen of the British aristocracy had done more than a century before them.

Some of the nation's richest citizens (and some of its most notorious) have been members of the Jockey Club. Many have held high government positions, elected offices, and ambassadorships. Many are famous for their philanthropy. It remains true that those admitted to membership are often wealthy, influential, and of high status.

I talked with some descendants of the industrial barons themselves. Alfred Gwynne Vanderbilt II, a great-great-grandson of Cornelius "the Commodore" Vanderbilt, was admitted to the Jockey Club in the 1930s, when his name was on the society page every day. Regarded as a Young Turk then, he for decades regularly challenged, even flouted, the traditions of his social set. For instance, the upper echelons of society considered it a scandal when Vanderbilt squired jockey Robin Smith around (Smith later married his friend Fred Astaire).

I also talked with Paul Mellon, for years reputed to be the wealthiest Jockey Club member. Mellon contributed $100 million to a number of worthy causes, most notably the National Gallery in Washington, D.C. The art gallery was founded with funds from the estate of Paul's father, Andrew Mellon, founder of Mellon National Bank and secretary of the treasury in the 1920s and 1930s. Paul Mellon also left a legacy to racing: In addition to breeding a number of excellent horses in the United States and abroad, he made generous donations to equine research.

The power of the Jockey Club over the decades has not gone unchallenged. Two colorful men who were never members play large parts in the Club's story. Jule Fink and Howard Jacobson were among the very few who ever publicly questioned the Club's right to rule the racing industry. Fink owned a string of successful horses and reputedly had ties to bookmakers. When the Club, whose sole prerogative it was to issue owners licenses, refused to issue him a license, Fink took the case to the courts.

Howard (Buddy) Jacobson rocketed to the top of the sport of kings by racing cheap horses, but his run as the most successful trainer in the world would be short-lived. His fall was even more meteoric than his rise. In his fight on behalf of pensions and other job benefits for stable hands in 1969, Jacobson chose the wrong strategy. He trampled racing's traditions, attacking the State of New York and the bluebloods, and called for a boycott of racing at Aqueduct Racetrack. It failed, Jacobson was denied stalls for his horses on New York's tracks, and he took the powerful New York Racing Association to court for misuse of power. His was an even more aggressive attack on racing's establishment than Jule Fink's.

Horse racing has existed in a world of its own in the United States for decade upon decade. *The Right Blood* explores the power of influence and wealth in that world—specifically, that of the Jockey Club and its members, from 1894 to today. I lay out the evidence I gathered and then share some of my conclusions at the end of the book. You are invited to draw your own.

1

JOCKEYING FOR POWER

From the time Achilles arranged a chariot race through the daily double at Aqueduct, . . . horse racing has been 'the sport of kings.' "[1] The designation has a long tradition. For centuries, though commoners owned horses, it was kings who traditionally raced them. When kings were not riding horses into battle, they were proving themselves in races. Few other people could afford such an expensive pastime.

In America, where there was no hereditary throne, certain men were establishing their own brand of royalty—as princes of finance, industrial barons, and railway kings. Some of them, who would start the Jockey Club, build the racetracks, and oversee the sport for decades, carried names like Lorillard, Morgan, Harriman, Whitney, Widener, and Vanderbilt.

THE SPORT OF KINGS

Early Roman emperors raced chariots. Caligula drove the chariots himself, and Claudius gambled in his chariots as his slaves drove. Over the centuries, men discovered the excitement of riding horses in races, rather than just driving them. By 500 A.D., a British poet wrote of a princess who was awarded as a prize in such a race. By the Dark Ages, horse races were common in Ireland.

It was not until the early eighteenth century, however, that British nobility and royalty began to take a serious interest in racing horses and in breeding them to race.[2] That was when they began to develop a breed of horse that could not only carry the weight of a man but run fast at the same time. They called this breed the thoroughbred. During this same era, Queen Anne chose the racecourse at Ascot as the place she would run her horses. King George II increased the number of royal races. By the 1760s, a noble group of dukes, earls, viscounts, and barons seized power over racing at Newmarket; they called themselves the Jockey Club. Within a few decades, their Jockey Club had so grown in influence it could dictate even to the Prince of Wales—at least about how he could run his horses.

Racing came to the colonies in America in the late 1600s and brought its traditions and the descendants of Britain's thoroughbreds with it. The first British governor established a racecourse on Long Island and named it Newmarket after its English counterpart. In the colonies, although horse ownership was common and racing was a regular part of town life, British law permitted only gentlemen to race. Consequences for violators varied. On one occasion, a gentleman who allowed a commoner to race was punished in the stocks. On another, a tailor who rode his horse in a race was brought before the colonial court in Williamsburg, Virginia, and found to have violated the law that proclaimed racing a sport only for gentlemen.[3]

With the Revolutionary War and the institution of democratic government, the traditions and patterns of racing in the former colonies entered a state of flux. While some commoners, including Andrew Jackson, both bred and raced horses, neither they nor the commoners' sportsman tradition they represented were typical. The upper classes still had the upper hand in the sport.

Jockey clubs with local and limited authority appeared by the mid-1800s. Tracks across the country were managed by these clubs, comprised "only of gentlemen of highest respectability and moral worth."[4] Match races between two competing horses had become common, and some of the most notable matches pitted the North against the South. Until the Civil War, it was customary for landed

gentry to raise and breed racehorses and for slaves and farm workers to ride and train them. There was a reported practice on the part
of some plantation owners to force particular slaves to mate, in
hopes that their progeny would be small enough to ride the owners' horses.[5]

When racing in the South went into a decline during the Civil
War, the sport followed the money north to New York. John Morrissey, an Irishman from a family of commoners, brought it to Saratoga
Springs, where he built the town's first racetrack and casino.[6] A
pugilist and gaming-house proprietor in New York City, Morrissey
bore the nickname "Old Smoke" because, in a fight over a prostitute,
his opponent temporarily pinned him down near open coals.

Morrissey's connections to Tammany Hall may have helped
him secure legitimate backing for the Saratoga Springs track.[7] However he managed it, three prominent New Yorkers lent his enterprise their financial support: lawyer, publisher, and financier
Leonard W. Jerome; stockbroker and society wit William R. Travers;
and sportsman and socialite John R. Hunter. Though Morrissey
continued to own most of the track's stock, his name did not appear on the deed when the Saratoga Springs track was incorporated
in 1865.

AMERICA'S ROYAL FAMILIES

New York was then home to America's greatest fortunes.[8] This was
wealth newly accumulated, fortunes made possible largely by the
Civil War and the rise of industrialization. At the time, govern-
ment-owned land (in some of which lay precious metals), including railroad rights-of-way, could be bought; sometimes the land, as
in the case of land grants, was even government subsidized. The labor needed to mine the metals and build the rails could be imported freely. With Wall Street in its infancy, rich traders could buy
in and corner the market on new industry.

Those who made the fortunes, called "robber barons" by their
critics, divided among themselves the wealth of the emerging in-
dustrialized nation.[9] Aggressive and ruthless, the robber barons
took the land, monopolized the means of transportation, controlled the sources of energy, and spent the profits lavishly. Immigrant laborers worked their mines and railroads for a pittance.

America's new royalty lived ostentatiously in their widespread kingdoms. Each had, at the least, a Fifth Avenue mansion in New York City—some of these stretched over entire city blocks—a castle on the gold coast of Long Island's North Shore, and a summer cottage in Newport, Rhode Island. They were also inclined to own yachts and Pullman cars and to keep large stables of race horses. During these gilded days for these golden families, at weddings the bride and groom could expect to receive a million dollars each. The men of the families often took trips to Scotland solely for the hunting, a sport that in this case entailed a roundtrip cross-Atlantic voyage.

The robber barons have been called poor boys who made good through hard work and ingenuity. [10] (This plot line, though not new, had been revived at the time by Horatio Alger's stories.) Among the self-made barons were Andrew Carnegie and Henry Phipps, both of poor Scottish immigrant background, who were childhood friends in Pittsburgh and later partners in Carnegie Steel Company. (Four generations of Phipps's family have been members of the Jockey Club.) But perhaps the humblest born of the robber barons was Thomas Fortune Ryan, of Irish stock, and a future member of the Club. [11] Ryan was penniless and orphaned at age fourteen when he went to Baltimore, where he took the first step on his rise to fortune via a dry goods establishment. Before his death, he had acquired substantial interests in New York City's transit and subway systems, American Tobacco Company, and Equitable Life Assurance Society, and he held large amounts of stock in the diamond, gold, and copper mines of the Belgian Congo.

While some of this wealthiest of classes could trace their lineage to America's forefathers, most were nouveau riche and lacking in social graces—at least as defined by New York's contemporary Knickerbocker society, who viewed them as usurpers. Possibly as a result, the new Fifth Avenue families tended to become preoccupied with a quest for old-stock roots. [12] Another road to higher social standing, they hoped, was to assume the manners and life-style of those already entrenched there by right. It was not uncommon therefore for the nouveau riche to join exclusive men's clubs, convert to the Episcopal church, marry into a higher social bracket or into British gentry, build ostentatious, European-style mansions, and accumulate the art treasures of Europe. Some, of course, took up the sport of kings.

THE FOUNDERS OF THE JOCKEY CLUB

For most of the families of the Jockey Club founders, by the late nineteenth century horse racing had become both an integral part of their leisure life and a source of social status. They now bred and raced horses. Twenty-seven members of this elite, mostly new monied group founded America's Jockey Club in New York City in February 1894.[13] Their intention was to control horse racing, primarily on tracks in the Northeast. Their assurance that they would succeed owed a great deal to their power, fierce competitiveness, and financial influence. Most would graduate from Yale, live on Fifth Avenue, join the most prestigious New York men's clubs, attend an Episcopal church, and "marry up." Only six belonged to Mrs. William Astor's Four Hundred, the crème de la crème of New York society.

William K. Vanderbilt

One of the founders of the Jockey Club, William K. Vanderbilt, was a grandson of Cornelius "the Commodore" Vanderbilt. Among the industrial barons of his grandfather's day, the railway kings were foremost, and the Vanderbilts were said to be the most exploitative (and successful) of them all. Although William Kissam Vanderbilt had a head for business, he would prefer racing thoroughbreds to running corporations. This preference may in part account for his reputation as the "most charming of the Vanderbilts."

Of Dutch origin, the Van Der Bilts were miserably poor squatters on Staten Island in the seventeenth century.[14] William Vanderbilt's grandfather Cornelius had no formal education. He set out as a teen in 1800 to make his fortune in steamboats. Tall, handsome, and profane, he married his first cousin, who was similarly uneducated, and sired thirteen children.

The Commodore's business tactics—first in steamboats and then in railroads—have been characterized as violating both the law and morality. When competition for steamship travel in New York and New Jersey was fierce, Vanderbilt at first operated unlicensed vessels. Later, he crushed or bought out his competitors, thereby monopolizing the market, which allowed him to raise his prices.

During the Civil War, the Commodore charged the government as much as eight hundred to a thousand dollars a day to charter his steamboats—some of which had rotten timbers. Although a Senate investigation found that he had extorted money from smaller steamship lines in return for not taking over their businesses, he was never sued or prosecuted in any court. Some historians suggest that he bought off judges, public officials, and legislators. He is reported to have boasted about his apparent untouchability, "What I care about the law? Hain't I got the power?"[15]

As steamship travel declined, railroads came into their own. In a period of less than ten years, Vanderbilt acquired control of the Harlem, the Hudson, and the New York Central railroads and merged them into a line running from New York to Chicago. His railroad mergers were held to be similar to his steamship dealings—derived largely from blackmail, extortion, and bribery. He caused the stock of one line to plummet by failing to provide it with connecting service. He cornered the stock of another, driving out lesser speculators, even friends, in the process. He bought enough shares in a third line to become director and vote himself additional money and new stock—$6 million in cash and $20 million in stock. Then, to pay his stockholders, he charged exorbitant rates to ride his trains, neglected repairs, and cut employee wages.

His cutthroat approach to success carried over into sports. The Commodore liked to race horses on the unpaved streets of the Upper West Side of Manhattan. He was most fond of trotters, and he thought nothing of paying the high price of $30,000 for a single horse. So famous were his races that Currier and Ives commemorated one of them in an 1870 lithograph, "Fast Trotters on Harlem Lane N.Y."[16]

As a father and husband, the Commodore was viewed as indifferent, sometimes cruel. He reportedly rejected his eldest son, William Henry Vanderbilt, until late in life, and disowned another, Cornelius Vanderbilt II, for his gambling and extravagance. When his wife refused to move out of their modest Staten Island home into one in Manhattan, he sent her to a sanitarium, where, coincidentally or not, she reconsidered her reluctance. There is evidence that the Commodore pursued young women throughout his life.

At his death in 1877, Cornelius Vanderbilt had $100 million, which qualified him as the world's richest man—and possibly its most successful crook. In spite of this wealth, the self-made Commodore and his descendants have not always been well received by what is termed "polite" society. His own less than auspicious pedigree hardly qualified him as royalty. Nor were his aggression, hot temper, swearing, tobacco spitting, and pinching the posteriors of housemaids the manners of royalty.

The Commodore willed the bulk of his estate to a son, William Henry Vanderbilt, who may have adopted some of his father's business tactics[17]—an investigation into W. H. Vanderbilt's and John D. Rockefeller's dealings in Standard Oil found that the two had colluded to eliminate small refiners. He may have also inherited the Commodore's blunt manner and his evident disdain for the public welfare. He is quoted as responding to a journalist who asked him why he ran his railroads without apparent concern for the public, "The public be damned! I am working for my stockholders."[18]

William Henry Vanderbilt survived his father, the Commodore, by only nine years, a victim during his adult life of chronic insomnia and indigestion. In less than a decade he had managed to double his $90 million inheritance. He died sitting at his desk in his neo-Grecian library in his recently completed brownstone on New York's Fifth Avenue. The mansion's European furnishings alone cost $1 million, and his collection of contemporary French paintings amounted to another $4.5 million.

William Henry Vanderbilt's fortune was shared among his heirs. His son William Kissam Vanderbilt, a future Jockey Club founder, became the head of the New York Central Railroad and the seventy-three family-owned corporations.[19] Beginning as a teen in his grandfather's Hudson River Railway office, William K. Vanderbilt "worked his way up" to the second vice presidency, then to the presidency, and ultimately to chairman of the board.

This grandson of the Commodore married the woman who is credited with bringing the family into society. She was Alva Smith, a woman of proper Southern family, French education, and strong will. William Vanderbilt named his $500,000 yacht after her and built her a $9 million Newport cottage. They named it Marble House, for its primary building material, decorated it in Louis XIV style, and lit it with stained-glass windows set with depictions of

European knights. It was Alva, though, who shaped their $3 million Francis I chateau at 660 Fifth Avenue, designed by Richard Morris Hunt. So exceptionally tasteful was this mansion that society found its residents impossible to ignore any longer.

Shortly after he helped found the Jockey Club, William Kissam Vanderbilt was divorced by Alva for reasons of adultery. He moved to France, where he built a chateau with a stable nearby for his hundred thoroughbreds.[20] For years thereafter, a member of the French Jockey Club, he raced his horses abroad.

William Collins Whitney

Of entirely different stock than William K. Vanderbilt was his fellow Jockey Club founder William Collins Whitney, who could trace his pedigree via "old Yankees" to English parliamentarians and Puritans.[21] He was the typical upwardly mobile young New Yorker of his day: He went to Yale, became Episcopalian, and joined the best metropolitan men's clubs. Unlike Vanderbilt, he himself qualified as a robber baron.

His fortune was made, however, when he married the daughter of Cleveland Standard Oil magnate Henry B. Payne. She was the sister of his Yale fraternity brother Oliver Hazard Payne. Soon after the wedding, Whitney's father-in-law built the newlyweds a townhouse on Park Avenue. When Whitney was later admitted to the bar, he became the city's corporation counsel and John D. Rockefeller's link to Tammany Hall.

With national political ambitions, Whitney spent a small fortune on Grover Cleveland's presidential campaigns. In return, Cleveland appointed him secretary of the navy. At about the same time, Whitney's father-in-law, Payne, was elected to the U.S. Senate. His election was immediately clouded by allegations of bribery.[22] Though Whitney was rumored to be a possible presidential candidate before Cleveland's third campaign, he retired from public life and returned to New York. There, again, Senator Payne helped the couple with housing and bought them a Fifth Avenue mansion— across the street from one of the Vanderbilts.

In spite of his English ancestry, elite education, distinguished appearance, and suave style, Whitney earned his robber-baron status the old-fashioned way. He and his partner, Thomas Fortune Ryan (later a fellow Jockey Club member), began to take over the city's transit system by buying up all available franchises. When they bribed the city's aldermen in an effort to obtain the biggest franchise, they were outbribed, but only temporarily. The two disclosed their competitor's corrupt techniques, and he was jailed. They then quietly appropriated the franchise. Whitney and Ryan have been described as "the most gentlemanly of the Robber Barons," as well as "a conscienceless team."[23]

Whitney and Ryan now controlled a monopoly of the New York transit system, including trolleys, horsecars, and elevated railroads. They named their merger and reorganization of the transit franchises the Metropolitan Street Railway Company. Through this franchise—probably the first U.S. holding company—they were able to control securities, without financial or legal obligations. They "watered" the stock,[24] speculated on it, and ultimately dumped it, leaving the stockholders holding worthless paper. In less than a decade, Whitney made $40 million on the Metropolitan.

At the time, "few legislators, newspaper editors, reformers, and muckrakers saw anything wrong in the enormous robbery of the public and Metropolitan Transit stockholders."[25] The press generally alluded only to Whitney's appropriation of the transit franchises and subsequent misuse of the company's funds. It was John Pulitzer, publisher of the *New York World* and Whitney's onetime friend, who would label the actions criminal.

But Whitney had moved on. Over the next ten years, he spent $28 million on himself. He accumulated ten houses on 36,000 acres in five states, including an Italian Renaissance palace on Fifth Avenue that was remodeled by Stanford White, a lodge and a golf course on 70,000 acres in the Adirondacks, a farm in Kentucky and another in South Carolina—one that had a racecourse and 2,000 acres of hunting land. By the time the Jockey Club was founded in 1894, Whitney had developed an interest in horse racing. He bought the leading thoroughbreds of the day and, at the outset of the twentieth century, became the nation's foremost owner of thoroughbreds. One of his horses won the English Derby. "New York no longer knew what most to envy, his horses or his houses."[26]

Whitney would ultimately be the largest individual landowner in New York and Massachusetts. He was viewed as having "thrown [away] the usual objects of political ambition like the ashes of smoked cigarettes [and] turned to other amusements, . . . gorged every appetite, won every object that New York afforded, and not yet satisfied, . . . carried his field of activity abroad."[27]

His death in 1904 brought investigations into his transit system, as well as eulogies. The former ambassador to England Joseph Choate called Whitney's inflation of the Metropolitan's securities "the greatest enormity committed in New York."[28] The city's district attorney filed formal charges. Meanwhile, someone had destroyed the books on the company's reorganization. The grand jury deliberated but, under a foreman who was a director in one of Ryan's companies, found no evidence of crime. (Later, Ryan would admit that there had been considerable stock watering.)

Whitney has been called "the grandee of graft" and the worst of the robber barons—not so much because of his monopoly with the Metropolitan, the watering of its stock, and his desertion of it and its stockholders, but for leaving behind something of so little benefit.[29] His legacy has been called "that bankrupt ruin, that failure in public transportation, the Metropolitan Railway, which paid for the palaces and . . . horses."[30]

The Belmonts

All three sons of August Belmont I were prominent members of the Jockey Club, and two were among its founders—August Belmont II and Perry Belmont. A banker of German Jewish descent, the senior Belmont raced thoroughbreds. He and fellow financier Leonard Jerome founded a racetrack in the Bronx the year after Jerome had helped finance Saratoga Racecourse. To operate their track, Jerome Park, they formed the American Jockey Club, a precursor of the Jockey Club that thrives today.[31] Belmont senior died four years before the Club was founded, leaving his sons a fortune and a taste for the good life.

According to archival records, the Belmonts were among the wealthiest landowning families in the early 1800s in Alzey, Germany, near the French border.[32] As a young teen, August Belmont I went to work for the Rothschilds and later became their agent in Naples and Havana. With their support, he came to the United States, where he would take advantage of the financial panic of 1837 by buying stocks cheaply. He set up a banking firm on Wall Street, and by 1845, Belmont was worth $100,000. Within a decade his fortune had doubled.

From these beginnings, August Belmont became a banker and investor of considerable repute.[33] His background, however, was the subject of rumor in his day. Novelist Edith Wharton in *The Age of Innocence* modeled the mysterious upstart Julius Beaufort after him. In the novel, members of New York society in the late 1800s asked, "Who was Beaufort? He passed for an Englishman, was agreeable, handsome, ill tempered, hospitable and witty. He had come to America with letters of recommendation from . . . the banker . . . ; but his habits were dissipated, his tongue was bitter, and his antecedents were mysterious."[34]

In fact, Belmont wrote his own history. He designed his own family crest. He fought a duel, which was something that only gentlemen did, and came away with a limp that then became an indicator of his gentleman's status.[35] He married into a family of naval heroes. His bride was the daughter of Commodore Perry, who was famous for his expeditions to Japan. Their marriage in the Episcopal church was quite grand, and their children were baptized as Episcopalians. Marrying outside the Jewish faith and choosing spouses with social standing has become a tradition in the Belmont family.[36]

August Belmont would even become a political figure. President James K. Polk appointed him consul general to Austria, and President Franklin Pierce appointed him minister to the Netherlands. He headed Stephen Douglas's presidential campaign against Abraham Lincoln. During the Civil War, when a large segment of the Democratic Party supported the practice of slavery, Belmont chaired the Democratic National Committee.[37]

In contrast to the business practices of many of his wealthy contemporaries, Belmont's have been described as conservative. His reputation seems to have derived from his practice of making low-risk loans at high rates of interest, regardless of the applicant. When President Abraham Lincoln approached him for a loan, for example, the federal government was charged the same high interest rate as any other borrower. The robber barons went to Belmont to finance their cross-continent railroads when they needed a banker who could sell their mortgage bonds on the international market. With his Rothschild banking connections, Belmont was ideally situated for such transactions.

Although Belmont's financial dealings were conservative, his life-style was not—which did not endear him to either society or his fellow bankers. Society considered Belmont the personification of a snob and social climber. He had seven houses, and his mansion on Fifth Avenue was the first in the city to have its own ballroom. He would invite two hundred guests to his parties and is said to have coerced his way onto others' guest lists. His party attire on one occasion was a $10,000 suit of armor inlaid with gold. Belmont rolled out his own red carpet—at a time when others rented them. Further, he had a taste for elegant European cuisine, elaborately served.[38] His fellow German Jewish bankers found his behavior equally shocking. "It seemed to them dishonest. It was one thing to wish to assimilate, but quite another to deny a whole tradition; one thing to embrace a new culture, but another to betray an old."[39]

As was his custom generally, August Belmont I was flamboyant in connection with his horse racing. He had his carriages painted in his racing colors, maroon and scarlet. He required that his coachmen and footmen wear scarlet-piped and silver-buttoned maroon coats, and he insisted that his chief steward—similarly attired—change his uniform five times a day.[40]

August Belmont II, his father's namesake and a Jockey Club founder, took over as head of August Belmont and Company.[41] In 1900, New York City's Rapid Transit Commission presented him with a financial plum when it authorized him to finance the building and operation of the city's subway system. He set up the Interborough Rapid Transit Construction Company to fund the West Side subway, and he very shortly had a monopoly on the city's subways.

Enterprises beyond New York City also looked to August Belmont II for financial support. When the nation was in a financial panic at the turn of the century, banking giants Belmont and Company and J. P. Morgan and Company joined together to effect a rescue—by then, Belmont and Morgan were not only banking giants but fellow Jockey Club members. The two made a deal with President Grover Cleveland: They would give the U.S. Treasury $3.5 million in gold in return for government bonds. When they got the bonds, they promptly sold them at a 15 percent profit. Shortly thereafter, Belmont was involved in an even more far-reaching business transaction. He joined with two other banking giants—

Kuhn, Loeb, and Company and Levi P. Morton, father-in-law of another Jockey Club member—to form the Panama Canal Company of America.

Like his astute business practices, August Belmont II's personal tastes were akin to those of his father. He also raced thoroughbreds, and for nearly thirty years he was not only the fox set to watch the chickens, but the chickens too—he simultaneously served as chairman of the state commission charged with regulating racing and as chairman of the Jockey Club, whose rules the commission regulated. He was also a racetrack official and president of Belmont Park.

August Belmont's brothers were Perry and Oliver Hazard Perry. Besides being a founder of the Jockey Club, Perry Belmont was a lawyer, U.S. congressman, and minister to Spain, a politician ahead of his time: He advocated that political parties publish statements of their campaign expenditures. Oliver Hazard Perry (Harry) Belmont had given his parents a good deal to worry about. Harry did poorly in school, and they thought he would never be more than a wastrel. But, like his brother Perry, Harry served in the U.S. Congress. Even though the brothers were not congressmen at the same time, Harry's image was so impossible for people to reconcile with that of a man who could hold a seat in Congress, his congressional position was often credited to his brother Perry (the brothers did share the name *Perry*). A Jockey Club member, Harry is most often remembered for housing his thoroughbreds on the first floor of his mansion in Newport, Rhode Island.

The second generation of Belmonts became acceptable to New York's social elite, at least a generation sooner than had the Vanderbilts. August Belmont I's only daughter married a member of the Jockey Club, whose forebears included a Puritan leader on the Mayflower. Harry Belmont married the ex-Mrs. William Kissam Vanderbilt. Perry Belmont married the beautiful Jessie Robbins Sloane, the day after her husband divorced her.

Further, the Belmonts went about securing their place in society with some astuteness. They followed the practice of others of New York's nouveau riche, establishing their own institutions rather than waiting for acceptance from those controlled by the Knickerbocker old guard. August Belmont II had first married the daughter of the governor of New York. When she died, he married the actress Eleanor Robson. She is reputed to have been influential in the founding of the Metropolitan Opera Guild—in part because the reigning opera house of the day turned down William Henry Vanderbilt's offer of $30,000 for a box seat.

The Original Twenty-seven

Twenty-three more men joined William Kissam Vanderbilt, William Collins Whitney, August Belmont II, and Perry Belmont in founding the Jockey Club. All were colorful, very wealthy, and nationally influential. Yet neither the Belmont brothers nor William K. Vanderbilt were among the new-money Jockey Club founders or subsequent members welcomed into New York society through invitations to the annual balls of Mrs. Astor.[42] Those she invited to the ball of 1892 became known thereafter as the original Four Hundred, that is, the cream of the city's social register. William Collins Whitney was invited, along with five future fellow Club members: Frank Griswold, heir to Lorillard Tobacco; Frank Knight Sturgis, New York financier and president of the New York Stock Exchange; William Seward Webb, president of Wagner Sleeping Car Company and William Kissam Vanderbilt's brother-in-law; George Peabody Wetmore, governor of Rhode Island and later the state's U.S. senator for three terms; and Richard Thornton Wilson, Jr., the son of a Confederate cotton broker.

Not all the Club's founders were New Yorkers or even born in America. From Pittsburgh, Samuel S. Brown was a Freemason and Civil War volunteer with several coal mines. From Philadelphia, Alexander Cassatt—the husband of a niece of former president James Buchanan—was president of the Pennsylvania Railroad, and Rudolph Ellis was one of the railroad's directors. William H. Forbes, son of the founder of J. M. Forbes and Company and associate of J. P. Morgan and Company, was from Boston. James Ben Ali Haggin was a San Francisco gold and silver investor with 150 square miles of land in California; his mining partner, not a founder, was fellow Californian U.S. Senator George Hearst, father of newspaper giant William Randolph Hearst. Cleveland resident Oliver Hazard Payne was treasurer of Standard Oil and W. C. Whitney's brother-in-law.

Among the Club founders who were immigrants to America were German-born John O. Donner, superintendent of the American Sugar Refining Company; Irishman James Galway, who became New York City's fire commissioner; and London-born James R. Keene, silver stock magnate.

THE JOCKEY CLUB TAKES THE REINS

When the Jockey Club's twenty-seven founders assumed control of racing, they took the reins of power as if by the traditional divine right of royalty. They sought the permission of neither the New York legislature nor the governor. They were, after all, if not actual royalty, at least among the chosen in the United States and close to the national political scene. Many held positions of power themselves; many were related, often by marriage, to people in powerful posts. For example, Alexander Cassatt had married the niece of former president Buchanan. William Whitney was a former secretary of the navy and President Cleveland's chief patron. Benjamin Tracy had served as secretary of the navy under President Benjamin Harrison. Oliver Hazard Payne's father had just finished his term as a U.S. senator. William P. Thompson was the brother-in-law of then U.S. senator Johnson N. Camden. Perry Belmont had recently served as minister to Spain.

On its own (and following the British model), the Jockey Club wrote, interpreted, and enforced the rules that became horseracing law in New York and Delaware. Their rules were also honored by other states. The Club assigned racing dates, issued licenses, and appointed judges. Henceforth, the Club alone dictated who could train, ride, and own horses. In return for this power, the Club promised to save the sport from gamblers and bookmakers, from the absence of a set of rules held in common, and from horses of questionable pedigree.[43]

Within a year of the Jockey Club's founding, the New York State Legislature had rubber-stamped these prerogatives. There was support for the Club at the state, as well as the national, level. Club member Jacob Ruppert, Jr., was on the governor's staff. Club member Alfred Hennen Morris, of the steamship and telegraph Morrises, had been elected to the state legislature that same year. The legislature passed a bill that authorized racing as a sport, prohibited bookmaking therein, recognized the Club as the licensing power over racing in the state, approved the Club's appointing racing officials, and established the first racing commission to issue licenses to associations that conducted races.[44] The governor then appointed members of the Jockey Club to make up that three-person commission: Club chairman August Belmont II, Edwin D. Morgan—a distant relative of J. P. Morgan—and third-generation U.S. congressman John Sanford. Presumably in anticipation of these appointments, the Club had admitted Morgan and Sanford only two months earlier. Now Club members would issue licenses to Club members who owned racetracks.

The Jockey Club frowned on its members racing horses for profit—in fact, Club policy required members to be amateurs, not professionals, where racing was concerned. Of course, the fortunes of Club members did not rely on their racing horses. Still, some of the founders had made substantial investments in racing—they owned the tracks. Alexander Cassatt and August Belmont II co-owned New Jersey's Monmouth Park, and A. F. Walcott was its president. James G. K. Lawrence was owner, John Bowers was director, and John Bradford was treasurer of the Coney Island track. Philip Dwyer was the owner of Brooklyn's Gravesend Racetrack. Alfred Hennen Morris, state assemblyman, was the Yonkers track owner. John Hunter was founding co-investor in Saratoga Racecourse, and W. C. Whitney would soon assume its control. By 1905, Belmont joined with J. P. Morgan and James Keene to build Belmont Park, which he named for his father.

Betting and Bookmaking

There has probably never been a horse race on which someone did not bet money. By 1895, a year after the Jockey Club was founded, despite state laws against bookmaking, some two hundred bookmakers operating on New York tracks would "book" your bets and raise or lower the odds on the horses you were betting on.

Bookmaking had come to Saratoga Racecourse in 1865, when John Morrissey built the town's first track. He made himself the track's first betting commissioner, and he took a piece of the action for his services. Thirty years later, those two hundred New York bookmakers had bought their right to a place in the betting ring. Track and casino wagering was so widespread and out in the open in the city that John Pulitzer, publisher of the *New York World*, sent investigative reporter Nellie Bly to write about it. So common was bookmaking there that Club founder Philip Dwyer and his brother,

Mike (not a Club member), routinely took their own bookmakers with them when they raced at Churchill Downs in Kentucky, where state law allowed people to bet among themselves and on any horse they wanted. (The Dwyer brothers were self-made men. They began their lives as butchers and amassed a considerable fortune when they got into racing: Both owned successful racehorses, both made money betting on the horses, and Philip owned the Gravesend track. Mike's wagers were the more aggressive, apparently so large they sometimes paralyzed the betting ring.)[45]

At the turn of the century, Saratoga Springs was still a wide-open town, with wagering at the racetrack and other recreation available at casinos and houses of prostitution. John Morrissey's casino had reopened under the management of Richard Canfield, who required that patrons wear evening clothes and charged prices higher even than those at Manhattan's posh Delmonico's restaurant. (Canfield had traveled to Monte Carlo to educate himself on how aristocrats gambled.) Though the track was then in the hands of Club founder William Collins Whitney, it remained a haven for those who wanted to wager on the horses.

There remains the question of why these new-monied gentlemen, intent on *being* gentlemen, would have allowed bookmakers to operate—illegally—at their racetrack. In general, they tended to show a laissez faire attitude toward illicit entrepreneurs in Saratoga Springs, especially toward those who maintained a low profile. Perhaps the explanation is economic: Certainly the track and the casinos shared some of the same clientele; regulars at the races were often also regulars at the gaming tables.

Perhaps they turned a blind eye to wagering simply because some members of their families were avid bettors themselves. Commodore Vanderbilt, for instance, had frequented Morrissey's Clubhouse. Alfred Gwynne Vanderbilt I and Reginald Vanderbilt, his great-grandsons, wagered grand sums at the casinos. Reginald is said to have lost $70,000 on his twenty-first birthday, and he and Alfred were regulars at Canfield's casino in Saratoga Springs. Willie K. Vanderbilt, another of the Commodore's great-grandsons, according to one account,

> arrived [in Saratoga] one night . . . prepared to take a couple of ladies to dinner at the lake, but they hadn't finished powdering their noses or tightening their corsets, so he wandered lazily

across the road and down through the park to the Club House [Canfield's casino] to pass the fifteen minutes or so he would have had to wait. "Make a bit of money for dinner," he told himself with a whimsical smile, and then proceeded to blow $130,000 at the roulette wheel.[46]

Among the nouveau riche, the Vanderbilts were not the only patrons of the gaming tables at casinos. Club member Frederic Gebhard was a roulette man, winning $10,000 one evening and losing $90,000 another. Even the ultraconservative financier J. P. Morgan was said to have frequented Canfield's.[47]

Some Club members were, like the Dwyer brothers, themselves fond of taking a chance at the track. The Dwyer brothers used their own bookmakers, but at least one member—Club founder James R. Keene—let a nonprofessional bet for him. Keene had accumulated some $6 million on the San Francisco Stock Exchange and was a Wall Street competitor of W. C. Whitney, but he was shy at the track.[48] He chose a young financial genius of his acquaintance to place his bets for him. The youth was Bernard Baruch, who, it has been reported, "acted as a 'beard' for Keene—that is, he carried a great wad of money, amounting to several thousand dollars, to a New York racetrack where one of Keene's horses was running. Baruch circulated among the bookmakers, betting the money on Keene's horse a little at a time, to avoid jostling the odds."[49]

Although still in violation of New York statutes, bookmaking continued unabated until 1910, when racing itself was shut down by Governor Thomas E. Dewey as part of his campaign against vice. During the three-year shut down, several Club members, including William Kissam Vanderbilt, took their horses to Europe to race; some did not return on any regular basis. In 1912, the New York legislature decided that betting by word of mouth was not after all, in the strict sense, a violation of the law. Racing and wagering on races resumed.

Bookmaking on New York tracks continued for decades after 1912, though it remained officially illegal. Some have suggested it was possible because bookmaking served the interests of wealthy bettors. Indeed, one betting ring "head" made $50,000 a year presiding over what was called "the sanctioned hypocrisy of a trackside bookmaking ring in the service of wealthy sportsmen."[50] Apparently, bookmaking maintained the privacy of wealthy bettors better than did other methods of wagering. In light of the bookmaking sanctioned at New York tracks, the Jockey Club and its founders may have brought only the semblance of legitimacy to horse racing.

New Members

For the next few decades, the Jockey Club continued to admit the sons, brothers, nephews, in-laws, and associates of the founding members. Like their forerunners, these new members also had interests in transportation, mining, utilities, manufacturing, merchandising, oil, and—especially—finance. Among those invited to membership before the turn of the century were financier extraordinaire J. P. Morgan; Charles Oliver Iselin, a grandson of Swiss banker Adrian Iselin; William Astor Chanler, whose mother was an Astor; and Francis R. Hitchcock and Thomas Hitchcock II, sons of Thomas Hitchcock I, major stockholder of the *New York Sun.*

By the 1920s, Club members included Clarence H. Mackay, son of Comstock Lode magnate John Mackay; Robert Livingston Gerry, a descendant of Declaration of Independence signer Elbridge Gerry; Marshall Field III, the grandson of Chicago department store magnate Marshall Field; William Averell Harriman, a son of railroad baron E. H. Harriman; Pierre Lorillard (II), the son of tobacco magnate and Tuxedo Park builder Pierre Lorillard; transit baron Thomas Fortune Ryan; and Joseph E Widener and his nephew George D. Widener (II), descendants of Philadelphia transit magnate P.A.B. Widener I.

Among the illustrious admitted to the Jockey Club in the 1930s was James Cox Brady II, a grandson of utilities baron Anthony N. Brady I.

The social backgrounds of members of the Jockey Club remained the same as the social backgrounds of the Club's founders. Men who belonged to the Club were the nation's aristocrats who owned and raced thoroughbreds.

2

THE MYTH OF PEDIGREE

In 1896, the two-year-old Jockey Club committed itself to the protection of the thoroughbred, a breed that was in fact of mixed parentage. The event reflected Club founders' belief that success bred to success would produce progeny destined to accomplish greater things than progeny of lesser breeding. It was a belief not inconsistent with popular notions of the day regarding human achievement; this same year the U.S. Supreme Court affirmed the myth of human bloodlines when it maintained, in *Plessy v. Ferguson*, that separate but equal facilities for whites and blacks were not unconstitutional.

The notions of the time failed to recognize that progeny, whether human or animal, obtain, in addition to genes, other advantages from their breeding that might account for their success. They have the best nutrition, the finest training or education, the most extensive networks of opportunity, and the best care that money can buy. According to Mark Twain, even young Huckleberry Finn's "pap [who was of] no more quality than a mudcat himself [knew that being] well-born [was] worth as much in a man as it is in a horse."[1]

GOOD BREEDING (HUMAN)

When the Club was founded, its nouveau riche members could not take their own breeding for granted. Though some founders were of English, Dutch, and even Mayflower Puritan stock, others were of less highly regarded Welsh, Irish, German, Catholic, and Jewish backgrounds. No wonder many of these self-made men were concerned that they marry well. Good marriages, and the social standing that went with them, would enable them, a generation or so later, to feel, with other "of the old families . . . that their good breeding . . . [was] in their genes."[2]

The villains here, apart from the engrained snobbery that sometimes goes with very old money, were eugenics and social Darwinism. From the Civil War to the Progressive Era, the ideas of Charles Darwin, Herbert Spencer, and especially of Darwin's cousin Francis Galton—the founder of the eugenics movement—were welcomed with general interest in the United States.[3] Social Darwinism suggested that humankind owed its progress to the selection of the biologically fit; it predicted that in a free market, the fit would achieve and accumulate great wealth. This was of some comfort to new-money industrialists like steel baron Andrew Carnegie, who believed he had found the "truth" of evolution in Darwin and Spencer.

Some Americans were also swayed by the pseudoscience of eugenics, which suggests that humankind can be improved through the selective mating of certain fit groups. At the time, it even advocated the elimination or sterilization of those who were considered unfit. This was an era when popular thinking, and that of many scientists, favored "nature" over "nurture" for explaining behavior— that is, one's genes rather than one's environment set the course of one's life. Both social Darwinism and eugenics received support from some among the nouveau riche, including a believer with close ties to the Jockey Club.

Mary Williamson Averell Harriman, the widow of railroad mogul Edward Henry Harriman, apparently became intrigued with the possibility of improving the condition of humans, like horses, through selective breeding.[4] (E. H. Harriman had headed the Union Pacific and the Southern Pacific Railroads and had also bred thoroughbreds. He was infamous for hiring, as strike breakers, thugs armed with machine guns. The Harrimans' daughter became the second wife of Jockey Club founder William Kissam Vanderbilt. The Harrimans' son, William Averell Harriman, would become a Club member.) In the last quarter of the nineteenth century, some women of elite background, like Mrs. Harriman, actively involved themselves in causes that were seen as "progressive."

Mrs. Harriman was able to lend considerable financial support to eugenics concerns. For instance, she purchased the eighty-acre tract of land at Cold Spring Harbor on the North Shore of Long Island where the Eugenics Record Office was built. From 1909 to 1940, that office conducted the nation's major inquiries into human heredity. Cold Spring Harbor was also the site of Andrew Carnegie's Department of Experimental Evolution, and the organizations shared the same director.[5]

Mrs. Harriman lent her influence to other similar projects as well.[6] She joined gun-powder baron General Coleman du Pont and steel magnate Henry Clay Frick in support of the permanent institutionalization of the "feebleminded." She also joined John D. Rockefeller, Jr., to argue for the sterilization of women with histories of prostitution. Rockefeller's Bureau of Social Hygiene intended to remove from society those whose heritage was thought to incline them toward crime and other social problems.

At the same time that the doctrine of the survival of the fittest was gaining support, many of society's ills were attributed to the growing immigrant population.

Right Ethnic Heritage

In the 1870s, so-called polite society became blatantly anti-Semitic.[7] Banker Joseph Seligman, a founder of one of New York City's elite men's clubs, the Union League, was among those affected by this overt prejudice. In 1877, as was his custom, Seligman went to Saratoga Springs in August, and the Grand Union Hotel turned him away. It had a new policy: No Jews. About the same time, Seligman's son was blackballed from the Union League, the club that Seligman had founded and from which he himself would then resign. Men's clubs were among the worst offenders in adopting anti-Semitic policies, which often benefited their Anglo-Saxon members in pragmatic ways. White males apparently "realized that the club was an ideal instrument for the gentlemanly control of social, political and economic power."[8]

Equally discriminatory practices reached into elite neighbor-hoods, mountain resorts, ivy-league fraternities, and prep schools—and not surprisingly into the Jockey Club itself. The Lake Placid Club in upstate New York, frequented by the Harrimans, Vander-bilts, and Whitneys—all families whose names appear on the list of Jockey Club members—posted this rule: "No one will be received as member or guest against whom there is physical, moral, social, or race objection, or who would be unwelcome to even a small mi-nority. . . . This invariable rule is rigidly enforced; it is found im-practical to make exceptions to Jews or others excluded, even when of unusual personal qualifications."[9]

The application form at one New England prep school asked outright, "Is the boy in any part Hebraic?"[10] Anti-Semitism, which might have been predicted to infect fraternities at Yale and other elite colleges, became so common that even the Greek-letter soci-eties of the tuition-free City College of New York—a college that traditionally drew from immigrant populations—barred Jews.[11] So-ciety had drawn its lines, and the Jockey Club seemed to concur. August Belmont I, father of two Club founders, was said to be the last Jewish member accepted by upper-class society before the bar went up.

Right Family Origin

For many Jockey Club members and their social ilk, perhaps more than for people of another social rank, family origin is singularly important. The well bred are considered to be exactly that: the product, literally, of good breeding. This seems to be as true today as when the Club was founded. Members identify themselves, each other, and outsiders based on who their families are; it is a criterion by which a person may be differentiated and judged. Family origin carries with it a cluster of attributes, actors, and events that have special meaning within this inner circle.

Club members seem to be like others of their social set for whom blood relationship has come to confirm not only their iden-tity and their kin, but whom they can trust, and to whom they owe their first allegiance.[12] Among members of this set, it is the most important of the ties that bind. Their family origins carry with them the roster of relationships with leading families of the past, ties reinforced each time members of the set meet and talk. They "know that they are placed indefinitely in the social world by the strings which bind them to their ancestors."[13]

The importance of family origins to social discourse, specifically in privileged society, is clear in this excerpt from Stephen Birmingham's *The Right People:*

> In Real Society it is less a matter of which club, which school, which street, and what clothes, than it is a matter of *who. Who* will always count more than how, or how much. One does *not* ask, "Where are you from?" or "Where did you go to school?" or "What do you do?" Such questions are considered as tactless as "How much did it cost?" If you have to ask such questions, you have no right to the answers. On the other hand, you may ask without fear of rebuke, "Who . . . ?" "Who is she?" as a question may mean "What was her maiden name?" It may also mean what was her mother's maiden name, and what was her grandmother's maiden name, and so on.[14]

In the same way, many contemporary members of the Jockey Club wish to be known by their family origins. Most of those I talked with assumed I was familiar with their name and knew who they were, or who their family of origin was. In the event that I might not be aware of the origins of others of whom they spoke, they identified them for me.

> "He's a du Pont."
>
> "But, she isn't a du Pont, you know, [she only married one]."
>
> "He married Isabel Dodge Sloane's niece."
>
> "He married James Cox Brady's sister."
>
> "He's Nick [Nicholas F.] Brady's first cousin."
>
> "He married into the Phipps family."
>
> "She's Jock's [John Hay Whitney's] widow."

Right Spouse

Some Jockey Club members, aware that their family origin would fail to measure up in the society to which they wished to become accustomed, elected to "marry up"—into socially solid families in the United States or to gentry overseas. Others married women within their social group. Still others married "outsiders."

Club founders who married into families more socially acceptable included the sons of August Belmont I, who chose to marry women who did not share their Jewish heritage. James R. Keene, of rather humble London origins, was accepted into Southern society through his marriage to Sara Daingerfield, sister of Judge Dangerfield, of an old Virginia family.

Social standing and wealth both factored in such matches. More recent Club members Gifford A. Cochran and Harold E. Talbott, although wealthy in their own right, might have been viewed as improving their social standing when they married into fashionable Philadelphia society. The orphaned and once penniless Thomas Fortune Ryan married the boss's daughter. Ryan ran errands in the Baltimore dry-goods store of John Barry. Within a year of marrying Barry's daughter, Ida, Ryan bought his own seat on the New York Stock Exchange. William B. Leeds, a florist, married late in the nineteenth century into a Pennsylvania Railroad family. With their wealth, he founded the American Tin Plate Company, which had made him $40 million by the time he sold out to U.S. Steel.[15] Meanwhile, he had divorced his first wife, remarried, bought the Newport property of Frederick W. Vanderbilt, and in 1904 been admitted to the Jockey Club.

Some of the new-money elite who would join the Jockey Club improved their own social standing and presumably the "blood" of their descendants when their daughters married members of the European gentry. During the Gilded Age, these families commonly traveled to Europe and were presented at Court. The Americans who saw themselves as needing greater respectability and bluer blood often hobnobbed with European aristocrats who found their fortunes declining. Marriages, arranged or otherwise, could benefit both groups.[16] (Jennie Jerome, the daughter of racetrack builder Leonard Jerome, married a British peer in 1874 and bore him a son, Winston Churchill.)

Several members of the Jockey Club arranged such marriages for their daughters. The daughter of Richard T. Wilson, Belle, married the son of the first Baron Herbert. Pierre Lorillard's daughter Maude married the third Baron Revelstoke. W. C. Whitney spent a million dollars on the wedding of his daughter, Pauline, to Baron Queenborough. His stepdaughter, Adelaide, married the son of the ninth earl of Cavan. Henry Phipps's daughter Amy married the son of the first Baron Wimbourne, the Honorable Frederick Guest—both of their sons would grow up to be polo players and Jockey

Club members. Ogden Livingston Mills arranged for his daughter, Beatrice, to marry the eighth earl of Granard. James Greene secured his daughter's engagement to the prince of Denmark.

The best known of these trans-Atlantic unions, arranged a year after the Jockey Club's birth by a founder of the Club and his estranged spouse, was that of William Kissam and Alva (Smith) Vanderbilt's daughter and a British duke. Their story was one that would be repeated often. Its lesson seemed to be that the newly moneyed socially insecure could attain legitimacy by marrying up. The bride's feelings notwithstanding, one was obligated to marry the right stock and thereby to improve the family bloodline.

To set the stage, recall that the Vanderbilts had been on the margins of New York society for some time, and that Alva's exceptional taste in the design and building of their elegant mansion at 660 Fifth Avenue was said to have prompted a change in the family's social situation. With its completion, the Vanderbilts received an invitation to the elite 1881 Patriarch's Ball—but not to the 1892 ball of Caroline Astor. Inclusion among those invited to her annual ball was proof of one's acceptance into society. (The city's society had traditionally been ruled by women, and the lavish balls were where they reigned.[17] Caroline Astor was the society queen of the day—she was Caroline Schemerhorn of the New York shipping family, who had married William Astor, a grandson of fur-trade baron John Jacob Astor.)

Alva Vanderbilt was not one to be content with the most graceful and elegant mansion on Fifth Avenue or a husband who was one of the world's wealthiest men. She moved to divorce William Kissam, an almost unheard of act among the elite. Determined that her daughter Consuelo would marry very well, Alva chose for her the ninth duke of Marlborough, Charles Richard John Spencer Churchill, even though he was commonly held to be snobbish and petty.

In anticipation of the marriage, William Kissam Vanderbilt drew up a prenuptial agreement in which he pledged the income on $2 million in railroad shares to the duke and an additional $100,000 to the couple annually. The day before the wedding, he put another $4 million in trust for any children of the marriage. It has been estimated that the Marlborough title and, of course, any related blue blood was purchased for $10 million.

The *New York Times* described the wedding of Consuelo and the duke on November 6, 1895, as the most magnificent ever celebrated in the United States and supplied readers with the groom's entire genealogy. The six hundred invited guests, fifty-piece orchestra, sixty-member choir, and massive floral arrangements filled St. Thomas Episcopal Church. Although the press had expected the entire Vanderbilt clan, only the immediate family attended. According to writer Louis Auchincloss, who is Vanderbilt's grandson-in-law, Alva was feuding with the clan over her pending divorce of William and refused to invite them.[18]

The marriage was not a love match. Consuelo was not enthusiastic about her mother's choice; she had been held under constant guard and forbidden to speak to anyone on the day of her wedding. Clearly nervous, she leaned on her father when they arrived at the church, where thousands had gathered for a brief glimpse of her. She even delayed some twenty minutes before starting down the aisle. At the ceremony's completion, a formal contract was signed. It required the signatures of the duke, the new duchess, William Kissam Vanderbilt, a member of the British gentry, and the British consul general in New York. Vanderbilt then left the church through a side door and headed for one of his several men's clubs, the Metropolitan.

For thirteen years Consuelo remained in this arranged marriage to a man who once said, speaking of her, "I never could abide tall women." She bore him the tenth duke of Marlborough and Lord Ivor Spencer Churchill, bringing to the Vanderbilt line the very blue, highly socially acceptable blood of the English peerage.

The Right Set

Daughters of America's social elite, including those of Jockey Club members—or the members themselves—are no longer expected to marry European gentry. For that matter, there is little social pressure among the group to marry up at all, as these families have *become* the establishment. Both women and men are still expected, however, to enter into marriages that ensure the protection of family bloodlines and fortunes.

One way to accomplish this is to marry within their own set. Jockey Club members have regularly married into families with names as prestigious and powerful as their own, including Liv-

ingston, Astor, Mortimer, Rockefeller, Peabody, Lambert, and Goelet. They have also married into the Sears, Woolworth, General
Motors, and Dodge Motor Company families. Another pattern is
the marriage of Club members or others in their family into families of other members. Indeed, about one-fifth of the members of
the Jockey Club have been related by marriage.

No wonder that marriage within the group is blessed, for it
promises a financial, social, and family safety that many other marriages cannot. The pattern began as early as the marriage of William
Collins Whitney to the sister of Oliver Hazard Payne. When Whitney's son, Harry Payne Whitney, married the granddaughter of
Commodore Vanderbilt, the orchestra played "The Star-Spangled
Banner." (Recall that the Whitney and Vanderbilt Fifth Avenue
mansions were just across the street from one another.) O.H.P. Belmont married William Kissam Vanderbilt's ex-wife, Alva. (Alva out-
lived them both and became a militant suffragist.) William Seward
Webb married W. K. Vanderbilt's sister.

Lorillards married Griswolds. W. Plunkett Stewart married the
daughter of E. B. Cassatt. Thomas Hitchcock II married the sister
of the Eustis brothers, George P. and William Corcoran. William
Averell Harriman's first wife was the ex-wife of Cornelius Vanderbilt Whitney. Harriman's second wife, Pamela Digby Churchill
Hayward Harriman, was previously married to the son of British
prime minister Winston Churchill. Harriman's sister married the
brother of Peter Goelet Gerry.

One of F. S. von Stade's daughters married George H. Bostwick,
and another married W. Haggin Perry. George William Douglas
Carver married a Hitchcock. J. Simpson Dean married a du Pont.
Vincent de Roulet married John Hay Whitney's sister. Marshall
Field III married the ex-wife of Ogden Phipps. William Woodward
I's daughter married Thomas Moore Bancroft. Cortright Wetherill
married the daughter of P.A.B. Widener II. John W. Galbreath's
daughter married James W. Phillips. William McKnight's daughter
married James Binger. The Phippses have married the Mills, the
Bostwicks, the Janneys, and the Farishes.

William Stamps Farish II married the daughter of Bayard
Sharp. His sister, Martha, married Edward Harriman Gerry. His son,
William Stamps Farish III, married the daughter of Ogden Phipps.
The list goes on and on.

Just as the genealogies of Jockey Club members are frequently enmeshed, their lives are ones of almost seamless togetherness. They go to the same schools, serve in the same military units, join the same firms, and live in the same neighborhoods. The group, for the most part, also thinks, acts, and moves as one. This is not because its members are followers, but because they share a common view of the world, one that derives from common experiences and that rarely faces challenge. By virtue of position and wealth, these families seldom associate on a regular basis with persons of lesser position or less wealth—they are outsiders.

The rugged individualism often valued and subscribed to by the U.S. middle class is not necessarily a virtue here. Being a part of the group and of the family are more important. It is not surprising to hear a fifty-year-old Club member described as wishing to please his father or as handling his father's business well. There is little call for declarations of independence when security lies in maintaining group and family ties.

The Right to Be Wrong

Once Jockey Club members themselves became a part of society, they had the latitude to associate with outsiders if they chose to, without those associations destroying their social standing. Over the years, a few have become closely allied with actresses, artists, and showgirls, and some have formed permanent unions with them. August Belmont II took an actress for his second wife; his son, Raymond, also married an actress. Frederic Gebhard was rumored to be engaged to Lillie Langtry, to whom he gave a private Pullman car, Lalee. Clarence H. Mackay married a concert soprano the second time around, and his daughter married Broadway song writer Irving Berlin. William du Pont II's sister, Marion, married cowboy actor Randolph Scott. Jacob Ruppert, Jr., New York congressman and owner of the New York Yankees when they acquired Babe Ruth, was said to be a confirmed bachelor. He did bequeath one-third of his $45 million estate to Helen Winthrope Weyant, a friend and former actress, though.

In 1945, when Jockey Club member Alfred Gwynne Vanderbilt II married Jeanne Lourdes Murray, an amateur actress, his name was removed from *the* Social Register—the New York City annual listing of individuals of recognized standing, along with their college, clubs, societies, college clubs, addresses, and phone numbers. Being struck off the Register implies a judgment that, in the eyes of the compilers, improper behavior has occurred. (Similarly, a Supreme Court justice who married a twenty-three-year-old had his name removed from the Washington, D.C., social register, the Green Book.)[19] Alfred Gwynne was a great-great-grandson of Commodore Vanderbilt and the first in the family to be a member of the Jockey Club since founder William Kissam Vanderbilt. This was his second marrige, and he took an attorney with him when he married Jeanne Murray in the city hall in Philadelphia.[20] Though Murray was working as a publicity agent for the Stork Club in New York City, she was the daughter of a New York Port Authority commissioner and a cousin of Mrs. Henry Ford II. Her antecedents would seem to have been prestigious enough. Still, something must have offended the old guard. Vanderbilt took society's response gracefully, though, and named a horse Social Outcast in honor of his banishment.

One Jockey Club marriage outside the social fold had far more tragic consequences. Still, from the beginning, and in the tradition of the upper class, family members sought to cope well with the resulting scandals. When the son of William Woodward I (chairman of the Central Hanover Bank and Trust Company, member of the first Federal Reserve Board, and chairman of the Jockey Club) married Ann Eden Crowell, a model from Kansas City, his mother, Elizabeth Ogden Cryden Woodward, behaved with propriety. Even when the former Powers model, "a woman of ordinary lineage but of extraordinary beauty,"[21] shot and killed William Woodward II, his mother's upper lip was reportedly the "stiffest anyone had ever seen."[22] When questioned by detectives after the shooting, the senior Mrs. Woodward said she had thought the marriage was "quite compatible."[23]

The circumstances of the October 1955 early morning shooting got front-page coverage in the *New York Times*.[24] The Woodwards had just returned to their Long Island weekend home from a party given in honor of the Duchess of Windsor. While at the party, William Woodward II had received a call that upset his wife; they left shortly thereafter. Because a prowler had been reported in the neighborhood, they armed themselves with shotguns before retiring to their separate bedrooms. Ann Woodward awoke to their poodle barking, reached beside her bed for her British-made shotgun, turned on the nightlight, and opened the bedroom door. Not recognizing the figure she saw standing there, she fired a double shotgun blast. She killed her husband, silhouetted in the doorway of his bedroom ten feet away.[25]

The distraught widow testified for an entire day before the Nassau County Grand Jury, which on deliberation found the shooting accidental.[26] The Woodwards' night watchman testified that twenty minutes elapsed between the sound of the shots and Ann Woodward's screams. But after extensive questioning by police, the neighborhood prowler, a German immigrant with a history of local thefts, admitted to being at the Woodwards' home and on their roof when he heard the shots and fled.[27]

Lingering doubts about her innocence remained. Twenty years after the shooting, Truman Capote wrote a story about a woman in similar circumstances who hated her husband. Shortly after *Esquire* published Capote's short story "Mojave" in its June 1975 issue, Ann Woodward committed suicide. In less than a year, the younger of the two Woodward sons, James, who had reportedly had problems with drugs and who had spent time in a mental hospital, jumped to his death from an upper floor of a Central Park South hotel. In the 1980s, Dominick Dunne's fictionalized account of the Woodward tragedy appeared and was eventually made into a television movie, *The Two Mrs. Grenvilles*. Meanwhile, William Woodward III, the elder son, had become a *New York Post* reporter, had run unsuccessfully for public office, and had married and divorced. In 1992, still another book based on the Woodward story was published, *This Crazy Thing Called Love* by Susan Braudy. In 1999, apparently suffering from severe depression, William III too committed suicide.[28]

As with the American public in general, divorce among the elite, including members of the Jockey Club, has become more frequent and more acceptable since the nineteenth century. Some Club members have been married four and five times. Take, for example, Cornelius Vanderbilt Whitney, a grandson of W. C. Whitney and chairman of the board of Pan American Airways for forty years. C. V. Whitney was regarded as a playboy as early as his undergraduate days at Yale, when he was sued by a Ziegfeld Follies showgirl who claimed he was the father of her son. In his lifetime, he married four women. His fourth marriage took place the day after he obtained a Reno divorce from his third wife—and according to some, even before she knew about the divorce.[29] One of Whitney's close acquaintances at that time told me that the newly married man had to stay in California for awhile, because his third wife intended to have him arrested if he returned to New York. During this period, Whitney sold his horses and resigned temporarily from the Jockey Club.

GOOD BREEDING (HORSES)

As central to this story as the Jockey Club itself is one breed of horse. It is the thoroughbred. In 1896, the Jockey Club committed itself to protecting the thoroughbred line. The Club would become the official and absolute authority on thoroughbreds in a large part of the Western Hemisphere. For nearly a century, without its stamp of approval, no horse foaled in the United States, Puerto Rico, or Canada has been permitted to race on any thoroughbred track in the United States. At bottom, the Club is in the position of deciding which horses to let in and which to keep out.

Thoroughbred Genealogy

The English horse stock had been depleted during the fifteenth-century Wars of the Roses, and the remaining horses were not considered that consistent or swift.[30] To improve the stock, the English searched far beyond the British Isles and became especially interested in horses in Asia and North Africa—Arabia and Libya. While individual Britons had been generally inclined to breed their best horses to others with similar potential, serious attempts to breed for swiftness fell to kings, noblemen, and private landowners. With the rise of English public racecourses like Newmarket in the 1600s, the demand for swift horses became even greater.

So it was that the English developed a breed of horse just for racing.[31] They settled on three Middle Eastern sires. The Byerly Turk sire (imported 1688–1690) was Captain Byerly's charger in Ireland. The Darley Arabian sire (imported 1702–1704) was bought in Syria by merchant Richard Darley and sent to his brother in Yorkshire.

The Godolphin Arabian sire (imported 1728–1730), an Arab or Barb stallion rejected by the king of France, was bought by the second earl of Godolphin.

These three horses, notable in battle, were even more notable at stud. They were bred to the best available English mares—some owned by royalty, some not—and were found to produce exceptional racehorses. Their progeny were "hot-blooded" or high strung, capable of carrying greater weight and running at high speeds; they were called thoroughbred. After the importation of the Godolphin Arabian, it was claimed that other blood was no longer being introduced into the thoroughbred pool. In fact, however, mixing—even with horses of undetermined pedigree—continued for several generations. Ironically, the Godolphin Arabian was originally a "teazer"— a stallion used to bring mares into heat before they are covered by the preferred stallion. The Godolphin was bred to a royal mare only after the presumably better-bred stallion refused to cover her. It was some time after, when the resulting foal proved to be an exceptional racehorse, that the Godolphin would himself become a preferred stallion and eventually one of the three foundation sires.

In the United States, the thoroughbred story is similar.[32] Certain stallions, Medley (1783–1784), Shark (1788), Messenger (1788), and Diomed (1789), are credited with bringing the thoroughbred line to America. As in England, these sires did not drive out all unpedigreed stallions. The thoroughbred line was adulterated, and the actual business of pedigrees became a rather hopeless tangle of ignorance, hoax, and greed. Moreover, in these early years, American revolutionaries found a concern over pedigree, even in horses, almost offensive.

The American Stud Book

By the late 1800s, America's registry of thoroughbreds—the listing of the pedigrees of individual horses that were recognized as thoroughbred—was in chaos. The several attempts to keep complete and accurate records of all horses claimed to be thoroughbred had not been successful. Breeders often kept their own breeding and racing records. Colonel Sanders Dewars Bruce started *The American Stud Book* and, from the years 1868 to 1894, published a six-volume set of the pedigrees of all imported thoroughbred stallions and mares and their produce. After that time, he found the project too costly and asked the Jockey Club to take it over. The cumulative wealth of Club members would have made the task relatively easy.[33]

In 1896, the Jockey Club thus began to register horses as thoroughbreds.[34] Keeping the name *The American Stud Book,* the Club listed only American-foaled horses that were claimed to be validly descended from one of the original three English foundation sires. In spite of this requirement, the British Jockey Club for years refused to recognize the horses listed in this registry as thoroughbreds.

The American Stud Book placed a horse's breeding on record and admitted only horses that qualified as thoroughbreds. It "is the registry maintained by The Jockey Club for all Thoroughbreds foaled in the United States, Puerto Rico and Canada and for all Thoroughbreds imported into the United States, Puerto Rico and Canada from countries that have a registry recognized by The Jockey Club," according to the Jockey Club's 1993 *Principal Rules and Requirements of the American Stud Book.*[35] To race on any thoroughbred track in the United States, a horse foaled in this country, Puerto Rico, or Canada must be registered in the book. This has meant that the Club alone has the right to determine which horses are allowed to race, an important prerogative that it has protected and retained since 1896.[36]

Maintaining *The American Stud Book* confers on the Jockey Club great responsibility along with this power. It is a serious enterprise for the Club that impacts on racing generally. The task involves not only recording the births of all horses it determines by various identification procedures to be thoroughbred and all the descendants of specific registered thoroughbreds, but also defining exactly what constitutes the breed. In so doing, the Club, via the book, determines which horses will be included in the pool to be bred and raced as thoroughbreds and which will not.

Simply put, maintaining *The American Stud Book* means being obliged to make the determinations that keep some horses out and let some in. As horse-identification techniques become more accurate, there is less discretion involved or possible in making these determinations. Though not at all an application of eugenics to the equine world (there has been no move to keep any particular groups of horses out of the gene pool), the list is reminiscent of Caroline Astor's Four Hundred and of the concerns about human heritage and bloodlines that have preoccupied the privileged classes of the United States and Europe. Kings have been distinguished from commoners, gentry from peasants, masters from servants, whites from blacks, high society from the general public, and thoroughbreds from other horses—based on blood.

Getting in the Book

The Jockey Club has tried to ensure the continuing purity of the breed—and the accuracy of its listing—in part by employing more and more exact means of identifying horses. It has increasingly relied on scientific techniques and on refining those techniques. With each advance, the Club has also acknowledged that some horses had been misidentified by earlier methods.[37]

As early as the 1930s, the Club experimented with photographs and written descriptions of horse leg markings, called chestnuts or nighteyes, which are unique to each horse, much as fingerprints are unique to each human. In the 1940s, the Club consulted not only with noted veterinarians but with the head of the Bureau of Narcotics, Harry Anslinger, and mandated that horses that race must have a number tattooed on their upper lip. In the mid-1970s, the Club used a combination of the tattooed number and photographs of the horse with its nighteyes. By the late 1970s, the Club insisted on blood-typing for all thoroughbred stallions, foals, and dams. As of 2000, the Club was funding research on the use of DNA testing as the predominant way to identify thoroughbreds.

Regardless of the identification procedure, the Club has acknowledged that fraud in the registration of thoroughbreds has occurred. The press has sensationalized instances in which horses, known as "ringers," have raced under the names of other horses. There have also been "accidents" in the breeding shed when a mare was served by two stallions, throwing the foal's paternity into question.

Noted breeders and racing officials admitted as early as 1953, at the Jockey Club's First Round Table Discussion on Matters Pertaining to Racing, that there were instances in which foals had been "shifted" and breeding had been "falsified," and that the validity of any registration was only as good as the "integrity of the breeder."[38] At the eighth annual Round Table, in 1960, came the suggestion to routinely blood-type horses that race as a way to help establish correct parentage and eliminate "some honest mistakes where foals get mixed up [as well as] dishonest mistakes."[39]

Regardless of the method of identification or integrity of the breeder, it is still the Jockey Club that has the final word on horses whose names will appear in *The American Stud Book*. A story related to me by a veteran Club member suggests that this stewardship has not always been exercised without some discretion. The member told me about some action he once took in the face of soon-to-be-published information about horses that had been incorrectly identified in *The American Stud Book* as the progeny of a stallion handled by another Club member. Whether out of concern for the reputation of the Club, of the other member, or of the other member's horses, the man I spoke with persuaded a journalist to publish a story in advance that would avert the damage the information might cause. He explained to me that all progeny already listed in *The American Stud Book* were grandfathered in and would remain so listed.

The Breeder

Most members of the Jockey Club seem to welcome, if not seek, public recognition as successful breeders. I found that most were quick to identify themselves in terms of fine horses they had bred or as breeders generally. They also want credit for the success of those horses. The few members who failed to mention breeding were either closely associated with specific horses or were professionals in racing. To Club members, being known as a successful breeder seems to reflect favorably on their commitment to the bloodlines of the thoroughbred and on their identity as horsemen or horsewomen. Even more than racing, breeding appears to establish Club members' standing as belonging to a special class that is itself set apart by its breeding.

Yet in the most down-to-earth terms, neither the breeding nor the racing of thoroughbreds directly involves those designated as breeders. The breeder is seldom involved in the actual breeding process itself, and the actual racing of horses is the responsibility primarily of trainers. A breeder may select the stallion, although that is often left to trainers and other advisors. To further cloud the issue, one can qualify as a breeder simply by owning the dam when it gives birth, and not necessarily when it was bred. As the Club's rule book states, the "breeder of a foal is the owner of the dam at the time of foaling."[40]

For example, say an owner decides to sell a mare after it is in foal. Someone else buys the mare. This someone else knows nothing about stallions or dams, or even about the rudiments of breeding. This someone else now becomes the breeder of the foal simply by virtue of owning the mare when the mare gives birth.

Still, Club members see themselves as quite involved in the breeding of thoroughbreds. Some own both the mare and the stallion; the resulting foals are called "homebred." Others own the mare and select the stallion, perhaps one owned by another Club member. In these instances, the exchange may be the foal, rather than a fee. Christopher Chenery, for example, a Club member from 1951 to 1973, arranged to breed two of his mares to Bold Ruler, owned by Gladys Livingston Mills Phipps, the wife of Club member Henry Carnegie Phipps. They agreed to breed the animals for two consecutive seasons, with each receiving a foal. A flip of a coin determined who would get the first foal, and Phipps won the toss. By default, Chenery got the second foal the next year—which was Secretariat.[41]

Other members may sell the foals they have bred as yearlings, especially those that appear to have little potential for success at the track. Such may have been the case when August Belmont II, the breeder of Man o' War, sold him as a yearling—only to have the horse run twenty-two times in major races and be beaten only once. Similarly, Alice Headly Chandler, a Club member since 1989 and the daughter of the founder of Keeneland Racecourse, sold Sir Ivor as a yearling; the horse went on to win the English Derby. On the other hand, Club member Allaire du Pont played a greater role in the race performance of Kelso, a horse she bred, because she kept him while, as she told me, "he won everything."

This typical scenario will indicate the extent to which most breeders are involved in the breeding process: The owner of a mare begins to look for an appropriate stallion. She may look through the current stallion register. She may ask the advice of friends. Or she may look to sophisticated computerized breeding services. Of course, the mare must be acceptable to the owner of the stallion, the fee must be affordable, and the stallion must have an "open" season. (In general, each stallion has a limited number of times he can breed per year.) Then, she makes arrangements to have the mare shipped to the farm where the selected stallion "stands," or is housed. The mare arrives, comes into heat, is "covered" (mounted) by the stallion—perhaps several times—until she "catches" (becomes impregnated), and, barring any complications, delivers a live foal in eleven months.

Integrity, but Maybe Not Improvement

Jockey Club members take credit for the success of horses they have bred in part because they believe that bloodlines predict performance. It is indeed likely that the progeny of successful horses will also be successful. Even without serious research, few doubt that pattern.

Yet the importance of breeding may be exaggerated. Owners provide advantages to horses believed to have superior breeding, advantages that allow those horses to compete more favorably. They have the best care, nutrition, training, and jockeys. They have breeders and owners who can afford to enter them into the most prestigious races.

The belief that a horse's pedigree predicts its success in racing reaches mythical proportions; it is seldom questioned and ignores all evidence offered by objective reality.[42] While there is often a correlation between pedigree and success, the first does not guarantee the second. But the myth survives, and no wonder, given the advantages well-bred horses receive and the practice of these owners to breed the best only to the best. Each time a horse so bred wins the Kentucky Derby or another prestigious race, the public is presented with its bloodlines as proof of the myth. Should a horse of less notable birth win such a race, there is a search for signs of untapped ancestry, or the win is viewed as a matter of luck, a quirk, or a fluke.

A recent article in *The Blood-Horse,* racing's major trade magazine, illustrates the prevailing myth of breeding and the association of the members of the Jockey Club with the thoroughbreds. When Silver Charm won the 1997 Kentucky Derby, the article's author acknowledged the contributions of the owners, trainer, and jockey but gave ultimate credit to the horse's blood, which was associated with breeders of standing in racing. Silver Charm is a descendant on the top (stallion) side of a horse bred by Ogden Phipps, and on the bottom (mare) side of a horse bought by William Collins Whitney—though seven generations removed. The article attributed the horse's success especially to Whitney blood and breeding.

> The [seventh] dam [of] Silver Buck [the sire of Silver Charm] was . . . acquired by W. C. Whitney. . . . Following [his] death . . . his son, H. P. Whitney, took over the operation, and bred Silver Buck's next three dams. . . . After [his] death . . . , C. V. Whitney took over the horses. [He] bred Equilette . . . and bred [her] to Mahmoud [whom he bought from the Aga Khan]. Silver Fog was the resultant foal, and she produced stakes winner . . . Silver True [the dam of Silver Buck, the sire of Silver Charm].[43]

And despite the Jockey Club's real and longtime commitment to thoroughbred breeding, there is little indication that the breed has improved in the last century.[44] To the contrary, some veterinary scientists have suggested that it has grown weaker, with a substantial number of horses breaking down early in their careers.[45] One such scientist, in a late 1990s article in *The Blood-Horse,* makes the claim that "today's sire book, full of unsound horses incapable of winning at a mile or more or running in more than a few races, bears little evidence of any commitment to the improvement of the breed."[46]

These problems have been attributed to more recent breeding practices. The widespread practice of breeding for speed, so that horses may better compete in the increasing number of shorter races for two-year-olds, has produced "short-coupled" (short-bodied) thoroughbreds who bear little resemblance to their classic ancestors.[47] Yet these breeding efforts have in fact resulted in only minimal improvement in the horse's racing times, even with "advances in genetics, nutrition, tracks, and riding and training techniques."[48]

By comparison, during the twentieth century, humans improved their running times more than did horses. When world-record times of Olympic runners of mile races were set against times of winners of the Kentucky Derby for the years 1900 to 1996, the human runners reduced their times more than the Derby winners did.[49] Perhaps because the thoroughbred has not improved markedly, or perhaps because the Jockey Club's recommendations and breeding strategies have not improved the horse's performance, a Club official told me that the Club recently changed its commitment to the "integrity," rather than the "improvement," of the breed.

Zippy Chippy

A recent seminar in Kentucky kept people with a stake in horse racing glued to their seats. The discussion concerned an active gene that may go into an inactive mode and result in successful racing performance skipping a generation of offspring.[50] Such a gene would help explain the times when well-bred horses fail to produce successful horses or perhaps even fail to produce at all—another explanation that confirms the reliance on bloodlines.

This notion of performance genes becoming inactive and skipping generations may also explain what happened to Zippy Chippy, a grandson of the all-time leading sire, Northern Dancer (bred by Club member E. P. Taylor). Having not won a race in eighty-five starts, toward the end of the 1990s Zippy tied the record for the "losingest" horse in the history of American racing. So poor has been his performance that his usual jockey says he no longer wants to ride the horse: "It's making me look bad."[51] Zippy has so angered track officials at Finger Lakes, a "bush" track (the lowest-level category) south of Rochester, New York, that—to preserve racing's integrity—they have banned him from ever running there again. As of February 2000, he is back in training at Philadelphia Park.

On the flip side of this picture are the "nickle breds" who become major winners. The classic case is that of John Henry, a "$1,100 yearling with a throw-away pedigree" who went on to become racing's biggest money winner of all time.[52] Jockeys clamored to ride him, and tracks and fans nationwide could not get enough of him. Unless another stallion jumped the fence to breed his dam, there is nothing in John Henry's bloodlines to explain his success. But John Henry has no descendants to prove or disprove the bloodline theory, as the rank (that is, excitable and difficult to manage) colt was gelded as a two-year-old.

Real Quiet

The 1998 Kentucky Derby and Preakness winner, Real Quiet, who lost the Belmont by a fraction of a nose, further illustrates the dilemma racing faces when a horse defies the breeding myth.[53] So ingrained are the beliefs about the importance of blood for performance that challenges to those beliefs call forth explanations so convoluted as not to be credible. The process nonetheless reveals the depth of the beliefs about breeding and the ways they shape so much of what happens in thoroughbred racing.

In 1995, a businessman from Bogota, Colombia, sent his seldom-raced mare of unimpressive pedigree to be bred to an unremarkable stallion in Kentucky for $10,000. The product of this union was Real Quiet—a knock-kneed foal whose legs, even with corrective screws, remained crooked. Nicknamed "The Fish" because of his narrow appearance, he sold for $17,000 as a yearling, a figure nowhere near the exorbitant prices usually paid for Triple Crown entries.

With a trainer who had previously trained quarter horses and an owner who had made his money in McDonald's franchises, Real Quiet started racing. He did poorly and was sent out West to run, for awhile even on bush tracks, where he also lost. Then he finally "broke his maiden" (won his first race) at Santa Anita Park in Southern California.

With only two wins in twelve starts, Real Quiet went off in the Kentucky Derby as his trainer's second-string horse. Running against the most expensively bred horses in the world, he surprised nearly everybody when he won. Trying to make sense of the upset, a *Blood-Horse* writer attributed the outcome to the "staying power of Real Quiet's untapped pedigree."[54] A search of his bloodlines found well-bred horses to support the view, with credit going largely to Real Quiet's great-great-grandsire, Raise a Native. When the *New York Times* sports writers looked at the same pedigree, they called the Derby winner "blue collar," and another *Blood-Horse* columnist would later follow suit.

Even with breeding shares selling for $525,000 each to complete a $21 million syndicate, Real Quiet still did not get much respect. He nonetheless followed in the tradition of other recent Derby winners and went off in the Preakness as the second-favorite entry. He won again, this time by an even greater margin. "You never know where they are going to come from," was his trainer's answer to questions about the horse's unlikely success.[55]

Some sports columnists had a different explanation. The consensus was that a few well-bred horses had not run in the Preakness because of injuries, leaving Real Quiet with only mediocre competition. A former trainer for both Club member John Galbreath and the widow of Club member Warren Wright wrote of Real Quiet, "If you fight only pugs, you are only the best pug."[56]

On the off-chance that Real Quiet might win the Belmont, *The Blood-Horse* columnists continued to look to breeding to predict the horse's future success. One suggested, for example, that "Real Quiet's chance for victory in the one and a half mile race will be riding more on his pedigree than probably anything else."[57] As the race is the longest of the Triple Crown races, they looked to the horse's bloodlines for evidence of stamina. They found it in the same great-great-grandsire in which they had earlier found speed.

The grandstands for the running of the 1998 Belmont were packed with the second-largest crowd in history. They were there to watch the ugly duckling, underdog, Cinderella horse make a bid for the most prestigious prize in the sport of kings. In attendance was the trainer, a wisecracker from Southern California who the year before "wore" the Preakness trophy on his head; the owner, a small-town Indiana man with rowdy, beer-drinking friends; and the jockey, known to yell and scream after a win. Together, they defied all proper decorum. With Real Quiet and his entourage at the center of the racing public's attention, the sport of kings was, to say the least, a misnomer in 1998.

Real Quiet lost the Belmont by a nose. This was the smallest margin of loss ever in Triple Crown history. He must not have had the right blood after all, as a regular columnist for *The Blood-Horse* would conclude: Real Quiet's "pedigree [was] not really suited to that distance."[58]

3

OFF-TRACK
EXPECTATIONS

All men are expected to prove themselves in ways that are a matter of birth, and those born to wealth are no exception. A blueblood himself, Nelson W. Aldrich, Jr., speaks of such expectations for his set. In his book *Old Money: The Mythology of America's Upper Class,* he describes the ordeals that sons of society must endure to prove their fitness, determination, resourcefulness, and self-reliance.[1] Boarding school allows them to feel that they are pulling themselves up by their own bootstraps. Playing polo, fox hunting, sailing, and going on safari show that they are capable of handling difficult and uncertain situations. Going to war provides the opportunity to demonstrate character and therefore a rightful claim to the high position in which they find themselves.

Society also expects its sons to render public service and to be generous with their wealth. Members of the Jockey Club have served as politicans, cabinet members, and diplomats. And while the noblesse oblige tradition predates the founding of the Club, its members have also left a legacy of philanthropy. But for many, the enduring challenge has been the mastery of the horse.

LOVE OF THE HORSE

One Jockey Club member suggested to me that his fellow members, whether they had grown up with horses or not, were involved in racing because of the love of the horse. He called himself a traditionalist and characterized his own involvement in these terms: "For some, [the love of horses] is inherent in the individual. I was brought up in racing [and I am involved because of] my interest in the horse . . . as an animal with heart and courage . . . first. . . . My love of the horse [has been] a way of life."

Involvement in horse-related activities was a general way of life for those Jockey Club members whose racing stables dated back to the era of the Club founders. I found that Club members of an older generation were rather straightforward when they discussed their childhood, and their land and horses. While outsiders might tend to romanticize the idyllic nature of this experience, it was a given for them. One man who was born to this way of life described for me his horse-centered youth: "We had a place on Long Island. . . . We kept the horses there. My grandfather had a family polo team, which included his three sons [of whom my father was the oldest]. And we had Shetland ponies and were always into [riding] to that extent. My mother was a rider, and she took us out on lead and was adamant that we all learn to ride. And [of course] we would go to the races."

Theirs was a generation who could not recall a time when horses were not in their lives. They had learned to ride as early as they learned to walk. They became entirely comfortable with horses, foaling them, sleeping beside them in the stalls, and riding and showing them. The seasons of their lives were inextricably tied to the thoroughbred. Their families and the families of their friends traveled in August to Saratoga Springs to race, in the winter to California and Florida to race, and at various times during the year to Aiken, South Carolina, to train the yearlings.

For many, there came a point at which their involvement with the thoroughbred took on still more meaning. That point was often when their father became incapacitated or otherwise unable to continue as head of the stable, and when the son or daughter was then forced to decide whether to disperse the horses or continue the stable's operation. Some conveyed, as they spoke with me, what seemed almost a compulsion to continue the work and to assume charge of the family operation. From that point, some developed a particular niche, like racing on the turf or dirt or breeding a particular line; others continued to hire the same trainers their fathers had. This latter practice was one referred to as having "four deep on the bench." Not a few of these members saw their sons and daughters through to "the game," that is, racing.

These members found that somewhere along the way, their involvement with horses became much more than traditional and familial. It became personal. One assured me that while he had done well in a number of sports, nothing was as significant as the connection he had with his horses. He called it a "relationship." Another told of being "addicted to horses every breathing, waking minute" as a child. One declared with fervor, "There is nothing stronger than the bond between man and horse." Another used the term "caught" to describe how he felt after his first horse won its first race. Still another told me that he saw himself as "linked" to horses and did not know where he would be without them.

New-money members of the Jockey Club have also identified with the thoroughbred. Some have grown up with horses on Pennsylvania dairy farms, spreads in Missouri, and cattle farms in California. One man discovered that he could compete more effectively, even while he was young, while astride a horse. Others attended the races, worked with horses at the county fair, rode horses themselves, watched their grandfathers drive horses, or played polo in college. Still others developed their interest in thoroughbreds later in life, often through friends who raced.

These members, too, spoke of their love of and identification with the horse. One mentioned a certain "mystical connection between the human and the horse." Another suggested, obviously referring to himself, that "horses have a tremendous hold over men." Still another elevated the thoroughbred and deprecated other breeds. "Once the horse has bitten you, you're hooked. There is nothing as real as the thoroughbred," he told me. "I wouldn't go across the street to see a trotter. The thoroughbred is thoroughly spent at the end of the race; the trotter is not." One Jockey Club member was apologetic about having once bought—by mistake—a horse that was not a thoroughbred.

These rich and powerful members of postindustrial society

represent a modern-day clan of the horse. The close identification of Club members with the thoroughbred is not unlike the practice in what are sometimes termed "primitive" societies, in which natives divide themselves into clans, each taking its identify through association with a specific plant or animal. The clan's mythical ancestor, most often an animal or animal-like creature, is their "totem" and comes to represent the group.[2] Through rites that celebrate the totem, members of the clan intensify their sense of community.

In modern societies, a similar identification of human groups with animals may be socially driven by a desire for status and its attendant benefits.[3] Groups can establish themselves as superior when they associate themselves with animals that are viewed as superior. Viewed in this light, the close association of the members of the Jockey Club with the thoroughbred may suggest to some observers that the horse is for them a totemlike creature through which they reinforce their commonality and high social standing.

The Lure of Racing

Alfred Gwynne Vanderbilt II's sense of identify was less closely tied to the thoroughbred itself, compared to that of many of his fellow Jockey Club members, than to racing in general. A Club member from 1937 until his death in 1999, Vanderbilt went so far as to say to me, "When I go to the track, I know who I am." As he had explained to numerous journalists before, he told me that "over the years, so many times, I have tried to figure exactly what it was that attracted me to racing. It was not that I was in love with the horse but [it was that] the whole thing was fascinating. The paddock, the jockeys, the races, the colors." A few newer members likewise say they love the sport and its pageantry. One of them, who said he was "hooked," called racing a "passion" and a "natural high" and the total experience "magnetic."

Although Vanderbilt's father was a noted coach-horse racer, it was his mother who introduced him to racing. His father, Alfred G. Vanderbilt I, had gone down with the *Lusitania* in 1915. The story is told that the senior Vanderbilt, though he did not know how to swim, gave his lifejacket to a woman and bravely admonished others nearby to save the children. On the day following the *Lusitania*'s sinking, Vanderbilt's brother-in-law Harry Payne Whitney, a

Club member from 1900 to 1930, ran his filly Regret in the Kentucky Derby. She won.

Alfred Vanderbilt II's mother herself got into racing by chance. Vanderbilt told me that his mother "was a social lady—one who liked people and was attractive. A group of steeplechase people got the brilliant idea of sending somebody to Europe to buy horses. Everybody was to put up $1,000, and they would send a knowledgeable man to buy an equal number of horses as people who had put up the money. [Upon their return, horses would be drawn by lot.] My mother got a winner. . . . She was hooked."

Vanderbilt II was not much involved in athletic endeavors as a child. Having several bouts with illness, he spent considerable time in the company of nurses, as well as nannies. But when he was ten, his mother took him to the 1923 Preakness Stakes at Pimlico. When he bet on a horse that won, he was himself hooked. Vanderbilt went to prep school at St. Paul's School, where he coached the baseball and football teams and had the *Daily Racing Form* delivered to his room. As "the boy bookie" of St. Paul's, Vanderbilt took bets from his fellow classmates. He went on to devote his life to racing.

For some other Jockey Club members, too, racing—and often gentlemen's sports in general—became a way of life. Herman B. Duryea, who was reputed to have "never engaged in business, . . . gave his whole life to sport."[4] Duryea raced horses with one of the Whitneys, was president of the U.S. Field Trial Club, and also raced sloops. Frederic Gebhard, with a yearly inheritance of $80,000 at the turn of the century, went in "for racing and yachting, and . . . lived generally the life of the . . . leisurely man about town."[5] William Payne Thompson, Jr., "never entered business or a profession [but was] devoted . . . to social and sporting interests."[6] Following Jockey Club founder Prescott Lawrence's graduation from Harvard, Lawrence exhibited in horse shows and raced coach horses, where he took several ribbons.[7]

Fox Hunting, Polo, and Other Sports

The son of one Jockey Club member described his father's generation as one whose recreational lives centered around the horse: They fox hunted, played polo, and raced as amateurs. When he recalled the involvement of his father and his father's friends with the horse, he explained it as something with which they grew up. He did not claim for himself the same interest or involvement, because "society [and] everyone's life has changed . . . and there are . . . other things . . . to get pleasure from."

Yet upper-class fathers have, until recently, generally expected their sons to ride horses as well as to respect them.[8] The sports that involve the horse—fox hunting, polo, and steeplechase racing—also tie these families to the Old World and so take on additional virtue by their association with Europe and its aristocracy. For these reasons, several Club members continue to keep these ties alive by maintaining trainers and strings of horses in Europe as well. Some travel to Ireland and England to fox hunt, sometimes with the Prince of Wales. Similarly, when Queen Elizabeth comes to the United States, she often visits Club members. In recent years, Paul Mellon (a Jockey Club member from 1947 until his death in 1999) and William Farish III (a member since 1970) have entertained her at their farms. When the time comes that members dedicated to these sports are no longer able to ride, they often feel obliged to explain why—if they do not cite health reasons, it is becoming increasingly likely that the fault will lie with developers having taken over their hunt country.

From the 1880s through the 1960s, fox hunting was common for these families. It is a sport that dates from the 1600s, when Europe was overrun with foxes, and poor farmers got together to hunt them.[9] From this humble beginning, it has evolved into a regal activity in both England and America. The sport requires large tracts of land (or local landowners willing to allow the hunt to ride over their land), access to a pack of foxhounds (as few maintain their private pack), a master of the hounds to control them, and at least one fox. It is an ordeal of character and risk taking, and one of some grandeur. The riders dress gaily in riding britches, red jackets, riding boots, and caps. They arrive in the early morning, whiskey flasks handy; like the whiskey, the hunt is said to get "into the blood . . . and mind of [the riders] and contribute greatly to [their] well-being and happiness."[10]

For many Club members, fox hunting does seem to be in the blood. They grew up with it. John William Y. Martin, Jr., whose grandfather owned real estate in Chicago's Loop, grew up on his father's Baltimore County estate on which the Maryland Hunt Cup

Race was annually held. He is one among many Jockey Club members with such experiences in their backgrounds.

The social world of the 1930s and 1940s was dominated for these families by "hunts pursued through woods delightfully untouched except for the paths themselves, or across rolling meadowlands."[11] An entire section of the *New York Times* was dedicated to "society," and the fox-hunting crowd were the celebrities of the day. As a man close to them said, "They were the Marilyn Monroes, Clark Gables, and Cary Grants of that period"—they got that much national attention. They had dozens of servants, including butlers who stood in uniform at each end of the dining table, and they displayed farm animals, such as sheep, so as to create the image of a pastoral life-style, reminiscent of life in England before the growth of the middle class.

Several Club members—men and women—have been masters of the foxhounds, some of them playing this role at a most prestigious club on Long Island, the Meadow Brook Hunt Club. James Greene, son of the president of Western Union Telegraph, was a founder of the club. Thomas Hitchcock II and his brother Francis R. Hitchcock were both master of the hounds there. They were the sons of the *New York Sun* major stockholder, Thomas Hitchcock I, a descendant of Mathias Hitchcock, a London immigrant to Massachusetts in 1636. Thomas Hitchcock II hunted three days a week when he was in England preparing to attend Oxford. As a matter of course, he took a pack of his foxhounds along on his honeymoon. The brothers reserved some 8,000 acres of their land in Aiken, South Carolina, for the sport.[12]

Other Jockey Club families lived in the hunt country of New Jersey. There the land itself, the hunt, and the customary elaborate dinner parties that accompany it comprised the center of the aristocrats' world and of their social life in general. Anderson Fowler, the Brady brothers—Nicholas F. II and James Cox III—Reeve Schley II, and F. S. von Stade spent much of their lives in the Far Hills area. This part of New Jersey, about an hour outside Manhattan, was apparently settled by individuals who moved there specifically for the sport. It was customary for each family to own, at the least, an apartment in Manhattan and a country estate of several hundred to a thousand acres.

Now, developers have bought much of the old fox-hunt land,

corporate headquarters like that of Equitable Finance dot the countryside, and family farms are less likely to cover hundreds of acres. As one Club member told me, "The family [once] had three hundred acres. I sold most of it. . . . All the places where I used to . . . fox hunt are developments now."

Anderson Fowler, a Club member until his death in 1997, grew up with horses, rode the amateur circuit, and was master of the hounds for several years before he fought in World War II. His father was so involved in the sport that, following his graduation from Columbia University, he wrote poetry about it. Later, while in the coke and pig iron business in New York City, his father moved the family to New Jersey to ensure regular access to fox hunt country. In his eighties, Anderson Fowler was still riding, although then, he told me, it was to shoot quail in Georgia.

As challenging astride as fox hunting is, it is polo, considered by some to be "the most difficult game on earth," that requires "the horsemanship of a Genghis Khan, the anticipatory sense of a jockey, and the hand-eye coordination of a pool shark."[13] Jockey Club members of the older generation were likely to have played polo with family members, as well as to have played in national and international competition. Many played polo during their days at Yale, as they were quick to tell me.

The golden days of polo spanned the 1920s and 1930s, a time when sports in general were generating greater and greater media attention. A number of Club members were gentlemen players, among them Albert Carlton Bostwick and his brother George Herbert (Pete) Bostwick, descendants of Rockefeller Standard Oil associate Jabez A. Bostwick. Pete, who remained true to the sport all his life, died at age seventy-two in the middle of a game.

Probably the most well regarded polo player among the Jockey Club families was Thomas (Tommy) Hitchcock III, whose father had led the American team in the first international polo match in the United States.[14] It was Tommy, though, who became a polo legend. Some who follow the sport claim that no American ever played better. His teammates included Club members William Averell Harriman and William Jackson. Harriman, a distinguished rower at Yale before he took to diplomacy, was said to worship Tommy. Jackson told the story of how Tommy once saved him after causing his horse to fall—Tommy literally pulled Jackson back into the saddle with one hand while he hit a difficult shot with the other.[15]

Descendants of W. C. Whitney also proved themselves on the polo field. Payne Whitney built his own polo grounds. John Hay (Jock) Whitney made a name for himself in the sport. After his days at Yale, Jock captained the Greentree polo team, which he had named after the family's racing stable. Pete Bostwick and Tommy Hitchcock also played for Greentree. After the team won the U.S. Open Polo championship in 1933, Jock was pictured in polo attire on the cover of *Time*. He had a reputation as "the most unflaggingly roving back in the history of the sport," which meant that he "often found it intolerable to stick near his goal posts while the other players were wrangling at the other end of the field. . . . In one notable match he tallied seven goals for his team, and [Tommy] Hitchcock, who was expected to do the better part of his side's point-scoring, only six. So exuberant a participant was Whitney that after one victorious match in 1935 he pressed a drink of champagne upon one of Hitchcock's ponies."[16]

These were the years of Whitney's first marriage, to a Philadelphia Main Line horsewoman—he was said to have given her a wedding gift of $1 million. Having inherited from both his father, Payne Whitney, and his bachelor uncle, Oliver Payne, he had the wherewithal to do generally as he pleased. When Jock married for the second time, he chose a daughter of a Boston physician. One of her sisters was the second wife of Bill Paley, the head of CBS for thirty years. While not of the same magnitude, Whitney's own communications empire was substantial—a television station firm, Corinthian Broadcasting, that merged with Dunn and Bradstreet, as well as a private newspaper and magazine company, Whitney Communications Corporation.

Another Club member who played polo during these years was Gerard S. Smith.[17] The star of the Brooklyn Riding and Driving Club, which won the National Open from 1927 through 1929, Smith suffered numerous injuries on the field and often had an anxious physician watching from the sidelines. On the field, at various times, he broke his nose, both collarbones, one shoulder blade, five ribs, his left arm (three times), and his right thumb, right leg, and right ankle. He was known for coming back for more.

Contemporary members of the Jockey Club are less likely than their forebears to have grown up in the hunt country of Long Island, Maryland, or New Jersey or to have been gentlemen polo players.

And some members of the Club have broken the mold and involved themselves, if on the sidelines, with sports not related to horses. Several have owned professional teams. The four who have held ownership in professional baseball teams are Fitz Eugene Dixon, Jr., the Philadelphia Phillies; Daniel Galbreath, the Pittsburgh Pirates; G. Watts Humphrey, Jr., the St. Louis Cardinals; and Jacob Ruppert, Jr., who after failing in his bid for the New York Giants, bought the New York Yankees. Three members have had football interests: Henry Mangurian, Jr., as co-owner of the New England Patriots, and Townsend Bradley Martin and Philip Iselin as owners of the New York Jets. George Strawbridge, Jr., sits on the executive committee of the Buffalo Sabres hockey team. And Josephine Abercrombie is a boxing promoter.

Finally, besides his passion for racing, Alfred Gwynne Vanderbilt II liked to hunt big game. In his sophomore year at Yale, he received the first $5 million of his inheritance—and simply left school. On the ocean liner taking him toward a safari in Africa, he met another hunter, and thus began a friendship with Ernest Hemingway. In Kenya Colony, British East Africa, Vanderbilt killed two elephants and a lion, certainly among the most appropriate members of the animal kingdom to fall to a member of the Jockey Club.[18]

POLITICS AND PUBLIC SERVICE

Politician, cabinet member, and diplomat—members of the Jockey Club, their blood relatives, and their in-laws have served in all these capacities. As a rule, Club members have been Republicans, and often very influential in the party as Republican National Committee chairs as well as major fund raisers. A few have been from political families, among them the Gerrys. (Elbridge Gerry signed the Declaration of Independence and was governor of Massachusetts and James Madison's vice president, but made his fortune in Manhattan farmland located between Fifth Avenue and Broadway.)

Members who have been Democrats have tended to fall at the

conservative end of the party scale. William Astor Chanler, U.S. representative from New York, vehemently ridiculed President Woodrow Wilson's proposals, for example, and Peter Goelet Gerry, U.S. senator from Rhode Island, consistently opposed President Franklin D. Roosevelt's New Deal policies. Under the administration of Bill Clinton, no Jockey Club member held national office, either elected or appointed. Pamela Harriman, the widow of Club member and diplomat William Averell Harriman, was ambassador to France, though.

As U.S. congressmen, those closely associated with the Jockey Club have tended to serve in the House of Representatives and to have represented New York. As members of the cabinet, most have been secretaries and undersecretaries of the treasury and secretaries of the navy. As ambassadors, most have been appointed to England and its colonies, to France, Russia, and the former Soviet Union.

Members of the Jockey Club have in general supported a free market, private investment, and corporate interests; they are typically fiscal conservatives. Thus the expectation that members of the privileged classes should serve the public has often been beneficial to their own business interests. That they might see their own interests as in the best interests of the nation may often have been the case, especially as regards their advice on the nation's fiscal and military policies.

From McKinley to Wilson

When the Jockey Club was founded, the United States was emerging as an imperial power. The nation's capacity to wage war internationally developed considerably under Secretary of the Navy William Collins Whitney and his successor, Benjamin Franklin Tracy.[19] These two members of the Jockey Club were intent on building a major U.S. fleet—one able to compete with European nations in the quest for markets. Tracy's assistant secretary of the navy was the ardent militarist Theodore Roosevelt, a close friend and neighbor of Club members on the North Shore of Long Island. These three men set the stage for the Spanish-American War in 1898.

Others close to the Club were thought to be involved in keeping European nations neutral toward the U.S. action against Spain.[20] John Hay, outgoing ambassador to Great Britain and

Table 3.1 *Jockey Club Members, Relatives, and In-laws in National Office, 1840–1993*

NAME	TERM	SERVICE Congress	SERVICE Executive	SERVICE Diplomatic
John Sanford*	1841–1843	R—D/NY‡		
August Belmont I*	1844–1850			Austria
	1853–1857			Netherlands
Elbridge Gerry*	1849–1851	R—D/ME		
George Eustis	1855–1859	R—AP/LA		
James Buchanan†	1856–1860		Pres.	
Erastus Corning*	1857–1859,	R—D/NY		
	1861–1863			
Francis Kernan*	1863–1865	R—D/NY		
	1875–1881	S—D/NY		
Edwin D. Morgan*	1863–1869	S—R/NY		
John W. Chanler*	1863–1869	R—D/NY		
Stephen Sanford*	1869–1871	R—R/NY		
Henry G. Davis*	1871–1883	S—D/WV		
Stephen B. Elkins†	1873–1877	R—R/WV		
	1891–1893		Sec'y. War	
	1895–1911	S—D/WV		
Henry B. Payne*	1875–1877	R—D/OH		
	1885–1891	S—D/OH		
Thomas Ewing*	1877–1881	R—D/OH		
Levi P. Morton†	1879–1881	R—R/NY		
	1881			France
	1889–1893		Vice Pres.	
James B. Eustis	1876–1879,	S—D/LA		
	1885–1891			
	1893–1897			France
Robert R. Hitt*	1881–1882		Asst. Sec'y. State	
	1882–1906	R—R/IL		
Howell E. Jackson*	1881–1886	S—D/TN		
	1893–1895		Assoc. Justice Supreme Court	
James G. Fair†	1881–1887	S—D/NV		
Johnson N. Camden*	1881–1887,	S—D/WV		
	1893–1895			
Perry Belmont	1881–1888	R—D/NY		
	1888–1889			Spain
William E. Chandler†	1882–1885		Sec'y. Navy	
William C. Whitney	1885–1889		Sec'y. Navy	
Benjamin F. Tracy	1889–1893		Sec'y. Navy	
John Sanford	1889–1893	S—R/NY		
George P. Wetmore	1895–1907,	S—R/RI		
	1908–1913			
Rudolph Kleberg*	1897–1904	S—D/TX		
John Hay†	1897–1898			Great Britain
	1898–1905		Sec'y. State	
William A. Chanler	1899–1901	R—D/NY		
Jacob Ruppert, Jr.	1899–1907	R—D/NY		
O.H.P. Belmont	1901–1903	R—D/NY		

Table 3.1 Continued

NAME	TERM	SERVICE Congress	SERVICE Executive	SERVICE Diplomatic
William Woodward I	1901–1903			Sec'y. Court of St. James
Leslie Combs*	1902–1907			Guatemala
Thomas B. Davis*	1905–1907	R—D/WV		
Herbert Saterlee†	1905–1909		Asst. Sec'y. Navy	
Henry A. du Pont*	1906–1917	S—R/DE		
Simon Guggenheim*	1907–1913	S—R/CO		
R. S. Reynolds Hitt*	1909–1910			Panama
	1911–1913			Guatemala
Davis Elkins*	1911, 1919–1925	S—R/WV		
Peter G. Gerry*	1913–1915	R—D/RI		
	1917–1929, 1935–1947	S—D/RI		
Johnson N. Camden, Jr.	1914–1915	S—D/KY		
Jouett Shouse	1915–1919	R—D/KS		
	1919–1920		Asst. Sec'y. Treasury	
Raymond T. Baker†	1918		Dir. U.S. Mint	
Lawrence C. Phipps*	1919–1931	S—R/CO		
Thomas du Pont*	1921–1922, 1925–1928	S—R/DE		
Ogden L. Mills	1921–1927	R—R/NY		
	1927–1932		Undersec'y. Treasury	
	1932–1933		Sec'y. Treasury	
Andrew W. Mellon*	1921–1932		Sec'y. Treasury	
	1932–1934			Great Britain
Parker Corning	1923–1937	R—D/NY		
Harry F. Guggenheim	1929–1933			Cuba
Charles Adams†	1929–1933		Sec'y. Navy	
Richard Kleberg*	1931–1945	R—D/TX		
John W. Hanes	late 1930s		Undersec'y. Treasury	
Frances P. Bolton*	1940–1964	R—R/OH		
W. Averell Harriman	1943–1946			USSR
	1946			Great Britain
	1946–1948		Sec'y. Commerce	
	1963		Undersec'y. State for Political Affairs	
W. Stuart Symington†	1947–1950		Sec'y. Air Force	
	1953–1976	S—D/MO		
Thruston B. Morton	1947–1953	R—R/KY		
	1957–1968	S—R/KY		
George A. Garrett	1950–1951			Ireland
Prescott Bush†	1952–1962	S—R/CT		

Table 3.1   Continued

NAME	TERM	SERVICE Congress	SERVICE Executive	SERVICE Diplomatic
Harold E. Talbott	1953–1955		Sec'y. Air Force	
George M. Humphrey	1953–1957		Sec'y. Treasury	
Robert M. Guggenheim*	1953			Portugal
Oliver P. Bolton*	1953–1957, 1963–1965	R—R/OH		
John H. Whitney	1957–1961			Great Britain
William P. Rogers	1958–1961		Atty. Gen.	
	1969–1973		Sec'y. State	
Rogers C. B Morton*	1963–1970	R—R/MD		
	1971–1975		Sec'y. Interior	
	1975–1976		Sec'y. Labor	
Raymond R. Guest	1965–1968			Ireland
George Bush*	1967–1971	R—R/TX		
	1981–1989		Vice Pres.	
	1989–1993		Pres.	
Robert Eckhardt*	1967–1981	R—D/TX		
Vincent de Roulet	1969–1971			Jamaica
Pierre S. du Pont IV*	1971–1977	R—R/DE		
Robert Strauss	1977–1979		Trade Rep	
	1991–1993			Russia
John Warner†	1979–1999	S—R/VA		
Nicholas F. Brady II	1982	S—R/NJ		
	1988–1993		Sec'y. Treasury	

*Denotes a relative of a Jockey Club member
†Denotes an in-law of a Jockey Club member
‡R or S in the first position denotes a member of the House of Representatives or the Senate; R or D following the hyphen denotes membership in the Republican or Democratic Party; letters following the slash denote state.

father-in-law of Payne Whitney, apparently facilitated neutrality on the part of the British. In the same way, James Biddle Eustis, outgoing ambassador to France and the uncle of two Club members, reportedly helped keep France from interfering with U.S. actions.

Before war was declared, though, the public and the business community had to be convinced that such a move would serve their best interests. New York businessmen, for example, had substantial investments to protect in Cuba. The most influential Wall Street financier, J. P. Morgan, whose firm had become a fiscal agent for the allied governments, thought negotiation with Spain would be ineffectual. The City's yellow journalists reported horror stories about young Cuban women being accosted by Spanish soldiers. So it was that cabinet members, Wall Street, and the press agreed that the country should go to war against Spain.

American forces were victorious in what Theodore Roosevelt, then assistant secretary of the navy, called this "splendid little war." In the charge up San Juan Hill, Club member Craig Wharton Wadsworth was among Roosevelt's Rough Riders, an all-volunteer group of cowboys, miners, and Eastern dandies. So successful was the war, for the United States, and so instrumental in its success was Theodore Roosevelt, that he rose in little more than four years from president of New York City's Board of Police Commissioners to the nation's presidency.

Of the eighteen multimillionaires in Congress at the beginning of the twentieth century, six were Club members and another seven were their relatives or in-laws (see table 3.1). Theodore Roosevelt, their close friend, was in the White House.

The politics of the early twentieth century are nearly impossible to separate from Wall Street, itself dominated by members of the Jockey Club.[21] The New York Stock Exchange was comprised almost exclusively of banking institutions and their representatives. The dominant bankers were August Belmont II and J. P. Morgan and the head of the First National Bank of New York, George F. Baker (whose daughter and granddaughter married Club members). Morgan was undoubtedly the single most powerful member of the Jockey Club over time in terms of economic clout. By a recent measure of wealth that evaluates it in proportion to the gross national product of its era, Morgan emerges as the fifteenth richest individual of the twentieth century—the highest ranked of any member of the Club.[22]

In the century's first decade, the Pujo Committee of the House of Representatives determined that Morgan, Baker, and the Rockefeller-dominated Chase Bank held a near monopoly on the nation's purse strings. The control had been effected through the bank partners' directorships in other financial institutions, insurance companies, transportation systems, and public utility corporations. J. P. Morgan died in 1913, the year after the committee's findings, and the Federal Reserve system was created. Not until Franklin Roosevelt's administration, after the stock market crash, were regulations enacted to prevent such power from falling into the hands of individual bankers. In the 1930s, bankers were no longer allowed to hold seats on the Stock Exchange, and banks, financial institutions, and insurance companies were to remain separate entities.

World War I was profitable for the descendants of the robber barons, who at the time owned the factories as well as the raw materials. A prime example is the du Pont family, whose ability to amass profits during wartime is well known.[23] Soon after Pierre Samuel du Pont de Nemours came to America from France in the early 1800s, he got involved in making gunpowder near Wilmington, Delaware. By the beginning of the twentieth century, the du Pont empire, then comprising one hundred corporations, made all the military powders and three-quarters of all explosives used in the nation. By World War I, it supplied nearly half the explosives for the Allied forces.

The Jockey Club too sought to profit from the war. It had maintained a breeding bureau for some time and was interested in having the government purchase its horses for the military. In 1917, Senator Key Pittman from Nevada sponsored a bill for the government's purchase of stallions. He had ties in racing circles in a rather roundabout way: He was a close friend of the director of the U.S. Mint, Raymond T. Baker, who had just married the widow of Alfred G. Vanderbilt I.[24]

President Woodrow Wilson's War Industries Board, headed by Bernard Baruch, awarded government contracts to private industries for needed war materiel. The largest industries, including Meyer Guggenheim's American Smelting and Refining Company and Andrew Mellon's Aluminum Company of America, were often the recipients of the War Industries Board's most lucrative contracts. The Whitneys had substantial investments in American Smelting, and Harry Payne Whitney was himself director of one of its subsidiaries. Wilson appointed future Club member Richard Howe to the nation's Aircraft Board, and the president's personal physician was Club member Cary Travers Grayson. According to Baruch, Grayson was confidant and companion to the president, as well as his naval advisor, for the last few years of his administration.[25]

From Harding to Truman

Jockey Club members continued to be part of the political scene when the war ended. Warren G. Harding's cabinet has been called the oil administration because the president made three cabinet appointments with ties to the oil industry.[26] The Supreme Court had broken the monopoly of Standard Oil, and Jockey Club members held stock in a number of oil companies. Recall that Vanderbilts, Paynes, and Bostwicks were partners with Rockefeller in the original Standard Oil Trust. Harding appointed a Standard Oil attorney as secretary of state and a Sinclair Oil attorney as postmaster general. Harry Sinclair, president of Sinclair Oil, and a regular with Club members at the track, bribed the secretary of the interior to give his company a lease on the navy's rich oil reserves in Teapot Dome, Wyoming. The bribe was for half a million dollars and some prize animals, including a fine thoroughbred horse. Sinclair was subsequently jailed for a few months for contempt.

Harding appointed another oil magnate as secretary of the treasury, Andrew W. Mellon, the father of future Club member Paul Mellon.[27] Andrew Mellon owned Gulf Oil, Standard Oil's major competitor, as well as Alcoa Aluminum Company. Following in his own father's footsteps, he founded Mellon National Bank with his brother, Richard B. Mellon. Though both were active in the family companies, Richard was also given to fox hunting on his 18,000-acre Rolling Rock Estate, near Pittsburgh. Paul Mellon would inherit his uncle's interest in horses and the hunt and become a member of both America's and England's Jockey Clubs.

At the time of his cabinet appointment, Andrew Mellon was second only to John D. Rockefeller in power, wealth, and influence in the nation. He reportedly resigned from the boards of fifty-one corporations to avoid conflicts of interest. Yet Mellon had a very low profile with the general public. Few knew that he was worth between $1 billion and $2 billion or that Congress had investigated possible price fixing and price controls by his companies in their supply of aluminum during World War I.

As secretary of the treasury under Harding, and later under presidents Calvin Coolidge and Herbert Hoover, Mellon supported the interests of the rich. When he asked Congress to reduce surtaxes on those earning a million dollars, it did—reducing them by 50 percent. When he asked Congress to repeal corporate taxes, it did.[28] These actions were part of a political climate supportive of the rich, a climate that is held to have contributed to the Great Depression. (Before the 1929 stock market crash, the richest 1 percent of the U.S. population owned nearly 60 percent of its wealth.) Also during the Hoover administration, Club member Ogden Livingston Mills was undersecretary of the treasury, and a man who would come into the Club in later years, Harry F. Guggenheim, was ambassador to Cuba.

In the last years of his life, Andrew Mellon was charged with tax fraud for allegedly manipulating millions of dollars to appear as losses and concealing taxable income—dividends of $4 million and $90 million in stock profits in 1929 alone. The charges were dropped at his death in 1937.

On balance, those associated with the Jockey Club were less likely to hold national office during the Franklin D. Roosevelt administration than during earlier ones, although some were cabinet appointees and some were influential on the national and international scenes. Mills moved up to secretary of the treasury, though only for one year. Jouett Shouse, former Democratic congressman from Kansas, aligned himself with Pierre du Pont to oppose Roosevelt's programs.[29] With du Pont's direction and endorsement, he headed the Association against the Prohibition Amendment and became president of the American Liberty League, an isolationist group that opposed Roosevelt's social programs. While this alignment with du Pont signaled the end of Shouse's association with the Democrats, it may have facilitated his entry into the Jockey Club in 1956.

During the late 1930s, John W. Hanes was undersecretary of the treasury and a member of the newly formed Securities and Exchange Commission. With an inherited fortune in North Carolina textiles, Hanes had been a director in Cornelius Vanderbilt Whitney's Pan American Airways, then the foremost foreign airline in the country. He was also a director in the Harriman-dominated Aviation Corporation.[30] Hanes's prior associations, like Shouse's, may have stood him in good stead in the early 1950s when the Club was considering him for admission.

The Jockey Club's best-known diplomat, William Averell Harriman, began his career under Franklin D. Roosevelt. He was the son of railroad baron Edward Henry Harriman.[31] As was customary for a son of society, William Averell Harriman played polo, attended Yale—where he was a member of the prestigious fraternity Skull and Bones—and rose to head his father's company. He also launched his own investment firm, W. A. Harriman and Company, and appointed as president Club member George Herbert Walker. The company later merged with Brown Brothers to become the investment banking firm of Brown Brothers, Harriman, and Company. Unlike many of his social set, though, Harriman changed his political affiliation to Democrat.

W. Averell Harriman's first diplomatic appointment was as ambassador to the Soviet Union. It is likely that his background prepared him for the demands of diplomatic office. Spanning four presidencies, the length of his service is testimony, at least in part, to this factor.

His was a career directed largely toward managing relations with the Soviet Union. Before heading the embassy in Moscow, Harriman had negotiated for mineral concessions with the USSR and headed the Lend-Lease Program that sent needed supplies to that country. Though he seldom agreed with Soviet premier Joseph Stalin, Harriman graciously received the premier's gift of two thoroughbreds. After World War II, Harriman grew increasingly convinced that the USSR would move against its neighbors, a view that, some have contended, contributed to the cold war.

Although Harriman had resigned earlier from the Jockey Club, as governor of New York during the 1950s, he apparently had some difficulty disregarding the Club's interests. His firm was headed by a Club member, his sister had married another Club member, and his second wife was an ex-wife of still another, C. V. Whitney. It is not surprising then that Governor Harriman supported the Club's plan to reorganize racing in the state and that he further mandated a certain number of racing days each year for Saratoga Racecourse.[32]

Others with ties to racing were involved in the political scene during the years of World War II. Thomas Moore Bancroft was a member of the War Production Board, and William Stamps Farish II, then head of Standard Oil of New Jersey, was a member of the Petroleum Industry War Council. Still another, Reeve Schley, followed Harriman as head of the Lend-Lease Program.[33] Schley was then vice president of Chase National Bank—when there was only one vice president. Chase had been a leader in the Soviet credit business for many years, and had established a close connection with the Soviet government in the 1920s and 1930s. Schley had

also headed the American-Russian Chamber of Commerce, representing mercantile, as well as banking, interests.

Immediately after the war, Schley became vice president of
Monmouth Park. On one of his several trips abroad, it was reported, he had seen a type of racetrack box in which individuals
could dine in privacy. He brought the design for that box to the
Monmouth track. A childhood friend of several Club members,
Schley came into the Club in the 1950s. (His granddaughter, Christine Todd Whitman, rose to political prominence in the 1990s as
governor of New Jersey.)

The Eisenhower Administration

In the decade following World War II, Club members gained influence on the national political scene. The public was then increasingly concerned with Communism and the threat of enemies
within. U.S. Senator Joseph McCarthy, a Wisconsin Republican,
raised the specter of Communism as an omnipresent threat and
headed investigations, telecast nationwide, of individuals accused
of un-American activities.

Given this climate, it is not surprising that World War II general Dwight D. Eisenhower would be elected president. Eisenhower
was closely tied to members of the Jockey Club. He golfed and va-
cationed with them, and they paid the expenses on his farm while
he was in the White House.[34] Treasurer of the National Citizens for
Eisenhower was George Morris Cheston, Club member and the
husband of a General Motors heir. The president's regular golfing
companion was Club member W. Alton Jones, president of Cities
Service Company and one of the three independent oil men who
financed Eisenhower's Gettysburg farm during his eight-year administration. Eisenhower was especially fond of John Hay Whitney, whom he appointed ambassador to Great Britain. Later, he
several times urged Whitney, who took the president quail hunting
in Georgia, to run for political office, once for governor of New
York, and later for mayor of New York City. Whitney had little taste
for politics, though, and declined to be a candidate in either race.

Eisenhower also appointed two members of the Club to his
cabinet. One was George Macoffin Humphrey as secretary of the
treasury.[35] Humphrey had headed M. A. Hanna, a major iron-ore
shipper during World War II. He was himself a partner in the Na-

tional Steel Corporation and on the board of directors of Texaco (along with Club member Ogden Phipps). One story suggests how deeply engrained were Humphrey's conservative policies: The word was that he would have been inclined to dismiss his own grandmother, if she were not performing satisfactorily—though he would provide her with a pension. When he served on the National Security Council, he advocated the use of nuclear weapons, apparently on the grounds that they were less expensive than conventional ones.

The president's second cabinet member from the ranks of the Jockey Club was Harold Elstner Talbott, appointed to serve as secretary of the air force.[36] With money made initially in construction, the Talbott family and other Dayton businessmen established Dayton Wright Aeroplane Company, then among the thirty companies that comprised the Dow Jones industrials. Dayton Wright had been the largest producer of military aircraft in World War I—it had also been investigated for overcharging the government for wartime contracts. As a cabinet member, Talbott was required to divest himself of stocks that might compromise his decision making. A Senate subcommittee under Robert Kennedy disclosed that Talbott had solicited business for a company of which he was a co-owner. He had also secured new government contracts for Avco Manufacturing Company and Olin Industries, both firms in the hands of Club families. In light of the Senate investigation, Talbott resigned from Eisenhower's cabinet.

President Eisenhower again drew from racing circles when he appointed C. Douglas Dillon as ambassador to France. Dillon was senior partner in the investment banking firm of Dillon, Read, and Company, founded by his father, Clarence Dillon. Clarence Dillon had raced horses with Club member J. P. Morgan and had written a personal check for $146 million when he bought Dodge Brothers Auto.[37] C. Douglas Dillon, a member of the Council on Foreign Relations, the Committee for Economic Development, and the Business Council, was later appointed secretary of the treasury under Democratic presidents John F. Kennedy and Lyndon B. Johnson. Both Kennedy and Johnson received the financial support of Club member Charles William Englehard, in whose home Johnson was a guest.

Late Twentieth-Century Administrations

Those close to the Jockey Club continued their national political presence under Republican presidents. John Hay Whitney contributed $31,000 to the presidential campaign of Richard M. Nixon. Nixon appointed William P. Rogers, who had been Eisenhower's attorney general, as secretary of state. Rogers was later admitted to the Club and, in the early 1990s, chaired the U.S. Olympics Committee's Ethics Oversight Committee. Nixon also appointed the brother of a Club member as secretary of the interior. He was Rogers C. B. Morton, the brother of Thruston B. Morton, U.S. senator and board chairman of Churchill Downs. Nixon's successor, Gerald Ford, kept Rogers Morton in his cabinet, first as secretary of the interior and then as secretary of labor. Both Morton brothers chaired the Republican National Committee.

An exception to the mostly Republican Club members in public service—in addition to William Averell Harriman—is Robert S. Strauss, a Democratic Party chairman. Strauss, as an emeritus politician and well-regarded political advisor, is difficult to pigeonhole. Trained as a lawyer, he has been a special agent for the FBI and an associate of the Brookings Institute, a Washington-based organization for policy studies. Under Democrat Jimmy Carter, he served as special trade negotiator. Under Republican George Bush, he was ambassador to Russia. In the late 1990s, Strauss gained some notoriety simply because his Houston law partner was Vernon Jordan, who as a friend of President Clinton tried to obtain a position for former White House intern Monica Lewinsky.

Those in the Jockey Club also had some association with President Ronald Reagan. Late in Reagan's administration, second-generation Club member Nicholas F. Brady II was appointed treasury secretary. On the personal side, another Club member was said to regularly ride for pleasure with a group that included Reagan.

Former president George H. W. (Herbert Walker) Bush may be the chief administrator with the closest familial ties to the Jockey Club. His maternal grandfather, for whom he was named, was St. Louis banker and Jockey Club member George Herbert Walker. His father was Prescott Sheldon Bush, the son of a steel manufacturer who, following his graduation from Yale, married Walker's daughter.[38] His grandfather and father were both associated with William Averell Harriman's financial firm of H. A. Harriman and Company as president and vice president, respectively. Bush's father also raced thoroughbreds with Harriman.

Over the years, former president Bush has been close to another Texas oil family with ties to the Jockey Club—that of William Stamps Farish II. Farish was an independent oilman who went from head of Humble Oil to chairman of Standard Oil of New Jersey, at which time he was admitted to the Club.[39] William Stamps Farish III became a close friend of President Bush and was made trustee of the Bush Archival Library. The Farish family trust handles a blind trust belonging to George Bush as well as Farish money.

When George Bush was the nation's chief executive, he continued the cabinet appointment of Nicholas Frederick Brady II as secretary of the treasury. Brady was a great-grandson of utilities baron Anthony Nicholas Brady I.[40] With little education, huge ambition, and his marriage to a Vermont lawyer, Anthony N. Brady I went from owning tea stores in Albany to granite quarries and gas plants in Connecticut and New York and to street railways in New York City. In the latter venture, he was an associate of W. C. Whitney and Thomas Fortune Ryan in the city's transit system. At his death in 1913, Brady had sole control of Brooklyn Edison Company, the New York Edison Company, and the Brooklyn Rapid Transit Company; he was worth $50 million. His grandson, James Cox Brady II, became a member of the Club in 1939.

Nicholas F. Brady II was admitted to the Club in 1966, at about the same time that he occupied the presidency of Dillon, Read, and Company. August Belmont IV had just stepped down from the board chairmanship of the investment banking firm. (This was at the same time that the company's senior partner, C. Douglas Dillon, was treasury secretary.)

Brady in 1982 was appointed to fill out the vacated congressional seat of a U.S. senator convicted of accepting bribes from Arab sheiks. In 1988, Brady became secretary of the treasury. Among his proposals in that office was a major reform in U.S. banking that would allow financial firms to enter the banking business. Perhaps to avoid apparent conflict of interest, Brady resigned from the Jockey Club at the time. In this, he distinguished himself from Club members Ogden L. Mills and George M. Humphrey, who remained Club members during their terms as treasury secretaries.

PHILANTHROPY

The phrase "noblesse oblige" suggests that those of high birth are obliged to be honorable, responsible—and generous. The members of the Jockey Club, as members of the U.S. aristocracy, might be expected to have a tradition not only of public service, but of philanthropy. And such is the case.

Among those who bred thoroughbreds, the Harriman family acknowledged their responsibility in this regard. Railroad baron E. H. Harriman said: "Wealth is an obligation. Whatever you have to do with, you should try to improve it." His son, Club member Averell Harriman, in similar fashion said that "it is as indefensible for a man who has capital not to apply himself to using it in a way that will be of most benefit for the country as it is for a laborer to refuse to work."[41]

By virtue of the circumstances of their birth, members of the Jockey Club have felt obliged to make gifts to benefit society. Like others of their social set, their gifts have taken the form largely of philanthropy rather than charity, that is, to promote human welfare rather than to directly relieve the plight of the needy and suffering. They give to activities and organizations associated with the privileged classes as opposed to those connected with the masses and the poor. They have chosen to found and endow, for example, art museums, libraries, and foundations. Their pattern of giving defines who they are and binds them together as a special class.[42] For some, philanthropy may be a means of retaining respectability in light of bad publicity or merely a vehicle for sheltering wealth.

The Arts and Education

As early as the 1850s, there was a sense in the United States that wealth carried with it a mandate to contribute to the building of cultural and civic institutions, such as museums, universities, and libraries. But the New York nouveau riche of the day were less inclined in this direction than their counterparts in Philadelphia, Charleston, and Boston. By the turn of the century, however, J. P. Morgan, the Whitneys, the Schiffs, and the Guggenheims, among others of their set, had contributed so substantially to New York City's cultural institutions that they ranked among the premier such establishments in the country.[43] These included the Metropolitan Museum of Art, the Metropolitan Opera Company, the New York Public Library, and the Cathedral of St. John the Divine.

Yet a preoccupation with art had manifested itself among Jockey Club families during the Gilded Age, partly because new-money industrialists were seeking social status through owning art treasures of the Old World. The group had some legitimate claim to the art world, though, at least by kinship: The sister of Club founder Alexander Cassatt was Mary Cassatt, the only American admitted to the core group of French impressionists.

As W. C. Whitney, J. P. Morgan, William Henry Vanderbilt, and Peter Arnell Brown (P.A.B.) Widener I bid against one another for the riches of Europe, they "began to fill their own castles with the loot and plunder of the ages; and the paintings, the tapestry, [and] the china . . . began to flow as in a torrent to the western shores of the Atlantic [assuming] proportions both huge and grotesque." When these private collectors died, their descendants established museums to house the art they had amassed. (At a recent auction at Sotheby's in Manhattan, impressionist art from the collection of Club members John Hay Whitney and his wife, Betsey, brought sums far in excess of those estimated by experts.[44] The new-money bidders may have had motivations similar to those of the robber barons.)

Jockey Club families have founded some of the finest and best-known private art museums in the world. The Whitney Museum of American Art in New York City owes its origins to Gertrude Van-derbilt Whitney, a sculptor in her own right, as well as a grand-daughter of Commodore Vanderbilt and wife of Harry Payne Whitney. The funds for establishing the National Gallery of Art in Washington, D.C., came from the estate of Andrew Mellon; the art collection with which it began had belonged to P.A.B. Widener I. Then the largest private collection in the United States, it was do-nated by Widener's son, Joseph E. Widener. (His failure to give his father's collection to Philadelphia has been attributed to the less than gracious treatment Wideners received at the hands of Main Line Philadelphia society.)[45] In recent years, the National Gallery has displayed the private collection of Club member Robert E. Meyerhoff. The Corcoran Gallery of Art in Washington, D.C., be-gan with a donation from the estate of William Corcoran, banker and associate of Lehman Brothers. The gallery's first director was

Corcoran's maternal grandson, Club member William Corcoran Eustis. Guggenheim family donations have also flowed into their art museums in New York City, as well as around the world. Club member Francis A. Kernan founded the city's Lincoln Center for the Performing Arts.

Club members have also invested in less well known cultural institutions. Near the turn of the century, for example, Harry Payne Whitney opened the New Theater, an alternative, noncommercial theater in New York City.[46] His partner in the venture was Otto Kahn, executive of Kuhn, Loeb, and Company, owner of the nation's second largest private estate, and father-in-law of Club member John Barry Ryan, Jr. But the theater productions were not well attended, and even reducing admission in 1910 to a dime for residents of New York's Lower East Side could not save Whitney and Kahn's investment.

Club members and their families have also been prominent donors to elite educational institutions. J. P. Morgan was a major supporter of the Groton School. Alexander Smith Cochran left a quarter of a million dollars to St. Paul's School. The Sages gave to both Cornell and Yale. The Pratts founded Pratt Institute. Marshall Field I donated the land for the University of Chicago. The Widener family dedicated Harvard's Widener Library, among the world's five greatest libraries, to George D. Widener I, who died on the *Titanic*. The Widener family allowed its name to be used at a former military college near Philadelphia—now Widener University—where the nephew of George D. Widener II, Jockey Club member Fitz Eugene Dixon, Jr., has been board chair. William Arnold Hanger's gifts to the University of Kentucky enabled it to establish a medical school. The Mellons have given to Carnegie-Mellon University. John M. Olin made substantial contributions to Washington University in St. Louis. Jesse Mack Robinson gave $10 million to build Georgia State University's College of Business Administration.

Another contributor to Harvard was Club member Charles William Englehard. He was a precious-metals executive and international financier with companies in Johannesburg, South Africa.[47] He was also credited with providing the inspiration for Ian Fleming's villain in his novel *Goldfinger*, but it was his support of South Africa's apartheid regime for which his name was removed from a Harvard library.

Commodore Vanderbilt gave to the university that bears his name, though largely in response to the urging of his second wife. She was a distant cousin forty-three years his junior, and she persuaded him to give no less than half a million dollars to help her friend, a Methodist bishop, establish a university in Nashville, Tennessee.[48] This was the Commodore's single recorded act of philanthropy. While subsequent Vanderbilts have been similarly inclined in their giving, they have apparently not been hypocritical and have earned a reputation for spending their money on themselves "without recourse to the sanctimonious attitudes implicit in vast charities and in family foundations devoted to good works."[49]

Foundations

It has become customary for the wealthy to set up trusts and foundations to handle and protect family fortunes from estate and gift taxes and to channel some portion of them to causes that they deem worthy or in their own economic interest.[50] Philanthropic foundations in the United States currently number in the tens of thousands. Among the largest one thousand operating today are at least forty-three associated with at least fifty-three Jockey Club members who have been founders, board trustees, and major donors. (Some Club-associated foundations no longer exist, such as the one set up by John Hay Whitney after World War II to foster knowledge that promised to improve social welfare.)

Club members are associated almost exclusively with foundations that fund a range of issues of some status, mainly higher education, high culture, and medical research. That is, members of the Jockey Club, like others of their social set, most often give to causes associated with privilege. Some of the members' large foundations have the potential to exert tremendous influence on public policy.

Few of their foundations focus on specific issues or are directed toward human and social service concerns. In the last category, two foundations are especially noteworthy—the McKnight Foundation and the traditionally liberal David and Florence Gugggenheim Foundation. In general, Club-associated foundations limit grants to specific geographic regions and to organizations—often those that its board members have preselected. The only foundations that award grants to individuals are the four that were established to aid those who have worked in the racing industry (see chapter 6).

The Club-associated foundations vary considerably in size. Four rank among the nation's one hundred largest by assets: the Andrew W. Mellon Foundation (eleventh) with more than $3 billion; and the McKnight Foundation (twentieth), the W. M. Keck Foundation (twenty-sixth), and the John J. and James L. Knight Foundation (thirty-fourth)—each with more than $1 billion. Another four foundations have assets that range from $100 million to $370 million. Most are considerably smaller, with average assets of between $8 million and $9 million.

To maintain their tax-exempt status, charitable foundations must by law donate 5 percent of their principal, and recent studies have concluded that their "giving could actually rise to 8 percent . . . without reducing the value of foundation assets." Club-associated foundations vary considerably in the percentage they give—they average 8 percent. Nearly one quarter of the foundations donate more than 10 percent, including the Dreyfus Charitable Foundation (39 percent), supporting research on the drug Phenytoin; the Whitney Foundation (23 percent), supporting research on AIDS and substance abuse; the Duchossois Foundation, a company foundation (17 percent), on arts and AIDS; and the John M. Olin Foundation (17 percent), on institutions supporting the government and free enterprise. (The Olin Foundation, regarded as highly conservative and recently headed by former treasury secretary William E. Simon, has been a major contributor to the Heritage Foundation and the Center for Strategic and International Studies.)[51] The remaining three-quarters of the foundations give on average the required 5 percent, with the four foundations highest ranked by assets donating less.

Foundations that give away fewer of their assets generally stay in business longer than those that give away more. One foundation that did not observe this practice and so had a relatively short life was that of Club member Marshall Field III. Field was regarded as a traitor to his set, in large part because of his liberal politics.

The Marshall Fields and the Field Foundation

Marshall Field I was the nineteenth-century "merchant of merchants."[52] He started out as a Philadelphia dry-goods store clerk and went to Chicago where he built Field's, the world's largest department store. It became his custom to buy out his partners until he was the sole owner. Though regarded as frugal, Field had Richard Morris Hunt design his palace, the first residence in Chicago to have electric lights. In 1905, by which time he was the largest individual taxpayer in the country, his son Marshall Field II died, an apparent suicide.

The death of Marshall Field II was the subject of much speculation. Local scandal sheets said that he was shot by a young woman, possibly a prostitute, in Chicago's Everleigh Club, where he had been a visitor. The family's public statement was that he had died accidentally while cleaning a gun at home. Still, the pistol was regarded as a type nearly impossible to discharge accidentally. Another account was that he had intentionally shot himself—the account said to have been accepted by his son, Marshall III. Marshall Field I died shortly thereafter. Twelve-year-old Marshall Field III inherited both his father's and grandfather's fortunes—$150 million—and became the richest boy in the world.

As an adult, Marshall Field III pursued the lavish life characteristic of his set. He raced thoroughbreds, was admitted to the Jockey Club in 1922, and lived in the largest Long Island estate of the day, valued at $15 million. (It was grander even than Henry Carnegie Phipps's $1 million and Nicholas F. Brady's $2 million estates, as well as the 200-acre estate of Ogden Phipps, with its racetrack, numerous greenhouses, and indoor tennis court.)[53] After extensive psychoanalysis and a third marriage, this time to Ruth Pruyn Phipps, the former wife of Ogden Phipps, Field resigned his directorships in nearly two dozen corporations, founded the liberal newspaper *PM*, and became active in child welfare reform.

He and his wife became involved in Wiltwyck School for Boys, in the 1940s the most progressive program for delinquent youth in the nation.[54] The school was located on land that had passed from John Jacob Astor to Club member Oliver Hazard Payne and finally to his nephew Payne Whitney, also a Club member. In 1933, the property, as part of Whitney's estate, was donated to the Protestant Episcopal Mission Society of New York City, which converted some buildings into a school for the city's disadvantaged black youth. At the time, these youth were not housed by Catholic or Jewish private agencies, which served only children of their respective faiths. In 1942, the school was taken over and reorganized by Eleanor Roosevelt. She founded the modern Wiltwyck, which took in delinquent, as well as neglected, youth. Among the most active of the celebrities and aristocrats who helped in the reorganization and fund raising were Marshall Field III and his wife, and Alfred G. Vanderbilt II, who briefly served on the advisory board.

Wiltwyck applied the most progressive approaches of the day. It forbade corporal punishment, focused on rehabilitation, and housed the boys in cottages, each of which had a counselor and social workers. It was Eleanor Roosevelt's custom on the Fourth of July to entertain the boys at her home in Hyde Park, across the Hudson River from the school. She had the one hundred or so boys from Wiltwyck brought there by bus; fed them hot dogs, baked beans, coleslaw, and ice cream; and then read to them from Rudyard Kipling's *Just So Stories*.

When Marshall Field III set up his own foundation, the Field Foundation, it was to fund liberal causes, including those that dealt with child welfare and social and interracial problems. A civil rights pioneer, the foundation supported racial integration in the South as early as the 1950s. It was later active in describing the effects of the Reagan administration's cuts on programs for the poor. It also parented organizations such as the Children's Defense Fund. In 1989, the Field Foundation was only forty-nine years old and had "spent out" its funds. This was as the foundation's founder would have wished it—and, in the main, apparently counter to the way some Club members choose to operate the foundations with which they are associated.

SOLDIERING, THE ULTIMATE RISK

War, of course, is the ultimate challenge and ordeal. In each generation, Jockey Club members have had at least one war to enlist in, should they choose to. At least four volunteered in the Civil War: Samuel Brown, S. Howland Robbins, Oliver Payne, and William Thompson, a Confederate colonel. At least two Club members—Perry Belmont and Craig Wadsworth—served in the four-month-long Spanish-American War; Wadsworth went up San Juan Hill with Theodore Roosevelt.

Club members of the World War I generation, like many of their fellow Americans, viewed serving in that war as a most honorable endeavor. In the service, they could ride their beloved horses, and they could fly in the Lafayette Escadrille, an all-volunteer squadron funded by members of the elite themselves. As were young men of other social backgrounds, society's sons were eager to join the fight even before the United States officially entered the war in April 1917. Hundreds of young men from St. Paul's School volunteered, and many died.

One volunteer was Tommy Hitchcock, who was just sixteen at the time.[55] Former president Theodore Roosevelt, a Hitchcock family friend, pulled the necessary strings to get him in. The youngest to fly with the Escadrille, Tommy had downed one or two German planes when he was shot down behind enemy lines. After he escaped from a German prison, he walked more than a hundred miles to Switzerland and freedom. Tommy became a hero to his set.

Another St. Paul's alumnus from racing circles who risked his life in that war was Alexander Smith Cochran. Forty years old, he had volunteered to carry dispatches between the U.S. embassies in London and Berlin.[56] His was a short military career, though, as he was arrested on his first trip and spent the night in the guardroom. Subsequently, he donated his steam yacht to the British navy and was commissioned a captain in the Royal Naval Reserve.

Two Club members were captured in caricature, in their uniforms (which apparently they were quite fond of wearing), in a commemorative painting of Saratoga Racecourse, along with several dozen regular race goers waiting in the infield there in August 1917.[57] The two were Captain Perry Belmont, who had also served in the Spanish-American War, and Major Thomas Hitchcock II. Though not in the painting, Captain Edward B. Cassatt, a second-generation Club member, is remembered for having introduced a new style of riding gear for the army, the officer's saddle.

Men of privilege considered service in World War II nearly as important as they did in the Great War, World War I. While they often wanted to ride in the cavalry—as had their fathers in World War I and their grandfathers in the Spanish-American War—the cavalry was disbanded soon after the United States entered the war. Several Club members who were close friends and had fox hunted together enlisted as privates. Anderson Fowler spoke for some of his cohorts when he said, "We enlisted as privates because [as such] we were able to pick which group we would belong to. I picked the cavalry . . . I was in the First Calvary Division, which became an infantry division as they took the horses away." Another Club member who was over the enlistment age received a special dispensation; he too volunteered for the cavalry. When he had to make a change, he elected intelligence service in the O.S.S. When he was dropped behind enemy lines, he wore his cavalry boots.

Tommy Hitchcock, World War I hero and polo player, was too old for World War II service, so he volunteered to test experimental fighter escorts that were not performing well. While flying one of these planes over London in 1944, he was unable to pull out of a dive, crashed, and died.

John Hay Whitney enlisted at the age of thirty-seven and was commissioned a lieutenant colonel. He served as a public relations officer in London. In some unrevealed capacity, he was behind enemy lines in France, where he was captured. While en route by train to prison, he and several others escaped and were rescued by French guerrillas.[58]

Six months after the Japanese bombed Pearl Harbor, and after the navy had received criticism for giving some glamour boys commissions, Alfred G. Vanderbilt II enlisted. To help with recruitment, he made public appearances in uniform. Until then, it had not been his habit even to vote, as he was often racing on Election Day. At first assigned to Washington, he was transferred to a patrol torpedo (PT) base in New Guinea. By 1944, Lieutenant Vanderbilt was a PT boat skipper, and his PT-196 of the Twelfth Torpedo Squadron was shot at by a Japanese shore battery. He was awarded a Silver Star for gallantry. When he returned home, he got his radar man a job keeping the grounds at Belmont Park.[59]

Though considerably older than the usual World War II recruit, Bayard Tuckerman, Jr. (the descendant of a signer of the Declaration of Independence), at fifty-three drove an ambulance in North Africa. At times, he was only slightly ahead of the advance troops of Field Marshal Rommel.

Not surprisingly, the Club recognized military service on the part of others. During the war, it admitted as its first "professional" in racing, West Point graduate and commissioned officer Captain Louie Beard. A veteran of World War I, Beard had become a manager at Keeneland Racecourse, stud farm manager for Harry Payne Whitney, polo player on the Greentree team, and beneficiary of

$50,000 in the will of Whitney's sister.[60] A longtime Club member explained that Beard was a logical choice for the Club because he was "at ease" and could "pass."

At least one Jockey Club member who never bothered much about news happenings outside a racecourse, including the war, was F. Ambrose Clark, grandson of the attorney for Singer Sewing Machine Manufacturing Company. Brose, as he was called, was the uncle of the polo-playing Bostwick brothers. Clark's wife, Florence Stokes, recalled his suggestion that they should bring back their horses from England before shipping was shut down because of the war. "'Why, Brose,' she said, 'how did you know there's a war going on?' 'Read it in *The Blood-Horse*,' Clark replied."[61]

The racetracks of Jockey Club members also played a part in World War II. Generally, racing shut down during the war years, including that at tracks on the West Coast. Santa Anita Park in Arcadia, California, owned by several Club members, served as an "assembly center" for Japanese Americans, beginning in 1942 and before their "relocation" to internment camps for the duration of the war.[62]

Some of the sons of high society did not view the ensuing wars—the Korean conflict and the Vietnam War—as honorable, compared to previous international conflicts. For a few, intelligence service was a viable option for proving character. Some would become CIA officials during the cold war, among them Club member William Harding Jackson, a descendant of the Howell Jacksons of General Motors. He resigned his membership in the Jockey Club in 1950 to become deputy director of the CIA.

4

THE BUSINESS
OF RACING

The business of America may still be business, just as Calvin Coolidge
claimed three-quarters of a century ago, and the business of most
Jockey Club members may even be business, but the business of the
Jockey Club itself has always been, above all else, racing. The Club's
style of doing business, as well as that of its members, reflects their
social set. It is the style of gentlemen, who sometimes have robber
baron roots.

THE EARLY DAYS

In the years before the Jockey Club was founded in 1894, and on
through the Depression of the 1930s, the business people who made
the most money in the United States often did so in ways that today
we consider unethical, immoral, and in some cases illegal. But they
were the rich and powerful of this country, and, then as now, some
in this democracy were more equal than others. Few Jockey Club
members or their forebears have been formally charged with violating the law. Their wrongdoings have been dealt with through ad-
ministrative agencies and congressional investigations more often
than in the criminal courts, even when their offenses have caused
grave social harm.

Examples of wrongdoing, alleged and proven, are plentiful. Though some nineteenth- and early-twentieth-century entrepreneurs were actually indicted, apparently none were convicted.[1] Recall that Congress found that Commodore Vanderbilt committed blackmail and that J. P. Morgan had established a monopoly of the banking system but that tax fraud charges against Andrew Mellon were dropped. W. C. Whitney's New York City transit activities were investigated after his death. His partner Thomas Fortune Ryan admitted there had been considerable stock watering but did not lose his seat on the New York Stock Exchange. Club member Oliver Hazard Payne, treasurer of Standard Oil, was charged with bribery of the Ohio legislature in order to secure his father's 1885 election to the U.S. Senate. The legislature submitted evidence to substantiate the charge, but the Senate refused to act. The uncle and namesake of Club member William Zeigler, the Royal Baking Powder magnate, came under indictment for bribery in Missouri. According to muckraker Lincoln Steffens, Zeigler admitted to a substantial amount of bribery and corruption, though he was incredulous that an activity he regarded as so prevalent should be condemned. E. H. Harriman was indicted by the Interstate Commerce Commission for monopolistic practices with his railroads.

The father of Club member Alfred Hennen Morris, John Albert Morris I, who built Morris Park Racecourse in 1899 in the Bronx, inherited a fortune from his father, Francis Morris, steamship mogul and telegraph partner of Samuel F. B. Morse. J. A. Morris made his own fortune after the Civil War when he gained control of the Louisiana State Lottery.[2] At his death in 1895, there were rumors that his neglect of Morris Park was due to the lottery's having had some legal problems, including mass bribery.

Sometimes the charges stayed inside the family. The father and the uncle of Club member James Cox Brady II were taken to court by their sisters for mishandling the estate of their father, Anthony Nicholas Brady I, a utilities baron and a member of the New York Stock Exchange.[3] In 1923, Brady's daughters alleged that their brothers, Nicholas F. Brady I and James Cox Brady I, had unlawfully and improperly administered their father's estate of $50 million for their personal advantage. The sisters contended that they had lost $8 million as a result, and they asked the court to remove their brothers as trustees and compensate them for the loss.

The inquiry focused on James Cox Brady I, who was vice president of Brooklyn Edison Company, a director of Maxwell Motor, Imperial Tobacco, and Continental Insurance companies, and an owner of other major utility holdings. The specific charges were that he had used funds from the trust to buy shares of companies in which he was a director, to protect personal investments, to purchase securities for himself, to pay for a stock exchange membership for a friend and former classmate at Yale, and to spend extravagantly on office furnishings and staff. To answer all these charges, James Cox Brady I was sometimes on the stand for entire days. He admitted to improper dealings—he had set up dummy accounts for his own stocks, loaned $2.5 million to Maxwell Motor Company when he was its chairman, lost $7 million, and used estate funds for personal purchases.

Certainly, those charged were not always guilty. Club founder Alexander J. Cassatt was falsely arrested on charges of "running a disorderly house"[4]—highly embarrassing for one of his station. According to his biographers, the false arrest followed the complaint of New York City poolroom operators that Cassatt and the other Monmouth Park directors, August Belmont II and Pierre Lorillard, had cut off their telegraph lines. In the battle between track owners and poolroom operators over who would control wagering information, the telegraph was a crucial tool. And of intriguing and more recent note is the story of gold magnate Charles William Englehard's trying to evade international trade restrictions by shipping gold out of South Africa in the form of jewelry and dishes.

Soon after Henry Phipps received $50 million as his share of the sale of Carnegie Steel to U.S. Steel, he set up two family firms to manage his wealth. (Phipps's descendants to the fourth generation have been members of the Jockey Club.) The oldest firm, Bessemer Trust, now the largest trust in private banking, has centralized control over the family money. Current assets are over $7 billion, and minimum portfolios are $5 million and typically more than $12 million. Here is how it has marketed itself to the racing public:

> Bessemer was founded by a captain of industry in 1907. . . . We continue to advise more than 700 families of substantial net worth and their heirs. . . .

Whether you call them magnates, moguls or entrepreneurs, for generations these successful individuals have relied on Bessemer's expertise in managing their total financial needs.[5]

The other family firm, Bessemer Securities Corporation, is a family holding company, with assets that are primarily stocks in other corporations. (Phipps gave each of his five children an equal portion of securities in the firm.) In the 1960s, 40 percent of the assets of Bessemer Securities was in real estate and the rest was in common stocks of International Paper, Mellon National Bank, Ingersoll-Rand, Gulf Oil, and the specialty chemicals company W. R. Grace. The firm—affectionately referred to by family members as "the office"—is comprised of more than six dozen subsidiaries and is overseen by family members, who sit on its board as well as on those of its subsidiaries. Phipps's heirs have no apparent need for cash or credit cards, as they send their bills to the office.

In what seems to be another case of family infighting over money, one of Henry Phipps's grandsons brought an $88 million suit against Bessemer Trust and its trustees in 1960 in New York State Supreme Court.[6] The grandson was Esmond Bradley Martin, first cousin of Jockey Club members Winston and Raymond Guest, Ogden Phipps (then chairman of Bessemer Securities), and Michael Grace Phipps, and the younger brother of Club member Townsend B. Martin. Esmond B. Martin charged Bessemer and its trustees (his relatives) with gross mismanagement and misfeasance, including using their position for their own economic advantage. He asked that the trustees reimburse Bessemer Securities and pay his individual trust more than $8 million in surcharges, that the trustees be removed, and that his $15 million stake in Bessemer Securities be liquidated. For whatever reasons, this case seems to have been totally ignored by New York City's major newspaper, the *New York Times*.

In 1997, according to *The Blood-Horse*, the California Insurance Commission alleged that Club member John C. Mabee's Golden Eagle Insurance Company lacked sufficient cash reserves.[7] The state commission was said to have put the company in receivership and removed Mabee from its management. The two sides apparently abandoned litigation when another company that bid for Golden Eagle set up a trust account, from which Mabee would receive some portion after the company's outstanding claims are settled.

THE RICHARD WHITNEY CASE

Richard Whitney was an exception to the norm among Jockey Club families suspected of breaking the law. In 1938, Whitney, a former president of the New York Stock Exchange and senior partner in his brokerage firm, Richard Whitney and Company, was arrested for theft of his customers' securities.[8] His brother, George, was a partner in the nation's premier banking house, J. P. Morgan and Company. His wife was the daughter of George R. Sheldon, a banker, associate of J. P. Morgan, and Republican National Committee treasurer. Before her marriage to Whitney, she had been the wife of a son of Mrs. W. K. Vanderbilt and her first husband.

Whitney admitted that for seven years, including the years when he presided over the Stock Exchange, he had stolen millions of dollars from his customers' securities (among them, those in trust funds for his wife and for Harvard University); falsified balance sheets to cover his dealings; bankrupted his company, leaving it with more than $7 million in liabilities; and stolen bonds from the New York Yacht Club when he was its treasurer.

The fall of Richard Whitney was high scandal. The *New York Times* covered the story from the day Whitney turned himself in to District Attorney Thomas E. Dewey until a month later, when he was sentenced to Sing Sing. This was swift justice, due in part to the recent passage of the Truth in Securities Act and the establishment of the Securities and Exchange Commission.

With the article reporting Whitney's indictment, the *New York Times* ran a photograph of him, well-dressed and sober, his hair parted in the middle. The story ran alongside: "Inside the station house [on New York's East Side] a group of Bowery derelicts arrested on vagrancy and drunkenness charges were herded away from the desk and into the back room while the once powerful Wall Street leader was being booked. . . . Mr. Whitney wore a dark overcoat with a velvet collar and a pearl gray fedora hat, which he removed when he entered the station address."[9]

Bail was set at $10,000, a pittance for one of Whitney's station. Whitney pleaded guilty to two counts of grand larceny for misuse of customers' securities. He made no apology but stated for the record that some of "the securities in my trust had no debit balances, they were free and clear. Without the authority of these customers, I pledged their securities in a demand loan made to me on my personal note. . . . The proceeds of this loan were [then] deposited in my firm."[10]

When Whitney stood before the court, he had much to lose: a townhouse and a five-hundred-acre country estate; a life-style that cost him anywhere from $5,000 to $25,000 a month; servants, the exact number of which he could not recall; and a liquor supply that included 219 fifths of gin, 196 quarts of whiskey, 169 quarts of apple brandy, 114 quarts of champagne, and a few bottles of wine. He was disturbed that those who took inventory were generally uninformed about the quality of his liquor. They listed his oversized bottles of champagne incorrectly and listed bonded Green River bourbon as rye.

Officials also inventoried forty-seven suits, eight pairs of shoes, four pairs of riding boots, and four red coats for fox hunting; Whitney was master of the hounds of the Essex Hunt. He estimated that his livestock, including Ayrshire cattle, Berkshire pigs, and thoroughbreds, would bring $25,000 at auction. While willing to give up his three 1938 Chevrolet sedans, he wanted his wife to keep the Buick limousine that he had surprised her with the year before.[11]

Many people offered explanations for Whitney's theft. Episcopal clergymen appealed to the public to withhold judgment. Psychiatrists labeled Whitney as rather stubborn. A probation officer characterized Whitney as deceptive, deliberate, and compulsive, when he concluded:

> It is . . . apparent that certain personality defects [in Whitney] were contributory elements. . . . Among such was a seeming duplicity in his makeup, best evidenced by the fact that while publicly condemning dishonest brokers, he was betraying a double trust as a reputable broker and a trustee of estates. At no point in the explanation he gives of his offenses is there evidence that in their earlier phases he had considered discontinuing them. From his explanation . . . it is also evident that he is possessed of a strong gambling instinct. Under its compulsion he appears to have continued his malpractices in the expectation of a successful outcome of his commitments.[12]

Explanations aside, Whitney was quickly convicted and sentenced to a period of from five to ten years in prison. Following sentencing, he was handcuffed for the first time. Whitney did not care for the lunch of frankfurters and sauerkraut served as he awaited transport to prison, but that evening, he ate all of his spaghetti with meat sauce. In Sing Sing, as prisoner No. 94,835, he was the object of some respect. His fellow convicts "stepped aside to let him pass in the yard, [raised] their caps in deferential, silent homage," and even lent him bed linen.[13] Whitney's name was removed from the membership roll of the Jockey Club that year, 1938.

Meanwhile, the newly established Securities and Exchange Commission was looking into the case. Joseph Kennedy was the commission's head, but in this instance New York banker John W. Hanes was appointed to be in charge of the case. (Hanes would join the Jockey Club in 1952.) This was not the only high-profile case Hanes was handling. He simplified the huge debt that publishing giant William Hearst presented by reducing Hearst's corporations from ninety-four to twelve and his total debt from $128 million to $4 million.[14]

The investigation of Whitney revealed that others, including fellow Jockey Club members, knew in advance of Whitney's dealings and even aided him with substantial loans. Those who knew included his brother George, his partner Edwin D. Morgan IV, several J. P. Morgan partners, and twenty securities business leaders, including two governors and two ex-governors of the New York Stock Exchange. George loaned him $3 million, and J. P. Morgan and Company loaned him half that. Jockey Club members G. H. Bull, W. Deering Howe, Marshall Field III, and William Clark Langley made smaller contributions.[15]

The Securities and Exchange Commission found that Whitney was doing what was general practice in the securities business. Borrowing from trusts and other securities was so common that brokers felt above accountability for the practice. The president of the Stock Exchange acknowledged that "the free balances of customers are used by brokers 'as a rule in the Street.'"[16] Perhaps most indicative of the extent to which this was accepted were the words of the influential financier J. P. Morgan II. When asked, "Did you give any consideration at all to your responsibilities toward the Exchange in this particular matter?" Morgan answered, "No, none at all." And to emphasize the operating principle, he said, three times, "Every man's money is entirely at [the broker's] disposal."[17]

The Richard Whitney who would have to "doff the double-breasted blue . . . suit of yacht club style [and] get into the gray shoddy" of prison garb was a little fish who happened to get hooked; others of the same ilk stood by unscathed as he was sent up the river, quite literally.[18] While free use of other people's money was common among brokers at the time, no other Wall Street financier was condemned, castigated, or indicted, much less convicted.

Whitney maintained a relatively low profile in prison. Within six months, at about the same time that his East Seventy-third Street house was auctioned for $90,000, he moved to a new cell block. He was visited monthly by his wife, and his old school headmaster, the Reverend Endicott Peabody of Groton, occasionally came to see him. During his first year in prison, the *New York Times* reported on a Sing Sing athletic event: "Wearing gray trousers, a gray sweater and a white shirt, Richard Whitney, former president of the New York Stock Exchange, played first base for the Sing Sing Prison School baseball team today. Guards said he made two hits in three times at bat, fielded well and ran the bases with proficiency."[19]

GENTLEMEN OF THE CLUB

Of some members I interviewed who were relatively new to the Jockey Club, one man expressed his thankfulness that though some members had been aptly described in the past as "stuffed shirts," such was no longer the case. Another new member remarked that at his first meeting with the Club he found members a lot more friendly than he had anticipated. He said that they greeted him and shook his hand in order to make him feel at ease, and that one seemed "humble" in this regard. A third new member described Club members on the whole as generally sincere and well-meaning, even though, according to him, some seemed to have lived in an isolated world for too long a time. In my own experience, Club members were generally approachable and gracious. As a group, they were intense, polite, and reserved.

Some Club members have been famous for exemplifying graciousness. Second-generation member John A. Morris II was described to me as

a wealthy man, but so down-to-earth. He just enjoyed life. [For instance, when he and his wife went to] the [annual] Belmont Ball,
they were [often] the last ones to leave. She had been a very tall
model at one time, [you know, and] the press liked them. I can remember some people from Buenos Aires . . . showed up at Belmont. They spoke very little English. [The man] had bred some very
nice horses. I had met them when I was down there. So, I took
them upstairs to the Trustees' Room [where John Morris and his
wife were. She] started speaking Spanish . . . "We'll be glad to
take you into [New York] City." . . . They were always that way.

In general, Club members, like others of their social set, are expected to maintain a low profile, avoid arguing, and avoid dis-
cussing money—at least not in public, where it is considered in
poor taste. Several people close to the Club described this style, typical of some members, as a "behind-the-scenes" style. It is clear that
maintaining a certain appearance in the public eye is desirable and,
at the same time, that the manner in which business is actually
transacted should be private. It has been customary for many Club
members to conduct business in social clubs, which are closed to
the general public. This has been the case at least since the year the
Club was founded, an era when J. P. Morgan was a member of nine-
teen such clubs and established two himself.[20] The first of these was
the Metropolitan Club, which Morgan founded to accommodate a
friend who had been rejected by the Union Club. In 1870, Morgan
founded a second club—one that has been called the most exclusive of all. It is the Zodiac, which, since its founding, has been limited at any one time to twelve men "of good genes." Of the present
twelve, three are from Jockey Club families—a Phipps, a Heckscher,
and an Iselin.

These social clubs were the settings Morgan chose for conduct-
ing his financial reorganizations of corporations. U.S. Steel was a
case in point. On December 12, 1900, the University Club in New
York City held a private dinner party to honor noted broker
Charles M. Schwab. Schwab invited Andrew Carnegie of Carnegie
Steel to the affair to meet with Morgan. This proved to be Morgan's
most infamous such dealing, with more than a billion dollars in
capital involved in the reorganization. He performed similar reorganizations with AT&T, GE, Consolidated Edison, Standard Brands,
Montgomery Ward, IT&T, American Can, Kennecott Copper, New
York Central Railroad, and General Motors.

But whether at their club, in a boardroom, or in the clubhouse at Saratoga Racecourse, Jockey Club members typically do business in a tradition and with a style that might still fairly be called Ivy League. Although some contemporary members have attended public universities, the favorite alma maters of the Jockey Club have traditionally been Ivy League schools, particularly Yale. Still recognized in the late twentieth century by those considered by some the "right people" as "the most important college, socially," Yale is the traditional school for Vanderbilts and Whitneys.[21] Club members have gone to other Ivy League schools, most notably Princeton, although the Belmonts have customarily gone to Harvard. The exception is O.H.P. Belmont, who attended the U.S. Naval Academy, was dismissed, reinstated, and finally graduated.

Still, a great many Jockey Club members have gone to Yale. It was something they often were expected to do; they shouted the school cheers from the time they were small children. As Yalies, they became members of the college's most prestigious fraternities—Skull and Bones, and Scroll and Key—known affectionately as Bones and Keys.[22] More have been Keys men. Birmingham claims that "of the two, Skull and Bones, . . . is the older and definitely the grander. . . . On the other hand, Scroll and Key, . . . having always, and with such perfect modesty, accepted second place, inevitably emerges occupying a place considerably in front of first. It is a fact that infuriates Skull and Bones, but there is nothing they can do."[23]

RACING GOES BIG BUSINESS

Until the Depression years, Jockey Club tradition held that members should race only for the sport, not for profit. But in 1929, Joseph E. Widener, the Club's vice chairman, and his nephew George D. Widener II appealed to the Federal Tax Board, on behalf of thoroughbred owners, for a change in that status. An observer might have forecast this development based on two factors: recent changes in Club leadership and the timing of the Wideners' appeal.

The man who had led the Jockey Club for nearly thirty years, August Belmont II, had died in 1924. Belmont had also headed New York's first and rather ineffectual racing commission. The

Table 4.1   Jockey Club Members Who Are Yale Alumni, with Fraternity Affiliation

MEMBER	DEGREE/CLASS	FRATERNITY
Oliver Hazard Payne	1863 (nongrad.)	
William Collins Whitney	BA 1863	Skull & Bones
George Peabody Wetmore	BA 1867	Skull & Bones
John Sanford	BA 1872	
Edward S. Moore	Ph.B. 1888	
Harry Payne Whitney	BA 1894	Skull & Bones
Parker Corning	BA 1895	
Henry Williams Sage	BA 1895	
Alexander Smith Cochran	BA 1896	
Andrew G. C. Sage	BA 1897	
Joseph E. Davis	BA 1900	
Crispin Oglebay	BA 1900	Scroll & Key
William F. R. Hitt	BA 1901	
Gifford Alexander Cochran	BA 1903	
William C. Langley	BA 1903	
Reeve Schley	BA 1903	
Walter M. Jeffords	BA 1905	
Harry Frank Guggenheim	1910 (nongrad.)	
William Averell Harriman	BA 1913	Skull & Bones
John W. Hanes	BA 1915	Scroll & Key
Cornelius V. Whitney	BA 1922	
Donald Peabody Ross	BA 1925	Scroll & Key
John M. Schiff	BA 1925	
John Hay Whitney	BA 1926	Scroll & Key
Joseph A. Thomas	BA 1928	Scroll & Key
James Cox Brady II	BA 1929	Scroll & Key
Paul Mellon	BA 1929	Scroll & Key
Thruston B. Morton	BA 1929	
Thomas Mellon Evans	Ph.B. 1931	
Reeve Schley, Jr.	BA 1931	
Raymond Guest	BA 1931	
Michael Grace Phipps	BA 1932	Scroll & Key
Alfred G. Vanderbilt II	1935 (nongrad.)	
William Ewing	BA 1935	
James H. Binger	BA 1938	
Walter M. Jeffords, Jr.	BA 1938	
Kenneth M. Schiffer	BA 1939	
James Butler III	1940 (nongrad.)	
James Gordon Grayson	BA 1940	Skull & Bones
John K. Goodman	BA 1942	
James E. Bassett III	BA 1945	Scroll & Key
Richard L. Gelb	BA 1945	
Wheelock Whitney	BA 1950	
Nicholas F. Brady II	BA 1952	
Edward S. Bonnie	BA 1952	
Baird C. Brittingham	BA 1953	
Donald Peabody Ross, Jr.	BA 1954	
John A. Hettinger	BA 1955	
James Cox Brady, Jr.(III)	BA 1957	Scroll & Key
Richard I. G. Jones	BA 1960	
Ogden Mills Phipps	BA 1963	
G. Watts Humphrey, Jr.	BA 1966	

Club would nonetheless continue to dominate thoroughbred racing. For the next few years, Frank Knight Sturgis, a member of New York City's original Four Hundred and partner in the Wall Street brokerage firm Strong, Sturgis, and Company, headed the Club. In 1930, leadership was turned over to New York banker and member of the Federal Reserve Board William Woodward I; he would hold the position for two decades. A man who referred to himself as a Victorian, Woodward was said to have flicked his cigarette ashes on those sitting in the grandstands at the track.[24] His vice chairman was Joseph E. Widener.

Widener made his appeal to the U.S. Board of Tax Appeals and a U.S. court of appeals within a few months of the stock market crash. Here was an appeal on behalf of the rich when the country was in dire economic straits. Others of Widener's set were also doing well. Club member Warren Wright, for example, whose father had invented Calumet Baking Powder, had sold the patent for $32 million to Postum; the sale made Wright one of the nation's wealthiest individuals at the outset of the Depression.

Joseph E. Widener

Joseph E. Widener, a Jockey Club member from 1901 until 1943, built and owned Hialeah Park in Miami and was the chief stockholder in Belmont Park. His father, Peter Arnell Brown (P.A.B.) Widener I, was of ordinary German descent.[25] The senior Widener had started as a butcher boy in his brother's shop in Philadelphia, gotten a contract to supply meat for Civil War soldiers, and later been appointed city treasurer. In this position, he joined with William Collins Whitney to buy into Philadelphia's transportation system—first into horsecars, then into electric streetcars. In a practice not uncommon for robber barons of their day, they were said to have used bribery, among other tactics, to gain control of the system. Ultimately, Widener owned more than five hundred miles of streetcar tracks in New York, Chicago, Baltimore, Pittsburgh, and Philadelphia. He then diversified, buying into railroads, Standard Oil, U.S. Steel, and American Tobacco. At a stockholders' meeting of a company that he, W. C. Whitney, and Thomas Fortune Ryan controlled, P.A.B. Widener reportedly told the minority stockholders, "You can vote first and discuss afterwards."[26]

Like other self-made men from the poor side of the tracks,

P.A.B. Widener I was snubbed by society. In his case, "society" was Philadelphia's Main Line. He had three sons. The first died as a teen. The second, George D. Widener I, went down with the unsinkable *Titanic* in 1912; as his wife was boarding a lifeboat, he put his emerald ring on her finger. Among the other wealthy passengers who died on the *Titanic*'s celebratory maiden voyage from South Hampton to New York were Astors, Guggenheims, Roeblings, and other Wideners.

P.A.B. Widener's third son was Joseph E. Widener. Like his father, and despite his marriage to a widow of fashionable Philadelphia background, Joseph Widener was apparently never fully accepted by Main Line society. Unlike his father, he preferred horses to art. He sold some of his father's extensive art collection to buy thoroughbreds, to build Hialeah Park, and to invest in Belmont Park. He was the first Widener to become a member of the Jockey Club.

By 1929, when Joseph Widener was the Club's vice chairman, Club members had decided they wanted racing to be treated as a business so that their expenses could be tax deductible. Widener and his nephew George D. Widener II managed to persuade the Federal Tax Board to rule in favor of their appeal. Joseph Widener himself would derive economic benefit from the change, even for the horse cemetery that he laid out on two acres of his Lexington farm that same year.[27]

Two years later, in 1931, Widener threw an enormous party in New York City. This affair was less spectacular than Club member C.K.G. Billings's 1903 feast, at which two dozen tuxedo-clad men dined on horseback at Sherry's Hotel on Fifth Avenue, but Widener's entertainment did feature horses.[28] The guests included New York governor Franklin D. Roosevelt, gunpowder baron William du Pont, Jr., auto mogul Walter F. Chrysler, and police department notables. The ballroom of the Biltmore Hotel was decorated to resemble Widener's Belmont Park, and "as the guests sat dining in the boxes there performed before them prize mounts of the New York City Police Department, of blue-ribbon artillery and cavalry regiments, and of wealthy private owners. The palatial room resounded with the thud of hoofs, neighing of steeds, popping of champagne corks, and laughing chatter."[29] Some historical context sets this party in perspective: Prohibition was still the law, and on

the street corners outside the hotel, some of the multitude of un-
employed were selling apples.

Widener was reputedly generous to his employees as well. One
man I spoke with recounted an occasion on which the multimillionaire gave gifts to the jockeys at his Hialeah Park. The story goes
that it was Widener's custom to use his own money if he wanted
something done immediately, and, in this instance, he wanted the
riders at Hialeah to be attired like those at England's Ascot. He gave
each jockey a box of stock ties and a gold-plated pin from Wanna-
makers department store in Philadelphia. The man concluded the
story, "That's the kind of fellow he was."

The New York Racing Commission

In 1932, Joseph E. Widener, still the Jockey Club's vice chairman,
made an announcement at the New York Turf Writers' Association
dinner that was quoted in the next day's *New York Times*. In typical
gentlemanly style, he said, "In New York we [those with stock in
the New York tracks] have no desire to make money out of racing,
but we do desire to keep it alive."[30] Here was a fine line, the distinc-
tion between writing off racing expenses on one's taxes and making money out of racing. Widener proposed that the legislature
legalize racetrack betting, rather than letting bookmakers continue
to handle bets. He argued that legalizing betting would benefit
New York itself and not the tracks, for the largest share of the pro-
ceeds would go to the state.

New York State was then in dire economic straits. Further, legislators and officials at the state level were concerned about widespread bookmaking and the drugging of horses. Since racing had
resumed in 1912, the state and elite track owners had turned a
blind eye to bookmakers operating illegally on state tracks. (Illegal
betting was reputedly also common at Widener's Hialeah Park. According to the son of a man who worked at the Miami track at the
time, the practice was called racing "on the fix." He explained to
me that, although illegal, the betting was allowed because a track
official paid off the governor.)

The New York legislature did not take Widener's advice—at
least for a few years. Instead, the legislature would legalize bookmaking and set up a racing commission to have general oversight
of the sport. The commission determined that bookmakers had to

be solvent, that inspectors would report on them, and that rules would govern the betting ring. A ringmaster was to supervise them and keep them from altercations that might draw the attention of law enforcement. Still, in 1935, when the district attorney of New York's Nassau County wanted to make an arrest in Belmont Park's betting ring, the commissioners prevailed upon him to issue a statement to the press that he "could find no violation of betting laws."[31]

Even before the three-member racing commission was established, the Jockey Club was successful in having appointed to it men likely to look favorably on Club interests. The governor appointed journalist, society figure, and brother of the president of General Electric Herbert Bayard Swope as chairman, and Club member John Hay Whitney and noted architect and designer John Sloan as the commissioners.

Herbert Bayard Swope had been a theatrical press agent, a Pulitzer Prize–winning World War I correspondent, and executive editor of the *New York World*.[32] His friends were not all members of high society. His colorful life had thrown him into contact with the famous as well as the infamous. He was a lifelong friend of Bernard Baruch, beginning as his speech writer when Baruch was chairman of the War Industries Board during World War I. The term "cold war" and the famous excerpt from Baruch's speech to the United Nations about the atomic bomb—"We are here to make a choice between the quick and the dead"—were actually Swope's words.[33] Swope also had some high-stakes poker buddies. He played regularly in a floating poker game, the Partridge Club, that included oil magnate Harry Sinclair—of the Teapot Dome scandal—and notorious gambler Arnold Rothstein. Swope had been Rothstein's best man when he married a showgirl in Saratoga Springs.

Rothstein was a gambler of considerable repute. In the 1920s, he had opened a club called The Brook at Saratoga, for which he reportedly paid the district attorney $60,000 in protection money.[34] He was suspected of fixing the 1919 World Series. Known also as a "bootleg tycoon," during Prohibition he smuggled liquor into the country and distributed it to various establishments, including several in which he had an interest. He was rumored to have bankrolled and schooled a number of young hoodlums who went on to make unsavory names for themselves, including Frank Costello,

Meyer Lansky, and Lucky Luciano. Lansky's biographer called Rothstein the J. P. Morgan of the underworld and "the first urban criminal to attain . . . the mythic status that America had . . . bestowed on frontier thugs like Jesse James and Billy the Kid."[35]

Rothstein also raced horses at Saratoga and bet on them. This did not please members of the Jockey Club, although they tolerated it until the 1921 Travers Stakes race. Originally only three horses were entered in the Travers—Rothstein's, Harry Payne Whitney's, and one that was later scratched. Rothstein is said to have bet heavily on his horse, which was not favored and had longer odds, because he had learned that Whitney's horse was not in top racing form. Only two horses left the gate, and Rothstein's horse won. Whitney and his friends must have been more than chagrined. The story is told that August Belmont II, head of the Jockey Club and the racing commission, met with Rothstein privately, after which the gambler never again visited the Saratoga track.

Despite Swope's early relationship with Rothstein, his publishing connections and society friends made him a natural for appointment to the New York Racing Commission. Club member John Hay Whitney could certainly be counted on to support the interests of the Club and of other wealthy New Yorkers. And it was likely that the third commissioner, John Sloan, would follow the lead of Swope and Whitney. So even though the legislature gave the racing commission "general supervision . . . of racing in the state of New York," this commission posed little threat to the Club's power.[36]

When the commissioners met weekly, it was in the Belmont clubhouse, the directors' room at Saratoga Racecourse, the Union Club, a private dining room in Rockefeller Plaza, one another's houses, or Swope's personal box at the track. Whitney invited the stewards of the Jockey Club to the commission's first meeting, the first of many times commissioners invited Club members to meet with them. Not long after that first meeting, Swope invited Whitney to his house (designed by Stanford White) in Sands Points, Long Island. There the two men decided to reduce admission prices at Belmont Park from $2.50 to $2.00.[37] In the mid-1930s, even that sum would have kept virtually all but the rich from the track.

One of the racing commission's responsibilities was to address drug use at the tracks. The drugs used to stimulate horses at the time were heroin, coramine, morphine, pilocarpine, and even caffeine. In developing methods of detection and punishments for violators, the commission consulted Bureau of Narcotics Chief Harry Anslinger. A former track official told me, "Harry sent word that if racing didn't do something about [drugs at the track], the national government would." For the commission's first two years, commissioners repeatedly dealt with testing procedures and with individuals under investigation.

But in this enterprise, not surprisingly, the commission played favorites. In 1935, when cocaine was detected in a horse's saliva, the commission immediately suspended the trainer and stabled his horses pending a hearing. When morphine was detected soon thereafter in another horse's saliva, the Hispanic trainer was arrested and held for a thousand dollars' bail.[38] By contrast, when a horse of George D. Widener II tested positive for cocaine that same year, the commissioners proceeded slowly. Recall that George's uncle, Joseph E. Widener, was the major stockholder in Belmont Park. (In 1944, George would become track president.) It was in this context that the commissioners examined the effects of the drug, read veterinary books, and consulted veterinarians and Harry Anslinger. A week later, they suspended the assistant trainer's license and issued a public statement in which they acknowledged Widener's prominence and cautioned other trainers to watch out for possible tampering with their own horses.[39]

A BALANCE OF POWER: THE COMMISSION AND THE CLUB

Within six months of the passage of the law that established the racing commission, the Jockey Club began seeking official clarification of its rights in light of the commission's superior powers. What was the Club's role vis-à-vis the commission's? When Club chairman William Woodward I invited the commissioners to his house for dinner, they brought the assistant attorney general with them. After the gathering, questions remained.

Club vice chairman Joseph E. Widener requested a second meeting. This time, the commission extended the invitation, inviting Widener, Woodward, a sympathetic state senator, and the assistant attorney general to lunch in "Private Dining Room 2, 65th

Floor, 30 Rockefeller Plaza."[40] There, they unanimously agreed that the 1934 law should be revised in favor of the Jockey Club.

In less than a year after the commission was established, it had returned to the Club much of the Club's original power. The commission waived its rights to write new rules and to have all the votes on the hearing board (they returned voting privileges to the two Jockey Club stewards who had lost them with the 1934 change). The Club had not in a strict sense taken advantage of the commissioners, as the two groups were almost one and the same. Swope was the Club members' friend and neighbor, and Whitney was their own son.

That they were in basic agreement did not mean that business between the Club and the racing commission always proceeded smoothly. In 1937, when Widener informed Swope of the Club's intention to change track officials, Swope publicly reprimanded Widener. At the time, the Club trained and appointed all track officials, regularly assigning individuals to positions on the New York tracks. Further, it "leased" them in various capacities to tracks in other states. Swope directed the Club to consult the commission "in advance" and reminded Widener that the commission was "fully charged with authority . . . in racing matters and . . . the Jockey Club . . . had only those rights delegated to it by the Racing Commission."[41] Widener said he "understood" and "accepted" Swope's interpretation.

The distribution of power between the two organizations gave the commission jurisdiction over betting and drug regulation, and the Club jurisdiction over the rules of racing, licensing, and appointing officials. It was a distribution that reflected their ongoing negotiations. In the 1940s, the commission still accepted this division as it "approved in all respects amendments to the Rules of Racing submitted by The Jockey Club [and allowed licensed persons to be sanctioned at] the discretion of said Stewards of The Jockey Club."[42]

The Jockey Club's discretion in one area had never been successfully challenged. It had remained able to license and sanction those whom it licensed with any measures it deemed appropriate. In 1936, a state court reversed the 1934 legislative decision that delegated licensing to the Club, but no action was taken on it.[43] Thus, in 1942, the Club could suspend jockey Eddie Arcaro indefinitely and require that he appear monthly at their Manhattan office. The cause for the action occurred when Arcaro and fellow rider Vincent Nodarse were "mixing it up" during a race, and Nodarse lost his mount. Arcaro was suspended for "rough riding." At the inquiry before the Club, a Club official commented to Arcaro that "it looked like you cut that rider off." Arcaro, obviously still upset over Nodarse's own actions, responded, "[Cut him off?] I was trying to kill the S.O.B."[44] Arcaro went on to win the Kentucky Derby five times and the Triple Crown twice, and he would relish telling the story of that confrontation in years to come. One can easily envision the small and fiery man appearing before the Jockey Club each month in the Park Avenue boardroom. The Club had sole power, and jockeys had no right to legal representation. And the next year, the appellate court upheld the right of the Jockey Club to act as an agent of the state to license jockeys.[45]

In the mid-1940s, after nine years on the commission, Lieutenant Colonel John Hay Whitney handed in his resignation to Governor Thomas E. Dewey. He was off to the war. The commission praised Whitney, whom they said had been "alert, progressive and enthusiastic in the performance of his duties and . . . discharged them with a single eye to the improvement and betterment of New York racing."[46]

The governor replaced Whitney with a man who did not always see things as the Club did. Corporate lawyer Ashley Trimble Cole wanted the commission's prerogatives with respect to the Club to be more clearly delineated. He also suggested that the commission's chairmanship should rotate. By then Herbert Swope had served as chairman for twelve years; he resigned the chair, and Cole became chairman.[47]

While the Jockey Club seemed to have lost some of its power over New York racing, the commission in 1957 still recognized the Club's "Rules of Racing" as "a very satisfactory scheme."[48] Further, as it had done years earlier, in 1965 the Club again got one of its own appointed to the commission. He was Vincent de Roulet, who was married to Whitney's niece. A longtime Club member told me about the incident. The story was that to avoid any apparent conflict of interest, the Club asked de Roulet to resign his Club membership before being appointed a commissioner by Governor Nelson Rockefeller. He resigned reluctantly, and only after he extracted a promise that he could announce publicly at a Club meeting that he did not wish to leave, a promise that went unkept.

Into the 1960s, while the Club no longer had the exclusive power to issue licenses, it wrote the rules of racing and appointed its officials. This seems to have been as much the product of tradition and precedent as because of the Club's expertise and interest in the sport.

THE ROUND TABLES

In 1950, George D. Widener II, Joseph E. Widener's nephew, took over as chairman of the Jockey Club. A man who knew the younger Widener for some years had only praise for him, describing him to me as very understanding, very generous, just marvelous, a real gentleman, and a beautiful man. Under his leadership, the Club began a series of Round Tables, public forums for the discussion of issues of concern to the industry.

The first Round Table was hosted by Widener, vice chairman Ogden Phipps, John Hay Whitney, and executive secretary Marshall Cassidy at the Club's Park Avenue Office on July 1, 1953. They had invited fourteen men, none of whom were really representative of the general racing public. Among them were J. Samuel Perlman, the owner of the *Daily Racing Form*; A. B. Hancock, Jr., who had traditionally kept the Phipps family horses; E. Barry Ryan, a grandson of Club member Thomas Fortune Ryan; trainers Hirsch Jacobs and Preston Burch, the latter of whom trained Club members' horses; and jockey Ted Atkinson, who rode their horses. In years to come, when even farm managers began to receive invitations to the Round Tables, they were more likely to be those in the employ of the Whitneys, the Wideners, or Warren Wright of Calumet Farm.

At the first Round Table, George D. Widener II, in classic Scroll and Key style, deferred to his guests: "Because of the complications and pace of racing today, we have never had an opportunity to hear what people who are in another branch of the activity other than ourselves think about various problems. The purpose of this conference is to get every element in racing together to exchange viewpoints."[49]

But the Jockey Club chose the issues and extended the invitations. Those who came were likely to feel privileged. When the

guests raised questions, they saw Club members display a willing-
ness to listen. At the end of the next year's meeting, vice chairman
Ogden Phipps announced that "Jock Whitney [as] the Chairman of
the United Republican Finance Committee of the State of New
York [came] in contact with [Governor Thomas E.] Dewey a good
deal."[50] His comment might have implied that the Club had an inside track. It was surely meant to reassure the guests.

Ogden Phipps was a grandson of Henry Phipps, childhood
friend and partner of Andrew Carnegie in Carnegie Steel.[51] Among
the wealthy families of Pittsburgh, the Phippses were said to be sec-
ond only to the Mellons and richer than the Carnegies. Henry
Phipps invested the steel funds in utilities, including New England
Power Association and International Hydro-Electric System, and in
Eastern real estate from New England to Florida. His son, Henry
Carnegie Phipps, married Gladys Mills, a horse lover who brought
the family into racing. She was the sister of Ogden Livingston
Mills, treasury secretary and member of the Club.

The Round Tables began as a way to give the Jockey Club more
exposure on the burgeoning national racing scene at a time when
the Club's influence was waning. The meeting moved the second
year from Manhattan to Saratoga Springs, and Round Tables have
been held there annually ever since. Through these meetings, the
Club has positioned itself as an advisor to the racing industry and
as willing to serve its interests. The early meetings had informal
agendas and provided opportunities for nearly everyone to participate. In comparison to the guests, Club members were less likely to
take the floor. When they did, they spoke succinctly. They asked
questions of others. Their behavior conveyed deference to the
opinions of those outside the Club.

The Round Tables continued to prove good public relations
and to provide a national forum for the discussion of racing-related
issues. The meetings became more formal; the format changed
from open discussion to panels and guest speakers, often political
figures; and the guest list expanded to more than two hundred.
The conferences themselves revealed a changing style over time on
the part of Club members. In the 1950s, few would be inclined to
either boast of their accomplishments or complain of any adverse
situation facing the industry. Within two decades, some members
at the Round Tables did both.

At the 1969 Round Table, the Club invited a Republican senator from Florida, fellow thoroughbred owner George Smathers, to
be their guest speaker. Smathers was on the Senate Ways and
Means Committee, which was considering a bill that would reduce
the tax credits horse owners received. To fight the bill, the Club
had helped form an industry lobbying group, the American Horse
Council, and Club members were among the group's founding
trustees. In earlier years, Club members would probably have been
inclined to use personal influence to secure their interests, without
involving the general public. Now, they apparently thought it
timely to get the support of horse owners in general. In the process,
though, they maintained their usual style.

Smathers told the guests about the Club's effort to get President Richard Nixon to consider their position on the tax bill. There
were four men who went with Smathers to meet with the president. They were Club members John W. Hanes and Ogden Phipps;
soon-to-be Club member Thruston Morton, the U.S. Senator from
Kentucky; and Governor Nunn of Kentucky. As Smathers recalled
the meeting: "A group of us talked to the President [and he] gave us
a very courteous and gentlemanly audience; in fact, an encourag-
ing audience, but he did say, 'I hope you will make my job a little
easier by giving something.' Then with respect to oil he even mentioned that a little bit to Ogden, and I must say Ogden did not re-
spond very enthusiastically at that point."[52]

The meeting with Nixon offered the Club an opportunity to
demonstrate its support of the interests of horse owners generally.
The tax reform bill that eventually passed was less disadvantageous
to horsemen than it had been originally, as far as limiting their de-
ductions for losses and having to show a profit.

One panel at the 1970 Round Table was devoted to how to
deal with the news media. In the late 1960s, the racing industry
had been the target of bad publicity, often in relation to labor
problems among its track workers, referred to as "backstretch workers." The Club member who chaired the panel was the head of the
major newspaper chain, Knight Newspapers, Inc., John S. Knight.
Apparently with reference to recent press coverage, Knight addressed the audience as those who "have endured and survived the
Internal Revenue Service [and] burgeoning bleats from the back-

stretch."[53] In years past, it would have been unlikely for individual members to as openly disparage the Club's situation.

The Club has continued to invite friends who hold political office to be guest speakers at their Round Tables. Like Smathers, these individuals often have had close ties to racing and have been sympathetic to Club interests. In the mid-1970s, New York governor Hugh Carey, the nephew of a betting commissioner at Saratoga, was also a guest speaker. Carey congratulated the New York Racing Association, which was in charge of operating the state's tracks and whose entire board was then comprised of members of the Jockey Club. He praised the NYRA as the state's largest producer of corporate tax revenue. On a personal note, Carey went on to tell of how his uncle had taken bets from Bernard Baruch: "I'm one of the few persons who knows that when the late beloved Barny Baruch sat on a bench in the park and ruminated in the sunshine, day after day, he wasn't really thinking about his investments, he was thinking about what he would do in the wager he placed with my uncle, who was his favorite betting commissioner at Saratoga in those days."[54]

In the mid-1980s, again with unfavorable tax bills looming, the Club invited two men highly placed in the U.S. government to speak, U.S. senator from Kansas Robert Dole in 1984 and secretary of the treasury James Baker III the next year. Both talked about tax issues facing the industry. Dole took questions from the floor, and Baker was introduced as an "old friend of many."[55]

While the official minutes of Round Table meetings reflect the Club's concerns, political influence, and operating style, they do not capture fully their essence, as I learned by attending the Forty-first Annual Round Table Conference on Matters Pertaining to Racing. These events have increasingly become public relations forums in which the Club is able to advertise its activities effectively and to a broad audience.

The Round Table that I attended convened on the morning of August 15, 1993. Mercedes and Lincolns were parked in the circular drive that fronts the grand Gideon Putnam Hotel in Saratoga Springs when I arrived. In the hotel's spacious lobby, men in conservative suits and ties and women in slightly more stylish attire gathered in small groups, talking seriously.

At 10:05 A.M., chairman Ogden Mills Phipps said, "Could everyone come in and we'll get started?" Nothing happened. After five minutes, he repeated his request. The men and women moved toward the conference room. Inside were fourteen rows of tables and chairs. Awaiting each of the two hundred guests was a placecard, a program, and that year's memorabilia—a black plastic desk clock inscribed "1993 Jockey Club Round Table Meetings." Later, a man would tell me that "the gifts were better in the past."

Within another few minutes, Phipps had extended a brief formal welcome. Vice chairman William Farish III took over, disparaging the doom and gloom that was being forecast for racing, enthusiastic over the $1 million donation of Paul Mellon to the Grayson Jockey Club Foundation for equine research.

A series of announcements followed. A Club steward recounted ways that the Club had supported the "cutting edge of technology" in the racing industry. A spokesman for the industry's lobbying group gave an update on the group's fight against the "threat" to racing posed by Native American casinos.

In keeping with the custom of inviting trainers to the Round Tables, Shug McGaughey, who trained horses for the Club's chairman, was among the guests. McGaughey arrived late. He had apparently just come from the track after supervising the morning workouts for his horses. He took a seat in the ninth row.

The year's Jockey Club Gold Medal was awarded to Kenny Noe, Jr., president of Florida's Gulfstream Park. He was described as having done any number of jobs and, also, as being "hard-headed." (A few years later, the Club would be influential in bringing Noe to New York as president of the New York Racing Association, which operated the state's tracks; he soon moved up to chairman of its board, the first non–Club member to hold that office.)

The guest speaker was the Marquess of Hartington, who was retiring as senior steward of the Jockey Club of England—the British equivalent of the Jockey Club's chairman—known as "Stoker" to his friends. In his address, the marquess referred to the English Jockey Club as an "entirely undemocratic body [of] self-appointed guardians of the turf accountable to none"—words that might have described America's Jockey Club in years past.

Near the end of the meeting, the president of the Thoroughbred Racing Association, an organization of track operators, outlined a proposed new organization for racing in the United States.

He suggested a marketing strategy that would promote racing, much as other professional sports are promoted. He called on the guests to "unite," "bury provincialism," "market the product," and "establish the official hot dog and soft drink of racing." (While such an organization would be established soon thereafter, it failed to sustain industry interest and folded quickly.)

In closing, Chairman Phipps said he was ready to do whatever was necessary to support this change.

It is evident from this description that what began in the 1950s as rather informal gatherings have evolved into state-of-the-industry presentations. The gentlemen of the Club often lend official support to what others in the industry seem to want. Today, the Club continues to realize the political and public relations benefits of its Round Table meetings. This has been accomplished by the access that they provide to others in the industry and by the opportunities offered to demonstrate the Jockey Club's openness to government and public interests.

THE NEW YORK RACING ASSOCIATION

In the 1950s, the Jockey Club initiated another effort that had lasting implications for racing in New York State. At the time, the state's racing was threatened; attendance and revenue had declined, and racing in other states was expanding. In 1955, the Club appointed a committee to attempt to revitalize racing in New York. The committee proposed a change in how racing would be operated. It decided that one nonprofit association, the Greater New York Racing Association, should run the Aqueduct, Belmont, and Saratoga tracks, and that Jamaica Racecourse should be closed. The association's stock was to be owned by Jockey Club members, and all its trustees would be Club members.

In by now familiar terms, the committee said that the new association would rescue the sport, save the state money, eliminate private profits, and provide no remuneration to Club members. The situation was unlike that in 1894, when the Jockey Club simply assumed control of racing. Now the association, comprised solely of Club members, had first to obtain permission from the state. The legislature and the governor, former Club member W. Averell Harriman, granted that permission.

In September 1955, the Greater New York Racing Association, whose name was changed in 1958 to the New York Racing Association, took over the operation of racing in the state. Until then, the tracks had been controlled by five racing associations, in four of which Club members were majority stockholders. The NYRA's twenty founding trustees were Jockey Club members: George Bostwick, James Cox Brady II, Christopher T. Chenery, John C. Clark, Walter Fletcher, Harry Frank Guggenheim, John W. Hanes, George Humphrey (then U.S. treasury secretary), Howell Jackson, Walter Jeffords, Robert Kleberg, Jr., Ogden Phipps, John Schiff, Whitney Stone, Harold Talbott (then air force secretary), Alfred Gwynne Vanderbilt II, F. S. von Stade, John Hay Whitney, George D. Widener II, and William Woodward II.[56] The NYRA operated out of the Jockey Club office at 300 Park Avenue in Manhattan.

The Club appointed as the NYRA's secretary general Marshall Cassidy, who was also the Club's executive secretary and assistant treasurer.[57] Cassidy had been a deep-sea salvage diver, taxi driver, oil rig worker, and surveyor on the Mexican border, where he was captured and held hostage by Pancho Villa. From childhood, he had heard his father, Mars Cassidy, a racetrack starter, praise the Club. Marshall Cassidy grew up wanting to work for the men who belonged to it.

As a young man, Cassidy was a friend of Alfred G. Vanderbilt II; they played tennis and went to the races together. Vanderbilt told me, "Cassidy was a very good friend of mine. . . . In those days, we used to race at Yonkers. There was no bridge from Long Island to Westchester. Cassidy had a little boat, and my mother had a house on the water [at Sands Point, Long Island]. He would pick me up, and we'd go to the races everyday."

The Club also gave Cassidy responsibility for handling improvements at Belmont Park. In this capacity, he reported directly to the NYRA chairman, John W. Hanes. I have been told by people who knew them that both were men of strong will.

In the 1960s, under threat of a strike by workers at Belmont Park and failing in his efforts to contact Hanes by telephone, Cassidy asked some horse owners, including F. S. von Stade, about the possibility of temporarily using their nearby barns to stable horses. Von Stade had headed the racing association that operated Saratoga Racecourse before its takeover by the NYRA. Hanes made it clear he did not approve of Cassidy's having assumed this initiative and chastised him in public, although he later apologized. Cassidy described the confrontation in some personal notes:

> As I came up to [Mr. Hanes] in the back of the winner's circle, he exclaimed in a loud voice, "Why the Hell did you consult with von Stade! You are not to talk to him. I don't want you to have anything to do with him!" His face was as red as a beet. I asked him who he thought he was talking to, a servant? and started to walk away from him before I lost my temper. He went with me to my office and I told him that I did not intend to continue in a position where I was abused in public and treated as a servant. If I was not supposed to use my best judgement in such an emergency then I had an entirely erroneous conception of my job and he had better get someone to take my place.[58]

Given his lengthy association with the Club, his strong sense of self, and his seeming unwillingness to recognize his "place," Cassidy expected some latitude and respect. Hanes apparently had no doubt about his own place, though he was evidently not that sensitive to the ways of gentlemen. After these episodes, Cassidy seriously considered resigning his position with the NYRA. He turned for advice to a man he considered his friend, Club chairman George D. Widener II. Though Widener initially encouraged him to delay his resignation, he later raised questions about Cassidy's loyalty to the NYRA. Cassidy, completely unprepared for such questions, resigned. Upon reflection, he wrote in his notes: "Widener's question of my loyalty nearly destroyed my love and faith in humanity. Mr. Widener had known me, I thought, very well, not only as an official, but as a friend. I was so shocked I was numbed."[59]

From its beginnings in 1955 until the mid-1970s, the New York Racing Association had been under the sole purview of the Jockey Club. For nearly twenty years, the NYRA's board of trustees was composed of influential Club members, often stewards, who held stock in the association. According to a former official with NYRA, "The Jockey Club [in earlier years] was the management of the NYRA," thereby having considerable influence over it. By the mid-1970s, the governor and legislature began to appoint some persons to the NYRA board who, while they had voting privileges, did not hold stock.

This change destroyed the Jockey Club's total control of the

NYRA board, but Club members continued to represent the majority of its members. And a number of the state's new appointees would become Club members. Of note among them were John T. Landry, former vice president of Phillip Morris and creator of the Marlboro Man; Richard Gelb, CEO of Squibb Pharmaceutical Company; and William Rogers, former U.S. attorney general and secretary of state.

This has meant that the Club has continued to have some control with the NYRA. Though this control is not always official, the views of Club members on the board often seem to be honored. An individual close to the Club talked about the time in the 1970s when NYRA trustee and Club member Paul Mellon made clear his preference for who "would head the NYRA" and who would "head the Jockey Club." According to my interviewee, Mellon told others who were in influential positions that he wanted Nicholas F. Brady II to be the NYRA chairman and Ogden Mills Phipps to be the Jockey Club chairman. Within a short period of time, Brady and Phipps would occupy these positions.

In more recent years, the state has apparently had some difficulty overseeing the NYRA. Some of the NYRA trustees are major political contributors. One close to the situation went so far as to suggest that the state's chief executive found himself in the dilemma of being obligated to oversee racing while also having to approach some NYRA trustees for needed reelection contributions. By the mid-1990s, some of the founding NYRA board members had been forced to "retire."

Gentlemen are not inclined to discuss influence, and if they do, they try to explain it away. Few Club members would acknowledge that they or the Club have influence of any kind in New York State. One member who admitted he had been powerful credited his family and an official position he held. Another speculated that any influence on the part of the Club was probably the result of longstanding custom. One man with considerable experience in the racing industry, though less in the Club, speculated that its influence was a matter of financial support. Still another member thought the Club might continue to dominate in the state because of their position as major contributors to the Republican Party there. One who had worked closely with the Club for several decades did speculate about the Club's national influence. He implied such influence was simply the result of its members' "contacts" in Congress and the corporate world.

NATIONAL ORGANIZATIONS

Over time, there have developed a number of organizations in racing that are national in scope. With these, too, the Jockey Club has been influential, in its characteristic style. As early as the 1950s, thoroughbred breeders and owners who were not members of the Club formed their own groups, the Thoroughbred Breeders Association (TBA) and the Thoroughbred Owners Association (TOA). By 1961, they had merged to form the Thoroughbred Owners and Breeders Association (TOBA), headed by Club member Arthur Hancock, Jr.

At about the time of the merger, the Jockey Club made an attempt to take over the TOA's magazine, *The Blood-Horse*, which was then and continues to be the industry's major publication. The TOA kept the journal, although Club members came to dominate the board of its later incarnation, the TOBA. At the time, Club member Alfred G. Vanderbilt II publicly opposed the action. Though a Yalie, Vanderbilt was somewhat lax about displaying a low profile, and his behavior was not without consequences for him. As he reflected on his opposition to the Club, he told me about his feelings, efforts at compromise, and subsequent loss of influence in the Club: "At the time I thought there should be an organization other than the Club that had some [national] input into racing. [After the failed attempt, a committee was formed to try to develop a compromise.] I represented the TOBA [and made the suggestion that the organizations] have joint memberships. [The Club] said, 'No way.' . . . At that time, I was fighting against the Jockey Club. I was [never] a steward . . . after [this]." He concluded by characterizing the Club's policy—not his—as "Don't rock the boat."

Over the years, the Club apparently maintained some of its influence in racing through the appointments of its members to other organizations' boards. As one man with years of track experience told me, "Virtually everyone on these other organizations has been appointed by the Club." Another, even closer to the Club, was more specific when he claimed that the head of the Thoroughbred Racing Association, then located in the same building in Manhattan as the Jockey Club, was hired personally by the Club's chairman. There is also some indication that the Club has funded research studies for other organizations that those organizations could not afford to fund themselves.

The National Thoroughbred Racing Association (NTRA) represents the most recent effort to consolidate and strengthen thoroughbred racing in the United States.[60] Founded in 1997, with its slogan "Go, baby, go," the NTRA would market the sport to attract more fans and enhance revenues, in light of competition from other sports and casino gambling.

The Jockey Club is closely tied to both the NTRA's initial development and its present governance. The organization's founding CEO is Club member Daniel G. Van Clief, Jr. Its founding organizations were the Jockey Club, the Breeders' Cup Limited (headed by Van Clief), Keeneland Association (headed by Club vice chairman William Farish III), Oak Tree Racing Association (whose founder and president is Club member Clement L. Hirsch), and the National Thoroughbred Association.

Half the NTRA's current ten-member board has direct ties to the Jockey Club. Three are Club members: Robert Clay, representing both the National Thoroughbred Association and the Thoroughbred Owners and Breeders Association; Robert Lewis, representing the Thoroughbred Owners of California; and Ogden Mills Phipps, representing the Jockey Club itself. Two other NTRA board members are presidents of racing associations that are overseen by Club members: Tom Meeker, president of Churchill Downs, whose chairman is William Farish III; and Terry Meyocks, president of the NYRA, the majority of whose board members are Club members. Further, the NTRA's general counsel is the law firm of Rogers and Wells, whose senior partner is William P. Rogers, Club member since 1975.

In what is by now familiar rhetoric, the Jockey Club nonetheless states in its *1999 Fact Book* that the "[g]overnance of the NTRA is representative and balanced."[61] And apparently, some in racing hold to this view. A recent discussion with a New York trainer close to the organization suggests that even insiders believe that the NTRA represents a grassroots effort with little influence from the Jockey Club.

5

QUALIFYING FOR THE CLUB

 The Jockey Club is tax exempt. Its executive office today is on East Fifty-second Street in Manhattan, and its registry office is in Lexington, Kentucky. The current membership cap is set at about one hundred. As has been the case since the Club's founding in 1894, candidates are nominated by current members and admitted only with the unanimous approval of all members. Nine stewards serve as a board of directors; one of them is the chairman. While stewards of the Club have continued to represent the northeastern old-money establishment, members today come from across the country and include some women; they otherwise continue to resemble the traditional Club member and to serve the interests of the membership as a whole.

Changes in the composition of the Jockey Club seem to have been the result of impetus from within the Club along with three outside factors: bad press, political pressure, and competition in the racing industry. There is little indication, however, that the Club has changed the way it operates to reflect its more broad-based membership. This may be due largely to its continued control by the more established old-money families. While the current general membership might suggest otherwise, the Club remains a bastion of white Anglo-Saxon power.

INSIDE THE JOCKEY CLUB

Between 1895 and 1999, the Jockey Club had only 347 members. Entry qualifications, beyond a tie to horse racing and a sterling character, appear vague. The Club's secretary/treasurer James Cox Brady III told me: "We select those who add something to the sport—whatever they [represent]—the racing end, breeding end, track end. . . when we need help with advice, professionalism, experience, and to contribute to knowledge to solve problems. . . . I think it has to do with the quality of potential members and the extent to which [they] are considered upright. It is how you conduct yourself, not what your bloodlines are. We are only concerned about horses' bloodlines. . . . We are not looking for names in the Jockey Club."

The Jockey Club operates like a fraternity, perhaps because so many of its members have belonged to fraternities. Personal likes and dislikes do enter into the selection process. An individual close to the Club told me that personal qualities were a part of choosing members of his fraternity and of how deals are made in getting others to support a candidate. He was a member of a preppy athletic society that had turned down an individual about whom negative comments had been made. He explained that if a member gave an impassioned speech in support of someone who was turned down, the group might reconsider. In this instance, a prominent member gave such a speech. He then went on to say that he had used this as a means of getting his own friend in, agreeing to support the somewhat unpopular individual in exchange for support for his friend. Ironically, the unpopular individual went on to great heights in one of America's most elite societies—the Jockey Club.

The process of admitting persons to the Jockey Club has undergone some change over time. It was a more informal process in the past. It was a smaller world then. The nominating process took place behind closed doors, and participants were prohibited from talking about what went on. News was leaked on at least one occasion, though. The *New York Times* announced before the fact that Alfred G. Vanderbilt II was to be admitted.[1]

Discussions of the early process suggest it was quite congenial. One longtime member reminisced about the leather-bound book in which were listed the candidate's name, along with the name of the man who nominated him and the man who seconded the nomination. He said that members were free to write in the book, offering comments or blackballing the candidate, and that before the vote was taken, a member who knew the candidate would make certain the individual wanted to be nominated.

The process today is more centralized, and membership decisions rest largely with the stewards, who both appoint the Membership Committee and have the final word on who may be admitted. The nominating and admission process occurs in five steps, from proposal to acceptance. A proposal to consider a person is given to the Membership Committee. If the committee thinks the person is appropriate, a member who knows the potential nominee tries to find out if he or she might be interested in being admitted. A letter goes to the general membership with the nomination. If no one raises any objections, the person is formally proposed to the stewards. If the stewards approve, the person is officially a member of the Jockey Club. A process that begins and ends with the stewards is one that for all practical purposes seems to put the decision in their hands.

Still, the process is not without its personal touch. Club members personally notify new members of their acceptance. One man recalled that he was at the racetrack and phoned his secretary in order to get the day's messages. The secretary told him that "some guy named Phipps called," having apparently mistaken the chairman of the Jockey Club for "some kind of salesman." Another new member said that after a member telephoned him with the news of his acceptance, it took several days for the reality of his nomination "to sink in."

Because nomination to membership involves sponsorship—one already in the Club must make a case for the potential nominee— and because that sponsorship is generally kept secret, new members inevitably wonder who might have put their name forward. A man whose father was a Club member said his own nomination came as a real surprise to him. He had known that he could not count on his family name to bring him a nomination, and that nominations must derive from the genuine personal convictions of others. Like other members I spoke with, he thought that upon speculation, he knew who his sponsor had been but would not with certainty identify his suspected sponsor. One exception among the members who talked to me about their sponsors (or rather, did not) was Paul Mellon, who was willing to speculate aloud about his nomination: "I remember being greeted by William Woodward [then chairman of the Club]. Everything was very pleasant. I was overawed to have been nominated. Jimmy [James Cox] Brady, a friend of mine, who was already a member, may have had something to do with [my nomination]."

The Typical Club Member

While it is true that an individual's conduct and integrity have been considered among their qualifications for Club membership, it is also apparent that bloodlines have had an influence on nominations. The record indicates that the Club has admitted first those related by blood, then those related by marriage, then friends, and, last, business associates. Half of the members are related either by blood or by marriage (at minimum, 40 percent are blood kin and 21 percent are in-laws).[2]

If one were to look closely at the list of members of the Jockey Club over time, one might come to believe that the Club has in mind clear criteria for the ideal candidate for membership. One might conclude that this ideal candidate would be male, of Anglo-Saxon descent, and related by blood or marriage to another Club member; that he would have been born and raised in the Northeast and have attended the right schools; that he would either be the self-made founder of a major corporation or have such inherited wealth that he need not work at all; and that he vote Republican and be an Episcopalian.

The wealth of the Club's early members derived primarily from transportation, mining, and utilities—all of which were sometimes controlled by individual families, such as the Vanderbilts, Whitneys, Wideners, Ryans, and Phippses. One could almost trace the history of the influence and wealth of these families through the companies that have comprised the Dow Jones Industrials over time. One could also look to a single industry in this category, such as the oil industry, and find Club members who had controlling interests in the major companies in it—in this example, companies that include Standard Oil, Superior Oil, Humble Oil, and Gulf Oil.

Other Club families have derived fortunes from manufacturing, merchandising, and publishing. The du Ponts are noteworthy among those who have mined chemicals and manufactured pharmaceuticals. More recently, the Club has included the heads of three major pharmaceutical companies in the nation—Bristol Meyers Squibb, Merck, and Smith, Kline, and French. In 1990, Du Pont and Merck established a joint global pharmaceutical company. As regards publishing giants, major New York, Pittsburgh, and Chicago newspapers have been controlled by Club members, and Knight-Ridder Publications was formed by the merger of the publishing companies of two Club members. Macmillan Publishing and Commerce Clearing House have also been in the hands of Club members.

A substantial number of Club families have built or added to their empires through the financial world as bankers, brokers, and investment managers. Not a few have been founders, partners, and directors of major financial institutions, including August Belmont and Company, Mellon National Bank, J. P. Morgan, Chase National Bank, Delaware Trust, and Central Hanover Bank. They have established and served on the boards of directors of several New York Stock Exchange–registered firms that offer comprehensive services. These include the well-known Lehman Brothers and Company, Kuhn, Loeb, and Company, Dillon, Read, and Company, and the nation's biggest brokerage house, Merrill Lynch, Pierce, Fenner and Smith.

It is a safe assumption that Jockey Club members continue to be well represented on major corporate boards. Its early members served on the first boards of Standard Oil, U.S. Steel, American Tobacco, and American Can, among several other major industrial, manufacturing, and financial firms. Further, not only were these men in control of the major industries, but each of them was likely to have held controlling interests in several industries. Recall that J. P. Morgan had control of the financial and industrial arenas, that Thomas Fortune Ryan was a controlling director in more than thirty corporations, that William Kissam Vanderbilt assumed control of the family's seventy-three corporations, and that Marshall Field III resigned his positions in nearly two dozen such companies.

Just as when the Club was born, I have found, its members today have controlling interests in the associations that operate major tracks throughout the United States, especially those in New

York, Kentucky, and California. The Club has admitted on a fairly consistent basis those who have been chairmen and trustees of the New York Racing Association, chairmen of Kentucky's Keeneland and Churchill Downs racecourses, and chairmen of California's Santa Anita and Del Mar racecourses. An object of considerable media exposure, Churchill Downs, currently headed by the vice chairman of the Jockey Club, controls four other racetracks, as well—Calder, Ellis Park, Hollywood Park, and Hoosier Park.[3]

At least 101 Club members (29 percent of the membership) have owned stock in associations that operate racetracks, serving as CEOs, chairmen, or board members; several have held stock in more than a single such association. Members of the Jockey Club have made substantial financial investments in the racing end of the sport. One Club member himself raised a question about possible conflict of interest on the part of his fellow members who, he said, "wear various hats."

To accommodate a changing society and sport, the Club has made exceptions to its unwritten rules regarding membership. The climate and circumstances under which exceptions have been made point to underlying values of the Club.

Even though the membership cap has doubled in the last half century, the number of total members in the Club has not grown substantially; membership remains the privilege of the highly elect. For years, there was a membership cap of fifty. That cap was lifted in the 1950s, though in 1952, there were only fifty-five members. By 1970, the cap was about seventy; and now it is slightly more than one hundred. Because members are inducted for life and few ever resign, and because of the cap on membership, openings are infrequent. The few members who have resigned have done so for reasons of military, political, or diplomatic service or ill health, or because they have left the country or sold their horses. Others have resigned because they were facing public scandal or they had lost interest in racing or involvement in the Club's business, or from personal conviction. These conditions make the few available spaces all the more coveted.

Benefits of Membership

The prize for being recognized by the rich and powerful in racing would seem to be nomination to the Jockey Club. Even though

Table 5.1   Members of the Jockey Club, August 1999

NAME	YEAR ADMITTED
Josephine E. Abercrombie	1994
Helen C. Alexander	1986
Joseph L. Allbritton	1991
John Ed Anthony	1993
Charles Baker	1975
William W. Bancroft	1976
James E. Bassett III	1985
John A. Bell III	1980
James H. Binger	1976
Edward S. Bonnie	1985
Frank A. Bonsal, Jr.	1984
James C. Brady, Jr. (III)	1973
Nicholas F. Brady II	1966
Baird C. Brittingham	1968
Alexander G. Campbell, Jr.	1989
Charles J. Cella	1974
Alice Headley Chandler	1989
Helen B. Chenery	1983
George M. Cheston	1965
Sherwood C. Chillingworth	1995
Robert N. Clay	1991
F. Eugene Dixon, Jr.	1958
Donald R. Dizney	1997
Allan R. Dragone	1988
Jack J. Dreyfus, Jr.	1969
Richard L. Duchossois	1987
Allaire du Pont	1983
William du Pont III	1981
Edward P. Evans	1996
Robert S. Evans	1991
William S. Farish III	1970
William S. Farish, Jr.	1996
Hugh A. Fitzsimons, Jr.	1992
Richard L. Gelb	1978
Edward H. Gerry	1956
Henry A. Gerry	1956
Martha F. Gerry	1983
M. Tyson Gilpin	1955
John K. Goodman	1978
Louis L. Haggin III	1997
Arthur B. Hancock III	1981
Dell Hancock	1995
Seth W. Hancock	1978
Joseph W. Harper	1983
John C. Harris	1988
George M. Hendrie	1993
John Hettinger	1983
Clement L. Hirsch	1994
Fred W. Hooper	1975
E. Edward Houghton	1976
G. Watts Humphrey, Jr.	1976
Stuart S. Janney III	1992
Richard I. G. Jones	1975
Russell B. Jones, Jr.	1989

Table 5.1   *Continued*

NAME	YEAR ADMITTED
A. Gary Lavin	1994
Robert B. Lewis	1997
F. Jack Liebau	1991
John C. Mabee	1985
James K. McManus (Jim McKay)	1987
William C. MacMillen, Jr.	1988
Kenneth L. Maddy	1993
Harry T. Mangurian, Jr.	1997
Frank L. Mansell	1995
J. W. Y. Martin, Jr.	1992
Robert E. Meyerhoff	1994
MacKenzie Miller	1997
Charles Nuckols, Jr.	1997
Allen E. Paulson	1996
John H. Peace	1991
Ogden Phipps	1939
Ogden Mills Phipps	1965
William A. Purdey	1979
David P. Reynolds	1976
Reuben F. Richards	1976
Jack K. Robbins	1995
Jesse Mack Robinson	1995
William P. Rogers	1975
Donald P. Ross, Jr.	1972
Timothy H. Sams	1989
Ernest L. Samuel	1989
Peter G. Schiff	1994
Bayard Sharp	1952
Joseph V. Shields, Jr.	1997
Viola Sommer	1988
Robert S. Strauss	1988
George Strawbridge, Jr.	1976
Dwight G. Sutherland	1997
Shirley H. Taylor	1989
Charles H. Thieriot	1978
Oakleigh B. Thorne	1981
Donald J. Valpredo	1991
Daniel G. Van Clief, Jr.	1991
Alfred G. Vanderbilt II	1937
Joseph Walker, Jr.	1956
Charlotte C. Weber	1994
Wheelock Whitney	1974
Charles Whittingham	1997
David Willmot	1996
Jacques D. Wimpfheimer	1985
Martin J. Wygod	1996
William T. Young	1989

one member who let me in on the benefits of membership was obviously downplaying its significance, he perhaps was not entirely joking. Nomination, he said, brings with it a notice in the paper, a parking sticker, and a pin—and if the man at the gates knows the pin for what it is, it will get you into the track. In addition, there is a black-tie dinner at Saratoga for members only, which on occasion has also been attended by the governor of New York and members of the European elite.

Naturally, some individuals (more often, new-money individuals), upon learning of their nomination, are curious about what lies ahead. One group of nominess posed the question of what they might expect to a man who had been in racing for nearly all his adult life and had a history of associating with Club members. He told me his reply was that they would not have to do anything "earth-shattering," an answer that he said left one of the new nominees quite "crest-fallen."

The top-heavy governing structure of the Club has negatively affected some new members, who are individuals of position and high regard generally. Their membership has seemed to bring with it an unaccustomed second-class standing. Still, few of those so disappointed would have their feelings known. Those few were often active in racing generally and had brought high expectations to their admission to the Club. Once inside, they found that they had little say.

One man was characterized to me by a fellow member as having wanted very much to be "accepted," who in spite of being admitted to Club membership had not found that acceptance. Another member told me plainly that he did more for the industry outside the Club than inside it and, as an afterthought, wondered why he had wanted to be a member in the first place. Still another said that membership generally was largely honorific and carried more prestige than it was worth. Some members have disengaged from Club activity and remain on the periphery.

Loyalty among Members

Being a member of upper-class society allows one considerable latitude in behavior. The more established one's family money, the greater the latitude one is accorded. As Stephen Birmingham suggests in *The Right People*, "[One's] grandfather may have been Ambassador to The Hague or an alcoholic suicide; it doesn't matter, if he belongs."[4]

Members of the Jockey Club are apparently no exception to this pattern. During the Club's early years, the nation was itself suspicious of and hostile toward its legion of new immigrants. It was also a time when society became blatantly anti-Semitic. Among the Club's then largely white Anglo-Saxon Protestant membership was one who was particularly vocal in this regard. He was William Astor Chanler.[5] His mother was an Astor, and his father was a long-time U.S. representative from New York. Chanler attended Phillips Academy and Harvard. He became a big-game hunter, raced thoroughbreds, served in the Spanish-American War, and, like his father, served in Congress. Chanler was notorious for his anti-Semitic and anti-Catholic views. He believed that the League of Nations was a Jewish plot; that Jews had written President Woodrow Wilson's Fourteen Points; and (in a remarkable contortion of thought) that Wilson intended to make Catholicism the national religion in exchange for using the Vatican's spy system.

In the 1920s, Chanler raced at Longchamps and was a regular at Maxim's in Paris. He had lost a leg in a bordello brawl and wore an artificial one. In an anecdote related by writer Stephen Birmingham, Chanler wanted to get a quick lunch at Maxim's one afternoon before the races and became impatient with a waiter when he was not served promptly. As disgraceful in his behavior as in his opinions, Chanler fumbled under the table, removed his artificial leg, "shoe, sock, garter, and all," and flung it across the room at the waiter, calling, "Now, may I have your attention?"[6]

William Astor Chanler's eccentricities may have been in the blood. His brother, John Armstrong Chanler, viewed himself as the reincarnation of Napoleon Bonaparte.

Of course, families at any social level often tiptoe around problem behavior—and the Jockey Club can lay claim to dysfunctions as varied and loyalties as deep as those in many family groups. Parker Corning, grandson of iron magnate and U.S. representative Erastus Corning was a Jockey Club member reputed to have been a heavy drinker, according to Erastus Corning's biographer.[7] A graduate of St. Paul's and Yale, and a U.S. representative for seven terms, Parker Corning had major interests in Albany Felt Company, owned five houses, and raced thoroughbreds. All was lost in the end, and he died essentially penniless. He was, however, like Chanler, never removed from the Jockey Club rolls.

Still, drinking seems to have contributed to some animosity among Club members. When Bull Hancock died in 1972, Arthur

QUALIFYING FOR THE CLUB   123

Hancock III had expected to assume control of the family farm, Claiborne. The farm passed instead to his younger brother, Seth. Arthur III, with some history of drinking problems, was alleged to have thought that Ogden Phipps, advisor to his father's estate, played a part in that decision.[8]

CLUB GOVERNANCE

The Jockey Club operates in much the same manner as a corporation does. The Club has a board that plans and executes its business. In the case of the Club, the board of directors are the nine stewards, including the chairman, vice chairman, and secretary-treasurer. It is a self-nominating body, as stewards make the decisions about who will sit on the board. Stewards serve four-year terms, though those who are also officers may serve beyond their term. The stewards appoint members to the three standing committees—the Executive Committee, the Nominations Committee, and the Audit Committee. Stewards meet six times a year and keep in touch much more frequently. By contrast, if general members attend any annual meeting, it is generally the one held at Saratoga each August. Members from outside the Northeast may find even this one difficult to attend.

Over time, most of the Club stewards have been from old-money families, and 80 percent have been northeasterners. It was not until the 1960s that someone from outside the Northeast became a steward, Kentuckian Louis Lee Haggin II. Given that the major breeding farms have always been in Kentucky, it is noteworthy that someone from the state had not been on the board of stewards earlier.

Two years later, John W. Galbreath of Ohio became a steward, and during the 1970s, Texan William S. Farish III began to serve. In the 1980s, a few westerners (from California and Arizona) served, often for single four-year terms. In the Club's entire history, no woman has ever been a steward. All those who have served for twenty-five years or more have been from northeastern old-money families.

Every one of the Club's chairmen has been old money and northeastern, and many have been Episcopalian. They are John Hunter (1894–1895), August Belmont II (1895–1924), Frank K.

Sturgis (1924–1930), William Woodward I (1930–1950), George D. Widener II (1950–1964), Ogden Phipps (1964–1974), Nicholas F. Brady II (1974–1982), August Belmont IV (1982–1983), and Ogden Mills Phipps (1983–present). With the exception of George D. Widener II, all the chairmen have derived the large part of their fortune from the financial world, as directors of banks and securities firms. Four chairmen (the two Belmonts and two Phippses) have been related by blood. Similarly, fourteen out of fifteen of the vice chairmen have been old-money northeasterners.

Family ties have apparently been central to the Club's organization. Cliques seem to be founded in families and extended to in-laws and close friends. One individual close to several Club families for years has used the term "mafia" to describe the phenomenon. The cliques appear to have varying degrees of power.

Probably the best current example is the larger Phipps family, which is well represented on the board of stewards, as well as in the general membership. Members of the Jockey Club who are descendants of Henry Phipps include his son (Henry Carnegie Phipps), five grandsons (Ogden Phipps, Michael Grace Phipps, Winston and Raymond Guest, and Townsend Bradley Martin), and two great-grandsons (Ogden Mills Phipps and Stuart Janney III). Those related to the family by marriage include Stuart Janney II, William Stamps Farish III, and William Stamps Farish IV. Ogden Phipps and his son Ogden Mills Phipps have been stewards and chairmen for a longer period than have members of any other family in the Club. The board of stewards is currently dominated by the Phipps family: Ogden Mills Phipps is chairman; his brother-in-law is vice chairman; and his cousin—and head of one of the family companies—is a steward.

Members are not inclined to criticize the Jockey Club, at least to outsiders. Still, there were indications that several members I spoke to were displeased with the Club's imbalance of power. Their comments in this regard were often matter-of-fact and understated. One member said that the stewards are in essence all-powerful. Another called the few men who run the Club a "dictatorship." Still another explained the manner in which the power of the few was conveyed. He said that although the stewards put forward their recommendations to the entire membership, the gesture is largely perfunctory. He further told me that the very tenor of the meetings suggested that the stewards' recommendations are not to be questioned, fully discussed, or otherwise challenged. The way in which one steward presented his viewpoint was described by a member as "presumptive close," as it conveyed to those listening that further discussion was unnecessary and therefore closed.

DEFENDING THE CLUB'S TURF

Once the robber barons had attained social legitimacy, they would separate themselves from the activities of those of lesser social standing, a pattern that has become customary among America's new-money elite. While some early members of the Jockey Club had gambled, and some families, like the Whitneys, Belmonts, and Vanderbilts, had been devotees of casinos as well as of the turf,[9] the Club officially stood for activities viewed by society as legitimate.

In the 1950s, the U.S. public became more sensitive to the long-standing and widespread discrimination against Jews in America. Concern over anti-Semitism extended to private as well as public sectors. At the same time, the U.S. Senate, via the Kefauver Committee, was investigating organized crime's involvement in gambling. All at once, the Club needed both to maintain to the public that its licensing practices were nondiscriminatory and to prove that its hands were clean in light of the congressional investigations. While the Club had taken a position against gambling—or at least against gamblers—it also had to avoid the appearance of basing its licensing decisions on ethnicity. Then a man of Jewish background with alleged ties to gamblers entered the scene.

Jule Fink

Until early 1951, the largely white Anglo-Saxon Protestant Jockey Club was all-powerful in New York thoroughbred racing. It wrote all rules, appointed all officials, and issued all licenses. Then a Cincinnati horse owner, Jule Fink, took the Club to court for refusing him a license to enter and race thoroughbred horses in the state, and (at first) won. A journalist and former employee of William Randolph Hearst who covered the story, Pat Lynch, was the racing correspondent of the *New York Journal American* and defended Fink in the paper on several occasions. Lynch felt that the Club had little more evidence for refusing Fink a license than hearsay and guilt by association.

As Lynch related the story to me, Jule Fink was "operating in New York," not only as the owner of the successful Marlet Stable, but as a "heavy player" whose "gambling operations caught the eye of the officials and the public." In Lynch's opinion, "Fink conducted himself with propriety except for his gambling activities. A funny thing, the racing business exists on the bedrock of gambling, but the people of the Jockey Club cloaked the sport in euphemisms."

According to Lynch, "Fink was ultimately ruled off [New York tracks] by Marshall Cassidy . . . the [executive] secretary of the Jockey Club. The members of the Jockey Club respected his rulings, usually proclaimed as being in the best interests of racing." At that time, Cassidy's "edict was self-sufficient, as the civil rights of people were never an issue. The Jockey Club was rarely hauled into court."

As Lynch's articles defending Fink came to the attention of "people in high racing places," Lynch said, "Ashley Trimble Cole, chairman of the [New York] Racing Commission, came to me one day. He blasted Fink and my attitude along with it. I said to the commissioner, 'You tell me one illicit thing Fink has done, and I'll get on your side.' 'I'm sorry,' said Cole, 'You'll have to take my word for it.' 'I'm equally sorry,' I said. 'The last time this happened, people were being thrown into the Bastille by French aristocrats, with little more than the infamous *lettres de cachet.*' "

Soon thereafter, Lynch said, "I received a call from Spencer Drayton, an ex-FBI man who headed racing's Protective Bureau. . . . Drayton said, 'We have voluminous files on Fink. I'll open them up to you.' I spent an entire day going through them. It soon became clear that all they had on Fink was guilt by association and vague charges which I doubted would stand up in court. Jealous trainers submitted odious tales of Fink's operations, and alongside the name of the sub rosa trainer was the hideous designation 'informant.' The case against Fink was largely hearsay."

Lynch went on, "Fink won a suit against the Jockey Club, resulting in them being stripped of their basic powers forevermore. The Jockey Club had such draconian power, they had become accustomed to never having their rulings contested, and hence the lassitude set in regarding the rules of evidence."

The Club had in fact previously licensed the successful Fink as an owner from 1944 to 1949. But he was known to be a gambler, and suspicions arose when his long-odds horses won. A man who had been relatively close to the case recalled for me a day at Belmont Park when, according to his recollection, Fink entered three horses ridden by a relatively unknown jockey. He said that when the horses went off at odds ranging from six to one to twenty to one, and all won by relatively wide margins, rumors developed that the races were "fixed."

The Club ostensibly refused Fink's 1949 license application because of his alleged ties to bookmakers. According to the Racing Commission's 1949 annual report, the Joint Hearing Board, which at that time consisted of the three members of the Racing Commission and two stewards of the Jockey Club, unanimously upheld the Club's denial.[10] The commission was made up of lawyer Ashley Trimble Cole, Wall Street investment banker William C. Langley (who would become a Club member within a decade), and Grumann Aircraft president Leon A. Swirbul. The Club stewards were Ogden Phipps and Joseph E. Davis. Even though Bernard Baruch, the highly respected statesman, appeared as Fink's character witness, the commissioners and Club members stood together against the owner.

A lieutenant in the Miami Police Department testified that Fink had a reputation as "the head of . . . the Speed Boys, which bet on supposedly fixed races [and] take bets, too."[11] Documents, including certificates of incorporation, were presented that indicated Fink had been a stockholder in a gambling enterprise handling pari-mutuel wagers in Covington, Kentucky. His associates in the enterprise were reputed to be bookmakers. In addition, he had failed to disclose to the Joint Hearing Board his arrest on charges of vagrancy, charges that were subsequently dropped. The board interpreted his lack of disclosure as a lie and an attempt to avert an investigation that might reveal any associations with bookmakers. Nevertheless, no substantiation of either illegal gambling or criminal activity—other than the dropped charges—was entered into the hearing record.

In 1951, Fink took his case to New York's highest court. His attorney was Charles H. Tuttle, former Republican candidate for governor of the state, the lawyer who had represented Club member Richard Whitney in his securities fraud case. The Court of Appeals of New York (*Fink v. Cole* 1951) annulled the 1949 Joint Hearing Board ruling and the subsequent refusal of the Club to consider Fink's application for the 1950 season.[12]

A front-page article in the *New York Times* reported that "the power of the Jockey Club to license owners, trainers and jockeys of race horses was wiped out yesterday by a unanimous decision of the New York State Court of Appeals. The state's highest court decided that the licensing power given by the Legislature to the social and exclusive group of sportsmen was an unconstitutional delegation of legislative authority."[13]

But the Club's decision not to license Fink was in essence upheld four years later when the Racing Commission denied him a license based on his having "undesirable" associates, a ruling affirmed by the appellate court.[14] Specifically, according to court records, the commission charged that Fink had "consorted with bookmakers in 1949" and that the ensuing five years were not sufficient time to excuse his behavior.[15] As far as Fink was concerned, he had to pay his attorney and still did not get a license. He can only take solace in his contribution to greater equality in the sport.

The Kefauver Committee Investigations

The Jockey Club's concern with undesirable associates seemed timely, given the simultaneous U.S. Senate investigations of organized crime in gambling. Central to the investigations, headed by a Senate committee chaired by Estes Kefauver, was the illegal transmission of wagering information from racetracks throughout the country. The Kefauver Committee's hearings were telecast nationwide. Notorious and unsavory characters, such as Frank Costello, Mickey Cohen, and Benjamin "Bugsy" Siegel's former girlfriend, Virginia Hill, testified before the committee while the public watched, glued to their tiny black-and-white television screens.

When the Kefauver investigations focused on Saratoga Springs, they revealed a panorama of gambling, racing, and aristocrats in the upstate New York resort town. The city had been a haven to gamblers since the Civil War days, when they frequented Morrissey's Club House. In the 1920s, they came to Rothstein's The Brook. Paul Mellon told me he could remember bookmakers when he and "[James Cox] Brady . . . were going to Saratoga in the early 1930s." (Brady was Mellon's fraternity brother in Scroll and Key and later his fellow Jockey Club member; he would eventually chair the New York Racing Association.) By the 1940s, it was widely known that the several casinos in Saratoga Springs were tied to organized crime. Mostly Italians and Jews and certainly not Yale graduates, the men who ran these places could not have been more different from the members of the Jockey Club. Yet they mingled with Club members and provided them with what members came to their places for: nightlife, gambling, and liquor.

A number of the clubs opened shortly after the repeal of Prohibition.[16] Saratoga Springs's politicians had suggested that these clubs were necessary to the depressed economy of the 1930s and that they were run by reputable bookies. Everyone in town knew about them, not excepting the police, whose headquarters were next door to the Chicago Club. The Arrowhead Inn and the Piping Rock had reputations as high-class operations.

As early as 1944, the New York State Liquor Authority held a hearing dealing with the elaborate Piping Rock casino and its owner, reputed New York organized crime member Joe Adonis. Adonis held the Piping Rock in partnership with notorious crime figures Meyer Lansky and Frank Costello. He also had an interest in the Arrowhead Inn. By 1947, the New York State Police had identified six casinos in Saratoga Springs, linked several to Adonis, and linked the Chicago Club to Lucky Luciano.

Local and state law enforcement agents were called before the Kefauver Committee. The superintendent of state police, John Gaffney, testified that when he received the report regarding the six casinos, he filed it and did not inform the governor, Thomas E. Dewey. He said he assumed Governor Dewey already knew about them, and admitted that it had been police policy at the time to ignore the gambling clubs. He further testified that if he had taken other action, he would have found himself out of a job.[17] The police chief of Saratoga Springs admitted to compliance, while two of the city's detectives admitted to transporting the day's profits from the Piping Rock and the Arrowhead to the bank every night in a police car.

Given the national press and television coverage of these hearings, those associated with racing in Saratoga Springs, including some members of the Jockey Club, might have felt the need to comment publicly. In September 1951, the U.S. attorney general appointed Alfred G. Vanderbilt II to a committee of sports leaders to look into the gambling issue.[18] (Like many others of the August regulars in Saratoga Springs, Vanderbilt probably went to the clubs there, if only to hear Sophie Tucker and Joey Lewis perform.) Three months later, Vanderbilt addressed the annual meeting of the Thoroughbred Racing Association, an organization comprised of racetrack operators nationwide. Racing, he assured the gathered members, "is in an enviable position; by keeping our own house clean and in order, . . . publicity and . . . investigation need cause us no fear."[19]

A BROADER CLUB MEMBERSHIP

Following the 1951 Fink decision, the New York State Legislature publicly criticized the Jockey Club's membership cap and policies. A joint legislative committee established to take a hard look at horse racing in the state recommended that the Club "immediately" broaden its membership and recognize men who are "representative" of those interested in racing and of "equivalent character and integrity."[20]

The Early 1950s

The Jockey Club may have anticipated the legislature's action. Three months after the Fink decision, Harry Frank Guggenheim, a member of America's wealthiest Jewish family of the day, was admitted to the Club.[21] He was a grandson of Meyer Guggenheim, the founder of American Smelting and Refining Company.[22] The Guggenheims were involved in the smelting, treatment, and production of lead, copper, silver, and bullion in thirteen companies worldwide, companies that were held to pay their workers very little. The family had for some time enjoyed a business association with the Whitneys, one of whom was on the board of directors of American Smelting, as well as with J. P. Morgan, with whom they controlled Kennecott Copper Corporation.

Harry F. Guggenheim had attended Yale, although he did not graduate, and had served in the navy in World War I. During the early years of the Depression, President Hoover appointed him ambassador to Cuba, when that nation was ruled by the reputedly bloody tyrant Gerardo Machado, who had been a local executive of

Morgan utilities.[23] Guggenheim was controlling stockholder in the rather conservative Long Island daily, *Newsday*. He married three times. But for his Jewish heritage, Guggenheim would seem to have fit the Club mold very well.

In 1952, John W. Hanes became one of the few Club members with roots outside the Northeast. As a Yale graduate and the director of Pan American Airways and Aviation Corporation, though, he already traveled in the right circles. More importantly at the time, he provided needed expertise for the Club. A longtime member told me that, in his opinion, Hanes was a politically smart appointment brought in for the specific purpose of heading the New York Racing Association. He was in fact one of three men appointed by the Club to the committee to reorganize state racing. The other two were Harry F. Guggenheim and Christopher T. Chenery, chairman of Southern Natural Gas Company. Another Club member, in referring to Chenery's admission, told me that the utilities chairman was said to have a number of contacts in the banking world.

By 1956, in the wake of the legislature's recommendation, the Club admitted twenty-eight new members. Most had backgrounds very similar to that of other Club members. Their family names and those of relatives and in-laws often had already been on the Club's roll. One of them, Amory Lawrence Haskell, later said, "Racing must have people who can afford to stay in the game without worrying about money."[24] All the new members fell into that category.

That same year, the Club admitted John M. Schiff, the grandson of Jacob H. Schiff, German-born and Jewish, who became the head of the brokerage firm Kuhn, Loeb, and Company.[25] Jacob H. Schiff's firm had close financial ties to Jockey Club members. It had financed the reorganization of W. C. Whitney and Thomas Fortune Ryan's Metropolitan Transit Company and of E. H. Harriman's railroads, and it was allied with August Belmont II in the formation of the Panama Canal Company of America. Though Schiff came under congressional investigation for knowledge of unscrupulous business practices, he was subsequently cleared of any wrongdoing.

Jacob H. Schiff, a religiously observant Jew, sought to have his son Mortimer exempted from Episcopal religious services at Groton

School upon making application for him there. Mortimer went elsewhere, however, perhaps because Groton was unwilling to make an exception. Mortimer Schiff's son, John, went to Yale and married, outside his religion, the wealthy Edith Baker, daughter of George F. Baker, Jr., chairman of the First National Bank of New York. As senior partner in his grandfather's firm of Kuhn, Loeb, and Company, John M. Schiff was a likely candidate for Club membership. By the 1970s, he was honorary chairman of Lehman Brothers after it merged with Kuhn, Loeb, and Company. His sister, Dorothy, married four times and was the publisher of the *New York Post*.

Bernard Baruch, however, who was closer to racing than Schiff or Guggenheim, was apparently never considered for Club membership.[26] Perhaps his antecedents, university of choice, or proclivities made him seem inappropriate. Baruch's father, an immigrant from Prussia, had been a doctor in South Carolina. Baruch turned down an opportunity to work as an ore buyer for Meyer Guggenheim to pursue his own ventures, including betting on the horses and placing bets for Club members. Rather than attending Yale or Harvard, he went to the City College of New York, where the tuition and books were free to youth who were academically qualified. His financial genius took him to the White House as advisor to presidents, although his advice was not without controversy. A U.S. Senate committee criticized his recommendation that the War Department do business with the industries of the Guggenheims and Andrew Mellon, largely because he had invested in these same industries and so stood to profit from the recommendation.

The Late 1950s and 1960s

Recall that in the 1950s, the Jockey Club began to reach out to others in racing through its annual Round Table discussions and to reorganize its operation of the state's major tracks. The Club was able to accomplish these ends and at the same time to appear to comply with the legislature's call for broader membership, in part by adding to the Club individuals with unique business and financial acumen, as had been the case with John Hanes earlier in the decade. These individuals provided the new blood the Club needed to survive, in light of the legal decisions and changes in the industry.

In the late 1950s, the Club recognized Leslie Combs II, who had been enormously useful to Club members for more than a decade. Combs had brought to the industry the syndication of thoroughbreds, that is, the division of ownership into shares that carry with them breeding rights (called "seasons"), the value of which is based on the horse's bloodlines, racing record, and ultimately, quality of progeny. In 1946, the business entrepreneur had developed such a syndicate for motion picture producer Louis B. Mayer's horse Beau Pere.[27] In 1955, he syndicated the Woodwards' Nashua for the record sum of more than $1 million. At around the same time, a major Wall Street insurance broker and relatively new member of the Jockey Club had purchased the nation's premier horse auction company, Fasig-Tipton. These two events signaled the beginning of a trend in the industry, one that anticipated the potential for making money by buying and selling thoroughbreds, rather than by simply racing them.

It would be an understatement to say that the changes occurring in the membership of the Club during the 1950s and 1960s were out of step with contemporary social changes outside the Club. Major league baseball had been integrated since 1947, when Jackie Robinson played for the Brooklyn Dodgers. Schools throughout the nation were required by the Supreme Court to integrate in 1954. By the 1960s, the nation was captive to free love, hippies, and Beatlemania. Gay liberation and the women's movement would quickly follow. By contrast, the Jockey Club in the 1960s opened its doors to Hollywood.

Aristocrats and the movie crowd had mingled—and married—for decades. Racing's aristocrats had traditionally gone to Santa Anita Park in the Los Angeles area ever since the track's opening in 1934. Motion picture producer Hal Roach was among the founders of Santa Anita. In the early years, Club members rode the train to southern California for the season there, which had all the trappings of a movie set, and one of them drew almost as much attention as a movie star himself. Alfred G. Vanderbilt II had come into the first $5 million of his inheritance.[28] These were the years when he resembled a young Jimmy Stewart, dated Betty Grable, was an acquaintance of Gene Tierney, had his photograph taken with numerous starlets, and started a friendship with Fred Astaire that would last a lifetime. Vanderbilt's horses put him on the sports page every day, and speculations about his romantic interests put him on the society page just as often.

But it was one thing to hobnob with movie people, and another to invite any of them into the inner sanctum. Not until 1962 was a member of the Hollywood set admitted to the Jockey Club. He was Gene Markey, a novelist, screenwriter, and occasional movie producer.[29] Markey had already been married to actresses Joan Bennett, Hedy Lamarr, and Myrna Loy when he married for the fourth time and finally settled down. His wife was the very wealthy Lucille Wright, widow of Club member Warren Wright, heir to the Calumet baking powder fortune. Wright had bred two Triple Crown winners, and admitting Markey into the group kept the winning horses of Calumet in the hands of a Club member.

The Late Twentieth Century

With near unanimity, Jockey Club members I spoke with said that the Club of the 1990s is a changed organization in terms of its membership. They talked about bringing in members from the West Coast, some professionals in the sport, some women, and even some who do not own horses but have been good spokespeople for racing.

Yet the Club certainly continues to invite into its ranks individuals who resemble the self-made entrepreneurs of the nineteenth century. In the 1980s, it admitted William Lester McKnight, who grew up on a South Dakota farm and went from bookkeeper to CEO and principal stockholder in Minnesota Mining and Manufacturing Company. His only daughter was married to James Binger, CEO of Honeywell, who would also become a member of the Club. In 1995, the Club admitted Jesse Mack Robinson, a college dropout who began as a used-car salesman and eventually became the major stockholder in the First National Bank of Atlanta.[30] In 1996, the Club invited into membership Allen Paulson, who at the time owned the Horse of the Year, Cigar. A former mechanic for Trans World Airlines, Paulson was chairman of Gulfstream Aerospace Company, a manufacturer of corporate jets, when it sold out to Chrysler. He also invested in resorts and made a $75 million offer for two casino holding corporations in Las Vegas.[31]

The Jockey Club has also admitted individuals who, like past members, made their fortunes in industries that do well during wartime. In 1978, James Kerr, CEO of Avco Corporation, joined the Club.[32] (Club member W. A. Harriman had been Avco's CEO forty years earlier.) Avco was a major government defense contractor for military engines, munitions, and tactical missiles. Among its major contracts were a type of air-launched munition used by the U.S. Air Force against Soviet tanks, and helicopter engines used by the army. Kerr was himself a member of the nation's Defense Advisory Council.

The Club has also continued to recognize those whose wealth originated in chemicals. John M. Olin, a Cornell graduate from St. Louis, Missouri, came into the Club in 1969. He headed Olin Corporation at the death of his father, the corporation's founder.[33] Beginning in the 1940s, Olin, in addition to its oil and gas subsidiaries, was a major producer of the insecticide DDT. The Olin plant was located at the army's Redstone Arsenal in Alabama. Twenty years later, DDT, discovered to have passed up the food chain, was banned. In the interim, it had contaminated the area surrounding the arsenal. The National Wildlife Federation and the National Audubon Society contended that the chemical had contributed to the declining bird population, local residents complained of health problems, and the federal government made demands that the company clean up the toxic waste. Olin settled with the residents out of court.

For nearly a century, the Jockey Club remained an old boys' club. Even the English Jockey Club, an organization not known for its egalitarianism, admitted women before the U.S. Club did. Paul Mellon, a member of both clubs, explained to me that "electing women was a big step forward. We were very late in electing women. I think we should have done that long ago. [When it did occur,] I thought—why didn't I push for this before? I was a little bit annoyed that the English Jockey Club was ahead of us. At least two or three years before we accepted women, they elected Lady Hallifax and Mrs. Hastings."

In 1983, the Jockey Club succumbed and admitted three women. Chairman Ogden Mills Phipps was said by several members to be instrumental in this radical change. One of the new members was Helen Chenery, the daughter of a former member and the owner of the 1973 Triple Crown winner, Secretariat. Another was Allaire du Pont, widow of Richard C. du Pont and breeder of Kelso, a champion in the early 1960s. The third was Martha F. Gerry, the wife of a Club member and the aunt of another. She was the owner of Forego, a champion in the 1970s. Since that time, the Club seems to have continued to favor women who are related to its male members—a criterion it also routinely applies to men. Charlotte Weber, ranked among the top two hundred richest individuals in the United States in 1999 and a member of the Campbell Soup Dorrance family, was admitted to the Club in 1997. Longtime Club member George Strawbridge, Jr., also belongs to the Dorrance family.

Another continuing pattern, which began in the 1940s, is to admit individuals to the Club soon after they assume major positions with other organizations in racing. This may be to honor such individuals, or, as one member suggested, a way to secure the interest and favor of these individuals for the Club. For example, the Club admitted a man shortly after he became head of another state's racing board, another after he became head of a national racetrack organization, one when he headed a national organization for regulators of the sport, and a fourth when he was made head of another state's breeders' association. In fact, one member told me he thought his membership in the Club was "to some extent to try to get the Club and [the organization of which he was the head] to try to work together. . . . [The two organizations had before this] been at odds."

The Club has extended its early practice of including those with substantial investments in racing to those who hold similar positions on major tracks in Canada. It has admitted with some regularity those who have occupied the position of CEO and others on the board of directors of the Ontario Jockey Club, which is the association that operates the tracks in Ontario, Canada. Bringing these individuals into the Club may have served to broaden its base of influence.

The Breeding Business

The business of breeding remains of major concern to Jockey Club members. In the past, it was more the case that members bred horses primarily to race. But beginning in the 1940s with the practice of syndication, thoroughbreds had for some members become investments as well as objects of sport. The hope of some breeders and owners would gradually change from simply winning the Kentucky Derby to making money from the syndication and standing of a Derby-winning horse. From the early 1970s on, "the dream . . .

was no longer just the glory of winning the Derby or earning the Derby purse of several hundred thousand dollars. . . . Now the incentive was the million-plus price tag that a top Derby performer and its progeny might bring in the marketplace for breeding and for syndication."[34]

The emphasis on breeding led to the "Bluegrass bubble" of the 1980s, when the prices of thoroughbreds were inflated, the number of breedings per year increased dramatically, and breeding practices became indiscriminate. When the bubble burst, many investors experienced a loss. By the late 1980s, two major farms declared bankruptcy—Calumet, formerly in Warren Wright's hands, and Spendthrift, owned by Leslie Combs II, who had brought syndication to the industry. The fall of both farms came under allegations of fraud by the stockholders.[35]

Contemporary Club members are more likely to be involved in breeding horses to sell them or in providing advice about breeding and selling. The latter activity is referred to as the "bloodstock" business. About 10 percent of the current membership of the Jockey Club are engaged in breeding to sell, the bloodstock business, or the selling of horses. This pattern parallels the fact that the nation's premier horse auction company, Fasig-Tipton, has remained in the hands of Club members since the mid-1940s.

THE IGNORED AND THE REJECTED

The Jockey Club claims to be an organization comprised of individuals who have made major contributions to racing. It also goes almost without saying that, following the pattern that began when W. C. Whitney bought the best horses of his day and August Belmont II bred Man o' War, those suited for membership should own or should have bred the most successful thoroughbreds. In fact, Club members have been among the most successful thoroughbred breeders and owners in the United States. But not all who have achieved such recognition belong to the Club. One contemporary member suggested to me that the Club's informal expectations keep some individuals from being admitted who might otherwise qualify for membership based on the success of their horses or their individual contributions to the sport.

That the most successful in racing are not always admitted is evident as early as the time of the Club's founding. Founder W. C. Whitney had hired John E. Madden, a man whose breeding advice was highly regarded at the time. He was also an athlete who was said to have sparred with boxer John L. Sullivan. Madden went on to breed several Kentucky Derby winners and was the nation's leading breeder from 1918 until 1927. But despite his athletic prowess, breeding success, and close association with the Whitneys, Madden was never admitted to the Club.

At least in the Club's early years, one's recreational habits and, in some cases, the source of one's wealth appear to have been used to determine one's appropriateness for admission. For example, the Club for a long time was not inclined to accept those with a history of gambling. An instance was Colonel Edward R. Bradley, who bred four Kentucky Derby winners in the early 1900s at his Idle Hour Stock Farm.[36] His profits from professional gambling and bookmaking allowed him to acquire large real estate holdings in Chicago and a lavish Palm Beach casino. Though Club members liked his style and frequented his casino, they did not put him up for membership. Yet so highly regarded were his horses that at his death in 1946, his entire stable was bought by Whitneys, Phippses, and Klebergs.

It's a different world now, and gambling seems to be viewed as a legitimate business endeavor for Club members. Indeed, a few members own and co-own casinos. Allen Paulson tried his hand at a partnership with Las Vegas casino mogul Steve Wynn.[37] Viola Sommer co-owned the Las Vegas Aladdin Hotel and Casino. The Ontario Jockey Club, which operates four tracks in the Canadian province of Ontario and whose board members are members of the Jockey Club, has joined with ITT Sheraton to try to acquire a casino in Canada.

One Club member told me that "if one is an alcoholic, he will not get in until he cleans up his act." At least one man was not nominated, according to another Club member, because he had a drinking problem. This is not to suggest that the organization objects to families making their fortunes in the liquor industry or that the organization is made up of teetotalers. Far from it. An appreciation of fine liquor and parties is central to the group's social life. Stories abound of August Belmont I's extravagant liquor bills, of W. C. Whitney's gifts of cases of champagne to Congress, of

Richard Whitney's well-stocked liquor cabinet, and of the parties that Joseph E. Widener threw during Prohibition and those that Mary Lou Whitney continues to host during the August season at Saratoga.

One mysterious case of rejection, or at least of overlooking, is that of Arthur Boyd Hancock, Sr., the owner of Claiborne Farm in Paris, Kentucky. In the 1930s, Hancock had led the group of Club members—William du Pont, Jr., Warren Wright, Jock Whitney, and Robert Fairbairn—who bought Epsom Derby winner Blenheim for $2 million from the Aga Khan. Though Hancock was himself the nation's leading breeder for ten years during the 1930s and 1940s, he customarily stood the horses of Ogden Phipps and longtime friend William Woodward I.[38] It was not until after both he and Woodward were dead, however, that the Club admitted any Hancocks. It was Arthur Boyd's son, A. B. "Bull" Hancock, Jr., who was invited to join the Club; he continued to stand Phipps's horses at Claiborne.

An outsider might have viewed California rancher R. C. "Rex" Ellsworth as a good candidate for the Club. Ellsworth became instantly famous when his horse Swaps beat William Woodward II's Nashua in the 1955 Kentucky Derby. It was completely unexpected for a California-bred horse to win that race. Further, Swaps set world-record times. Even after Ellsworth sold Swaps for $2 million to Club member John W. Galbreath, he continued to have successful horses in his stable. He was in fact the leading owner and breeder for several years in the early 1960s and mid-1970s.[39] Still, Ellsworth had several counts against him. He drove a pick-up truck, not the vehicle of choice for New Yorkers. And he was a Mormon, which may have given him status in some parts of the West, but not with the Eastern Establishment.

Another noted contender would seem to have been Louis Wolfson, owner of Harbor View Farm and the leading breeder in the early 1970s. His horse Affirmed won the 1978 Triple Crown and then syndicated for $15 million. In the entire history of the prestigious Triple Crown, only eleven horses have won the title; seven of these were bred and owned by members of the Jockey Club.[40] Because the Triple Crown brings with it such distinction, it is legitimate to wonder why the breeders of the other winning horses were not admitted to the Club.

The first horse to win the three races, Sir Barton (1919), was owned by a non-Club member, J.K.L. Ross. Club chairman William Woodward I bred the second and third winners, Gallant Fox (1930) and Omaha (1935). The fourth was Club member Samuel D. Riddle's homebred War Admiral (1937). Two homebreds of Club member Warren Wright, Whirlaway and Citation, took the Crown in 1941 and 1948, respectively. Mrs. John Hertz bred Count Fleet who won in 1943—one reason she was not a Club member, of course, was that at that time, no woman was. Club member Robert Kleberg, Jr., bred Assault, the 1946 winner. Not until 1973 would any horse again win the Crown—Penny Tweedy's (Club member Helen Chenery) Secretariat. The tenth and eleventh Triple Crown–winning horses were Mickey and Karen Taylor's Seattle Slew (1977) and Wolfson's Affirmed (1978). Affirmed raced neck-and-neck with Alydar, a horse owned by Calumet, founded by Warren Wright. While Affirmed was victorious in all three races, the margins were usually small—but perhaps significant as far as the Club was concerned.

While social differences might explain why some of these individuals were passed over, others simply may not have been interested. In spite of its status-conferring qualities, not everyone wishes to belong to organizations such as the Jockey Club. The Club has apparently made one error in judgment along these lines, admitting a man who then resigned. A longtime Club member told me the man had "no more interest in [the Club] than the man in the moon."

STILL A CLOSED WORLD

That there has been little change in the composition of Jockey Club membership or in the influence of some groups within the Club may also be a result of the closed nature of the world at this high social altitude. Members of the Club and their families have occupied a privileged position for generations. In an odd juxtaposition, in spite of regular press coverage of every aspect of their lives—where they go to school, whom they marry, which horses they race, and the amounts of their philanthropy—they move through the world relatively unrecognized; they are able to purchase the privacy that makes this so. Yet that same ubiquitous press coverage has led them to expect everyone to know them and to know about them.

The privacy that comes with privilege has meant that Jockey Club members and others of their social ilk regularly interact only with one another; only minimally do they mingle with others likely to present alternative perspectives on life.

The closed nature of their world became very clear to me one afternoon in the clubhouse at Saratoga. As I talked briefly with the son of a Jockey Club member, he reflected on the scene before us. "I can't believe another year has passed," he said, scanning the faces nearby. "And, these are people I see every day."

6

PHILANTHROPY AT
THE TRACK

In the racing world, the Jockey Club's dedication to the improvement and integrity of the thoroughbred line is widely known. This is in keeping with the Club's reason for being and the members' belief in bloodlines generally, as well as with the Club's role as keeper of *The American Stud Book*.

Less well known is the contribution of the Club and its members to the welfare of those responsible for the care of the thoroughbred. As owners of horses and racetracks and as organizers of racing in New York, they have demonstrated, to varying degrees, a sense of obligation for track workers' well-being. They have played some part in providing for minimum wages and overtime, medical coverage, and pensions for these workers. Yet track workers are up against a pattern in the history of thoroughbred racing in the United States of relying on inexpensive labor. In colonial days, slaves both trained and rode the horses. Payment for their services came in the form of board and keep. As racing became more organized and slavery was abolished, payment for handling the thoroughbred improved, but only somewhat.

The history of the treatment of workers on New York tracks under Jockey Club management—in comparison to the treatment of horses—dates to the days of Club founder W. C. Whitney. The grooms at Whitney's Long Island stables, which cost $2 million to build, were "told in no uncertain terms that their safety was a minor consideration in the event of fire compared with that of the horses."[1] O.H.P. Belmont, who joined the Club in its first year, housed his thoroughbreds on the ground floor of his Newport mansion, where he provided them with bedding of Irish linen sheets that were embroidered with the Belmont crest. Alfred Gwynne Vanderbilt I was said to have inscribed his horses' names in gold at the entrances to their stalls. Over time, it seems that the concern of Club members has sometimes extended more to horses than to those who care for them.

WHO WORKS THE TRACK

At the racetrack, there is a ranking of jobs, and therefore of workers.[2] At the top stand the trainers, who are paid by the owners to train and race the thoroughbred. In addition, trainers are entitled to a percentage of the purse when their horses "come in the money," that is, finish among the top four in a race. Jockeys have agents who negotiate with owners and trainers to get them mounts. They receive a dollar figure for riding, and, in addition, are entitled to a percentage of the purse when their horses come in the money.

At the bottom of the racing hierarchy are the backstretch workers—so named because they work and often live in the backstretch area of the track. Backstretch workers include grooms, who are responsible for the care and handling of the horses; exercise riders, who exercise the horses in the morning before the races; and hot-walkers, who walk the horse before and after its workout on the track. (In recent years, exercise riders have no longer been housed at the track.) All of these workers have historically come from working- and lower-class backgrounds; most have not finished high school and have developed few skills apart from their work with horses. They are usually members of racial and ethnic minorities. In New York in the 1980s, backstretch workers were Dominican, Puerto Rican, Cuban, Mexican, and African American. A longtime trainer told me that he estimated the present composition to be roughly 60 percent Mexican (largely from two towns in the Zamora province), 15 percent black, 10 percent Chilean, 8 percent white, 5 percent Jamaican, and 2 percent other. These workers have traditionally been paid minimal wages, with few guarantees and benefits, and they are entitled to no portion of the racing purse.

Grooms do most of the work at the track. Their job is to handle the horse—brush, wash, and feed it, and clean its stall. Grooms generally work every day of the year from 5:00 to 11:00 in the morning, 3:00 to 4:30 in the afternoon, and whenever their horses are entered in races. Although the state requires that they be licensed, most grooms have no contract, are paid wages set at the discretion of the trainer, and can be hired and fired on a minute's notice. Those who are paid in cash—as some trainers are known to do—are often without the benefits guaranteed under wage and workers' compensation laws. Grooms who are women and those who are in the country illegally are often paid even less than the going wage. In New York, grooms have never been unionized, though there have been several attempts at forming unions. Such has been the common lot of grooms on New York tracks, including those owned and operated by members of the Jockey Club.

Grooms work in the background. Though fans are likely to recognize jockeys and trainers by name, they are typically unaware of the grooms, who are visible to the public only as they lead horses in the paddock before the race. In the same vein, books on horse racing contain photos of prominent horses, jockeys, and trainers, but few of grooms. When grooms are pictured, they are seldom identified. An exception was Will Harbut, the black and reportedly loyal groom for Man o' War. When the great horse retired from racing in the 1920s, the story is told that its owner, Club member Samuel Riddle, allowed Harbut to go with him.

Sixty years later, two black grooms, father and son, were immortalized in a book by Norman Mauskopf, *Dark Horses*. Among the photographs by Mauskopf of the best tracks in Europe and the United States, like Chantilly, Epsom, and Saratoga, and of some of the lowest, like Charles Town in West Virginia, is a photo of the two men at Charles Town. Bill Barich, who wrote the captions that accompany the photos, described them in terms that evoke images of the difficult life of the backstretch: "Take the Joneses, father and son, who are grooms. . . . How dare they be so happy? Their armchairs appear to have been shredded with knives; their clothes are strictly retread; and their carpet is a blend of dirt, cigarette butts, and poptops . . . but the Joneses make no complaint. . . . Tired and sweaty, they've put in a hard day's work, and when they take a sip of cold Budweiser to wash the dust from their throats, it will hit them with the revitalizing power of a mountain stream."[3]

Barich has also written, in *Laughing in the Hills*, of his one-year retreat to Golden Gate Fields racetrack in California.[4] He found that people there work broken-down horses for years, against impossible odds, hoping to get a win, and that the very occasional win by such a horse makes all things seem possible. The dream of getting rich via a horse is compelling to many, as my own research on the New York backstretch found.[5] The dream also lies at the heart of the myth that surrounds the track.

Part of the myth is that poor workers enjoy their work—a belief that dates back to slavery. The myth of the track worker content with his lot hides the reality of poverty and exploitation. It also contributes to continued profit at workers' expense and gives consent to what have traditionally been deplorable working and living conditions. This myth, in all its moth-eaten fabric, is as alive at Saratoga as at Charles Town and Golden Gate Fields.

CONDITIONS BEFORE WORLD WAR II

It has been a matter of recurring debate as to who is responsible for backstretch workers on New York tracks—the owners and trainers who hire them, those who operate the tracks (historically members of the Jockey Club and, recently the New York Racing Association), or the state, which takes a percentage of track revenues. A look at laws governing the workplace and at the role the Jockey Club as well as its individual members have played in the sport sheds considerable light on this and other matters related to workers on New York tracks.

The labor laws include those that deal with workers' compensation and minimum wage and overtime. In 1908, Congress enacted a workers' compensation law that held employers accountable for employees injured on the job.[6] Although New York State developed a related law five years later, in part because of the horrific fire in the Triangle Shirtwaist factory that led to the death of more than a hundred young immigrant women, it was not until the 1960s that state regulators mandated that all track employees be covered by workers' compensation.

In the 1930s, the federal government passed the Fair Labor Standards Act, which entitled employees engaged in interstate commerce or in the production of goods for interstate commerce to minimum wages and a reasonable workweek. Since then, though, the minimum-wage law has been applied only in a limited way on state tracks.

The conditions of all backstretch workers were generally deplorable until World War II, although workers on Maryland tracks got some attention in the late 1930s. Vice president in 1938 of the Maryland Jockey Club, which operated Pimlico Racecourse, Jockey Club member Alfred G. Vanderbilt II had already built private quarters for his own stable help. At the time, he proposed a program for improving the living and working conditions of stable hands generally.[7]

Shortly thereafter, there was similar attention given to workers on New York tracks. A veteran of racing from coast to coast told me of the conditions at Saratoga when he arrived there in 1939. As an exercise rider, he had to sleep in the lofts of the barns and watch the races from "the louse ring," a place restricted from the public. At the end of that year, pari-mutuel betting was legalized and Alfred G. Vanderbilt II then became head of Belmont Park, as Club member Joseph E. Widener stepped down from the position. The major track stockholder at the time, Cornelius Vanderbilt Whitney, who was Vanderbilt's first cousin and also a member of the Club, had pressured the stockholders to put Vanderbilt in as president. During his two-year term, Vanderbilt proposed building living quarters for Belmont's track workers, a suggestion that brought him criticism from his set. This was not the first or last time that Vanderbilt would receive such criticism. Nor was he the only Club member to experience it. George Henry Bull, Vanderbilt's contemporary in the Club, was not considered a "genuine socialite" because he was a "little too friendly with the masses."[8]

In 1940, the Jockey Club helped to establish a foundation for the support of horse research. The Club, along with its chairman, William Woodward I, and John Hay Whitney, established the Grayson Foundation, named in honor of former Club member Cary

Travers Grayson. The Club raised one-fifth of the needed initial funds of $100,000.[9]

Three years later, the Club made its own effort to provide for track workers who were indigent. In 1943, it created the Jockey Club Foundation.[10] This time, all of the initial funds, $70,000, were provided by the Club, Woodward, and the racing associations operating the five tracks. Individual members of the Club headed four of the five racing associations in the state when the foundation was established: John A. Morris II headed the association at Jamaica; George D. Widener II headed that at Belmont Park; James M. Butler III headed that at Yonkers; and F. S. von Stade headed that at Saratoga Racecourse.

Racing flourished in New York during World War II. In good times, people often feel they have the luxury of losing some money. In bad times, they may feel they have little to lose and much to gain. Regardless of the economy, then, the odds are always with the tracks, but flush times are the most lucrative. In 1944 alone, state tracks took in four times as much money in bets as they had in 1939, on top of their receipts from general admission and clubhouse fees.[11] (The track associations were patriotic and gave $2 million to the War Relief Fund and another million to the American Red Cross and the National War Fund. Individual Club members, too, among them Harry Guggenheim in his capacity as president of a Guggenheim foundation, donated to the war fund and the American Red Cross.)

After the war, organized labor made demands in the workplace generally, and when the demands were not met, the major labor organizations—the American Federation of Labor (AFL) and the Congress of Industrial Organizations (CIO)—called for strikes. Labor organizations were apparently more interested in signing up the skilled laborers at the track than the backstretch workers. In 1946, the AFL threw up picket lines around Belmont Park and demanded that van drivers, ticket sellers, and electricians sign up with them.[12] The organization took no similar action for exercise riders and grooms.

At the same time, the track association operating Jamaica had stopped paying awards and bonuses to exercise riders and grooms when the horses they had exercised or groomed started in a race. The racing association there, then headed by John A. Morris II, increased the size of purses with the expectation that the owners and trainers would assume responsibility for payment to riders and grooms. After the riders and grooms staged their own one-day strike, the owners and trainers—though arguing that they had not asked for these awards and bonuses in the first place—agreed to pay them in the future.[13]

The next year, 1947, there was another strike in the back-stretch at Jamaica. This time, The International Brotherhood of Teamsters of the AFL backed some grooms and exercise riders in staging the strike.[14] The AFL asked that monthly wages for grooms (then $200), inexperienced exercise riders (then $225), and experienced riders (then $250) be raised by $50 each. It also asked for a six-day instead of a seven-day workweek, overtime, a cafeteria, dormitories, and an antidiscrimination clause regarding blacks. At the time, the Jockey Club asked the Racing Commission to transfer racing from Jamaica to Belmont Park on Long Island, so that racing could be "outside the jurisdiction of the authorities of New York City"[15]—and possibly further away from the heat of the union.

Most owners and trainers did not want to deal with the AFL and opposed the union's efforts on behalf of track workers. Some rationalized their position by arguing that such "itinerants" were generally uninterested in being tied down by contracts.[16] Those few who were interested in resolving the problem helped to draw up a code of honor (as opposed to a contract) to guide owners and trainers in the treatment of track workers. The code promised that the workweek would be five full days and two half days, that minimum monthly wages would increase by twenty-five dollars, and that there would be a goodwill gesture to improve living conditions. Signing the code was voluntary, and only a few trainers and owners, including Alfred G. Vanderbilt II and John Hay Whitney, another Jockey Club member, signed it. As a result, most workers saw no change in either their wages or their working and living conditions.

CHANGES IN THE 1950S AND 1960S

The 1950s was the decade in which the Jockey Club began to work at improving its public image. In 1952, *The New York Times* reported the Club's plans to build a home for "worthy" indigent horsemen whose age or physical disability rendered them unable to support themselves.[17] Despite the press coverage and the Club's noble intentions, no home was ever built.

The Club was nevertheless involved in the problems of backstretch labor during the decade. After the AFL and the CIO had merged, the federal government looked into whether racing was complying with the 1930s Fair Labor Standards Act. The U.S. Department of Labor actually conducted investigations at the New York tracks and found some violations of the minimum-wage, overtime compensation, and record-keeping provisions of the law.

Those in attendance at the Jockey Club's Fourth Annual Round Table, which met in 1956, formally discussed these issues.[18] Among employment practices at the track that were not in agreement with federal law was the pay rate: Many employers were still paying seventy-five cents an hours, six months after the minimum wage had been raised to one dollar. Employers were also commonly using a contract, the Belo contract, that allowed them to avoid paying overtime to backstretch workers. The Belo contract entitled employers to fourteen-week exemptions from overtime at each track in the state in which they raced during the calendar year. The attorneys for George D. Widener II, then chairman of the Jockey Club and head of Belmont Park, had developed this contract.

At the conclusion of the Round Table, a concerned Club attorney recommended that employers should not voluntarily settle issues regarding restitution of either wages or overtime. He said that such restitution "would establish a precedent for the collection of what the Department [of Labor] estimates to be in excess of two and one-half million dollars for the industry."[19]

While backstretch workers in New York apparently had some guarantee of minimum wages and overtime, a considerable number were without health and welfare insurance coverage. In the late 1950s, members of the Club who were the trustees of the New York Racing Association, proceeded to act on this situation on the state's tracks; California's racing associations had dealt with workers' health and welfare insurance a decade earlier. The NYRA set up a foundation with startup funds of $150,000 for such needs of New York's track workers. NYRA chairman John W. Hanes felt that, as the foundation's assets grew to several million, "the income therefrom would be more than sufficient to take care of all the needs that [are found] in the backstretch."[20] At the Club's Fourteenth Annual Round Table, in 1966, it was reported that the NYRA had been able to provide major medical insurance coverage for all regularly employed backstretch workers.[21]

More basic needs of workers were yet to be addressed. Many persons who had reason to visit the backstretch of most tracks in the 1950s could have viewed the inadequate living accommodations for workers; few commented on them. It was the head of the Horsemen's Benevolent and Protective Association in the state in 1958, Irving Gushen, who suggested that these conditions should be improved—and his proposal, presented at the Club's Round Table that year, seemed to point primarily to the benefits for racing. Only when heat was supplied in the middle of winter and sanitation facilities and decent food were provided generally, Gushen felt, would there be a "better class of people" working as grooms and exercise riders.[22]

The civil unrest and spirit of reform of the 1960s affected New York racetracks along with the rest of the country. Thomas E. (Tommy) Trotter was the NYRA's racing secretary when the Teamsters tried unsuccessfully to organize workers at Belmont. Trotter told me that the Teamsters used a number of persuasive tactics, including beating up some of the workers to try to intimidate them and setting fire to one of the horse vans. They failed in these efforts, though, Trotter said, because when thousands of horses were ready for transport from Belmont Park to Saratoga Racecourse for the August season, Nassau County and state police escorted them.

In 1964, the Racing Commission mandated that all jockeys and stable employees had to be insured by the owner or trainer who employed them.[23] Until that time, employers of backstretch workers had not been held to providing workers' compensation coverage. This state of affairs was somewhat remarkable, given that the law requiring such coverage had been passed nearly fifty years earlier and given the high risks involved in riding and working with 1,200-pound hot-blooded horses.

There was still no guarantee of pensions for backstretch workers on state tracks. In 1969, owners and trainers who were members of the New York division of the Horsemen's Benevolent and Protective Association (HBPA) staged a boycott at Aqueduct.[24] They withheld their horses from entering any races for nine days in an attempt to force the state legislature to approve a bill that would fund pensions for workers. The bill proposed adding four days to the racing schedule, with the state's share of the extra income to be used to set up a pension fund. As testimony to the invisibility of the backstretch workforce, one legislator, upon reading the bill, reportedly asked, "What the hell are backstretch workers?"[25]

The HBPA claimed that the state made $80 million a year by taxing racing and therefore should assume responsibility for the three thousand manual workers at the racetracks, nearly 80 percent of whom were black and Puerto Rican. The state held that the New York Racing Association, with its board of Jockey Club members, or the owners and trainers (the horsemen) who employed the workers should provide the money to start a pension fund. The NYRA claimed they had lost money the previous year; and the horsemen claimed that they made little more than the workers did and that only a small percentage of them make any profit at all. Again, no one assumed responsibility for the workers.

The Aqueduct boycott lasted for nine days, resulting in losses for the state and the NYRA. As part of his general efforts to end the action, the NYRA's racing secretary, Tommy Trotter, tried to get the trainers for the bigger stables to enter their horses; he failed. The Racing Commission obtained a court injunction to halt the strike, local police were called in, and some arrests were made. The next year, the NYRA's incoming chairman, Alfred G. Vanderbilt II, fired Trotter.

THE RISE OF BUDDY JACOBSON

The man who got the most press during the 1969 boycott was the newly elected head of the HBPA, the outspoken and nationally successful trainer Howard (Buddy) Jacobson. A young Jewish man from Brooklyn, Buddy had racing in his blood. Three of his maternal uncles were trainers, the most famous of whom was Hirsch Jacobs, the nation's leading trainer (that is, the trainer whose horses had won the most races) for eleven years during the 1930s and 1940s.

Jacobs's success was deprecated by those who claimed that he ran "cheap platers"—horses that run consistently but are seldom well bred and often run in claiming races.[26] The horses that run in claiming races are considered to be the lowest quality horses in racing. They are usually the least well bred and generally do not have the consistency of performance of horses that race in allowance, handicap, and stakes races.[27] Anyone entering horses at a meet may claim horses that run in claiming races by, prior to the race, placing a sealed bid in the amount of the designated claiming price. Running "claimers" is thus a risky business and garners little prestige. Ironically, Hirsch Jacobs became a leading breeder and was admitted to the Racing Hall of Fame.

To the street-smart and fiercely competitive Buddy Jacobson, his uncle Hirsch was someone to emulate.[28] At age eleven Buddy walked hots—horses fresh from workouts—and at twenty-one got his first trainer's license. Like his uncle, he became the leading trainer in the nation, making $150,000 a year in the 1960s, and the object of criticism. One journalist summed up Buddy in a *New York Times* article in late 1969: "Jacobson is a 37-year-old bachelor, a slim, dark man from Brooklyn who has made a great deal of money at the track through hard work, guile and skill. He claims horses, patches up sick horses, wins cheap races and runs an active public stable that is an Alexander's discount operation to the Bonwit Tellers of the so-called society trainers and owners."[29]

The racing elite also criticized his style, and no wonder. He trampled on the "old boy" traditions of New York racing. For Buddy, racing was a business—a way of making money. He once said, "I don't even like horses. . . . If they put on kangaroo racing, I'd claim some kangaroos."[30] He wore his hair long before it was fashionable, which offended some of the older generation. He wore jeans to the paddock, where tradition called for more formal attire.[31] And he broke the sex bar on state tracks when he named a female jockey to ride his horses.

This was the head of the HBPA who called for the boycott, whatever his motives—glory, conceit, demagoguery, or humanitarianism. He took this stand alone, with little support from the racing community. Despite claims to the contrary, there is no evidence that any state official, NYRA official, or Jockey Club member took a public stand on behalf of the workers—and against the establishment that had exploited their labor for so many years.

The boycott failed. But, in the process, it cost the state and the Jockey Club money and exposed ethnic disparities at the track.

"The race track," according to a *New York Times* article, is "a perfect example of the class system. . . . On top are the predominately WASP trustees and Jockey Club members, at the bottom are the black and Latin stable help. In between are the track administrators (many in New York are Irish), and the smaller owners and trainers, of whom many are Italians and Jews."[32]

Buddy would not refrain from speaking out even after the boycott failed. He told a *New York Times* reporter of his intent to continue working toward a pension plan and criticized racing's nobility in the process. "The little guys are racing," he said, "not the bluebloods." He described the contribution of the NYRA trustees and the Jockey Club as "negligible" and bragged that "the public bets more money on my horses, than on theirs."[33]

Jacobson predicted that there would be personal repercussions for his actions—that the state and the NYRA would try to "harass him into silence."[34] He said at the time, "Ever since I began to speak out on behalf of the little people in racing . . . I have been exposed to increasing attacks from wealthy and powerful men who rule the racing establishment."[35] Within two weeks of the boycott, the Maryland Racing Commission suspended Buddy indefinitely for selling a horse that he had claimed before the sixty days required for such a transfer in Maryland. Nine days later, New York's regulators suspended him for forty-five days for misrepresenting the prices of horses that he was buying and selling as a middleman, one of which he helped sell to a member of the Jockey Club.[36]

After his suspension, Buddy applied to the NYRA for stalls. The NYRA racing secretary, who was charged with making the stall allocations at the time, denied him. Buddy then appealed the denial, filing a $750,000 lawsuit that charged the NYRA with "maliciously and wantonly" punishing him for criticizing them.[37] Since he could not race in New York and while his case proceeded slowly through the courts, Buddy sold his horses and farm and bought a Vermont ski lodge. But for him, Vermont was Siberia. "Let's face it," he complained to a reporter in 1972, "I'm in exile. . . . They took away my stalls because I represented a threat to their control of thoroughbred racing."[38]

The NYRA tried to get Jacobson's case dismissed. By now the damage suit against the NYRA had grown to a claim for $4 million in compensatory damages and another $4 million in punitive damages.[39] A lower court denied the motion for dismissal and ruled that the NYRA, a "non-profit, quasi-public creature of the state [with] a virtual monopoly on thoroughbred horse racing," was not immune from justifying its conduct.[40] Upon appeal, a higher court upheld the decision in Buddy's favor but denied him the right to seek damages. Finally, the state's highest court overruled them all at the end of 1973, allowing him to bring suit for damages.[41]

The case finally came to trial in 1974. Appearing on behalf of the NYRA were former chairman Jack Dreyfus, Jr., chairman Alfred G. Vanderbilt II (both Jockey Club members), and racing secretary Kenny Noe, Jr. Noe testified that the NYRA considered the character of trainers in awarding stalls. What Noe considered to constitute bad character is not a matter of record.[42]

The jury took less than three hours to rule that the NYRA had acted in the best interests of racing when it had denied stalls to Buddy Jacobson. Within a year, the state legislature considered a bill making the racing secretary's responsibilities, including stall assignment, routinely subject to appeal to the state.[43] Buddy reapplied for stalls, and under Jack Dreyfus, Jr., again NYRA's chairman, he got them. But he would never rise to his earlier level of success at the track.

PROGRESS IN THE 1970s

When I interviewed backstretch workers at Saratoga, a Puerto Rican groom claimed to have helped try to form a union himself in the early 1970s. While unverified, his story is rich in detail and certainly plausible. The groom described some tangible successes as a result of organizing backstretch workers at another New York track.

> In 1971, my friend and I created the first union at Aqueduct. . . .
> At that time, we were trying to convince the blacks and the Hispanics that we would gain more power if we were united in the struggle. . . . Four thousand workers went to the polls, and my group won. . . . We got a day off and more money. . . .
>
> In 1972, I was thrown off the track because of my efforts to establish the union. In 1973, I began to work undercover . . . to convince people to join the union. . . . In 1975, I was thrown out again, because they found 478 letters in my room from the workers in support of the union.

Two years after Buddy Jacobson called for the boycott in 1969, New York's legislature considered a bill on a pension plan for track workers. Before the legislature could approve the bill, a majority of the horsemen had to agree to contribute to the fund. Three men associated with the Jockey Club were said to have played a part in getting their agreement. Two of them were officers in the Thoroughbred Owners and Breeders Association, Club member Reginald Webster and future Club member Jacques Wimpfheimer. According to a man close to the labor unrest, Club member E. Barry Ryan also supported the plan. Because Ryan's father had been disinherited by his father, utilities baron Thomas Fortune Ryan, and because Ryan was himself a professional horse trainer, he may have been more sympathetic to the workers.

About 90 percent of the horsemen on state tracks did agree to donate 1 percent of all purse winnings to a fund that would cover the pensions for regularly employed stable workers. The state legislature then mandated in 1973 that all horsemen participate in the plan.[44] To fund the pensions, the NYRA was required to withhold 1 percent of purses and give it to the horsemen's organization. There it was to be used for the operations of the organization, benevolent activities for employees—and horse research. This meant that stable-hand pensions would come from the purse winnings of owners and trainers and not from the income that came to the state and the NYRA from the sport—and, of course, it should not be surprising that money originally sought for workers' pensions would have to be shared with the horses.

Organizing labor on New York tracks has also proven difficult because some of the workers are undocumented aliens and live in fear of being found out. While in many ways the track has remained a domain unto itself, policed largely by private security forces, federal authorities have sometimes intervened. In these cases, it has often been to look for undocumented workers or to investigate whether employers were complying with federal laws. Some workers whom I interviewed experienced raids by federal agents personally. They told of seeing armed men, of running to hide, and of their friends being captured. (A female groom I came to know thought at first that I might be a federal agent investigating living conditions at the track dormitory where we met.)

THE FALL OF BUDDY JACOBSON

"Noted Racehorse Trainer Charged with the Murder of East Side Man" read an August 8, 1978, headline in the *New York Times*.[45] Buddy Jacobson, the former head of the HBPA, had been arrested for the murder of his former girlfriend's lover. After leaving the racing world, Jacobson had invested in Manhattan real estate, construction, and the modeling business. He had acquired several apartment houses on the Upper East Side and lived in a penthouse of the building at 155 East Eighty-fourth Street. He had shared his penthouse for five years with Melanie Cain, a twenty-three-year-old, $100,000-a-year fashion model, his partner in the My Fair Lady modeling agency. Cain was a familiar face to U.S. magazine readers—she had appeared on the covers of *Cosmopolitan* and *Redbook*.

The murder victim, John Tupper, had rented another penthouse in the same building. Two weeks before the murder, Melanie had moved out of Buddy's penthouse and across the hall into Tupper's. Tupper was shot seven times, stabbed repeatedly, bludgeoned with a blunt instrument, and then stuffed into a large wooden crate that was dumped in a lot in the South Bronx and set afire. A white Cadillac was reported leaving the scene, and its license plate number was identified. Shortly thereafter, the police stopped the Cadillac with Buddy and a young illegal Italian immigrant inside.

The prosecution argued that Buddy was insanely jealous over the very attractive model and in fear for his life because Tupper had threatened to kill him if he "so much as touch[ed] one hair on her head."[46] The case was built largely on Cain's testimony. She was on the stand for nine days and testified to seeing "blood and matted hair" in Buddy's hallway on the day of the murder, and also to seeing blood in Tupper's apartment.[47]

The murder victim, John Tupper, was posthumously named in a major drug indictment. He was implicated with several others following a nine-year federal investigation of a multimillion dollar drug trafficking and smuggling ring. Three of the conspirators also rented living quarters from Buddy.[48] Two of them, Allen Seyfert and George Miller, gained immunity and became witnesses for the prosecution in the murder case. Seyfert, who was with Melanie the day of the murder, testified that he saw Buddy in the building that

day. The third conspirator, Joseph Margarite, disappeared that day
and did not reappear until three years later when he was arrested
for smuggling hashish.[49] At that time, a spokesman for the Bronx
district attorney said that the D.A.'s office planned to question him
about the Tupper murder and admitted that the district attorney
had known all along there were two other men involved.

The argument in Buddy's defense was that he had been framed.
His lawyer argued that Seyfert and Miller killed Tupper over a drug
deal in the apartment of Margarite, who lived two doors away from
Buddy. Some corroboration came from the testimony of still another building resident, who said she saw blood and a bullet hole
in Margarite's apartment the day of the murder. Further, the defense lawyer tried to discredit Melanie's testimony, saying she was
bitter over Buddy's many infidelities. (And Buddy was indeed
known to be a womanizer. One longtime trainer I spoke with came
to Buddy's defense in a roundabout way: "Buddy liked women.
[But] you can't fault him for that.") After six days of deliberation,
the jury returned a verdict; they found Buddy guilty of second-
degree murder.[50]

Buddy was held in jail in Brooklyn to await sentencing. The
man to whom Buddy had sold his Vermont ski lodge (and whose
debt on the sale Buddy had forgiven) came to the jail posing as his
lawyer, using legal stationery that was forged by Buddy's new girlfriend, Audrey Barrett, a twenty-two-year-old model and Hunter
College student. Buddy then adopted the man's identity, "sign[ed]
himself out and [left] by the front door," wearing a gray tweed
suit.[51] He fled in a brand new Dodge Aspen and on his way out of
town picked up Audrey Barrett. They traveled to Des Moines, Iowa,
where they bought another car and took aliases from local tomb-
stones. They were able to finance the getaway with large sums
wired to them by friends and others in one state after another. It
was the stuff chase movies are made of: the two used elaborate dis-
guises, aliases, and coded messages, received help from friends, and
eluded the authorities for nearly forty days. Along the way, Buddy
apparently got in touch with writers to try to raise cash in exchange for his story; he also contacted California realtors regarding
properties there.[52]

Local, state, and federal law enforcement were at a loss until
they tapped the phones of Buddy's friends and relatives. The Bronx

district attorney sought and then reputedly coerced the coopera-
tion of several of these individuals in exchange for immunity from
prosecution. Buddy was finally arrested at a Manhattan Beach
restaurant near Los Angeles while on the telephone with someone
in New York.[53] Though Buddy said he had been betrayed, it was
never clear who his betrayer was. He spent the rest of his life in At-
tica and died of bone cancer in 1989.[54]

A reporter for the *New York Times* wrote around the time of
Buddy Jacobson's conviction for second-degree murder that his rise
and fall could be understood in two very different scenarios.

> In one version, an ambitious Jewish boy enters a profession dom-
> inated by a white, Anglo-Saxon Protestant hierarchy. He not only
> beats them at their own game—horse-racing—but a strong social
> conscience also drives him to take up the cause of underpaid sta-
> blehands. . . .
>
> He leads the stablehands to revolt, which further alienates the
> powerful aristocrats who control racing. At the first opportu-
> nity—when he commits a commonplace financial transgression—
> the hierarchy forces him out of the profession. Bad luck pursues
> him until, years later, he is framed and convicted of murder.
>
> In another version, a brash troublemaker and long-haired loud-
> mouth employs unsportsmanlike tactics to win races. He capital-
> izes on the issue of stable-hand dissatisfaction as a smokescreen
> for unethical maneuverings.
>
> He leads a boycott that stops racing for nine days and costs
> the state millions of dollars. But his deeds catch up with him; he
> is caught in a shady deal and brought to justice. Banned from the
> race track, he perpetuates his evil ways until, in a tawdry finale,
> he murders his girlfriend's lover in a jealous rage.
>
> Which version most closely approximates Mr. Jacobson's true
> story may never be completely determined.[55]

PROTEST FROM INSIDE THE CLUB

The Jockey Club has expressed some concern for track workers,
having set up one foundation to aid indigent workers and another
to provide them with health benefits. Individual members, too,
have lent their direct support to efforts to address the circumstances of workers at critical times. It is their wherewithal and the

extent to which they derive advantage from the labor that raise questions about the sufficiency of their support and the seeming reluctance with which they have sometimes extended it. Such questions have been raised even by Club members themselves.

Jim Ryan, the founder of Ryland Homes, a major home builder in the United States, retired early from the company's chairmanship, sold it through Dillon, Read, and Company, and got his master's degree in pastoral counseling. In the process of selling the company, he became acquainted with Club members August Belmont IV and Nicholas F. Brady II, who were then board members of Dillon, Read. Ryan was admitted to the Club in the early 1980s.

Belmont himself came to racing late in life. Because his father had raced yachts, there might have been less expectation that he race horses. When he did join the world of the track, he came to own a horse in partnership with Ryan. The horse was Caveat, a horse that won the Belmont.

Ryan's interest in racing had by then nearly been overshadowed by his concerns about track workers. The concern was precipitated when he and his wife attended a horse auction, and his wife called his attention to a man who was handling a horse. The man was unwashed, looked ill, and had no shoes. Ryan came to attribute the man's condition, in part, to alcohol use. He and his wife then set up a foundation to provide funds for organizations that would address substance abuse problems on tracks nationwide. He also became involved in setting up an alcohol and drug abuse counseling program for workers on Maryland tracks.

After Ryan became a member of the Jockey Club, chairman Ogden Mills (Dinny) Phipps appointed him to the committee that oversaw the Club's foundation for indigent track workers. In that capacity, Ryan suggested that the foundation give away more than 5 percent of its corpus—the percentage required by law in order for the foundation to maintain its tax-exempt status. Failing to persuade other committee members, he felt he should resign, and not just from the committee, but from the Club itself. Here is Jim Ryan's story, as he told it to me.

> I asked to go on [the] Foundation [Committee]. . . . I was on for three years. I did my homework and never missed a meeting. [The pattern of giving at the time was] at the level required to

maintain its charitable status. I said, "Charity begins after 5 percent." [Regardless,] I was voted down 85 percent of the time.

The Foundation Committee went over a number of programs [to consider which to contribute to, including the program for substance abuse on the Maryland racetracks]. Their response was, "That's beyond the 5 percent limit." I countered, "Let's go to 10 percent, then.". . .

Dinny Phipps said, "These meetings are acrimonious. If we can't get along, I'm going to ask you to resign." I said, "I'm not going to resign. You put me on. You can take me off." Dinny responded, "You make it hard. I'm taking you off." . . .

I appealed to Dinny to give away the corpus. "Let's give this away. Go back and make some more." . . . I said I would give a half million, and would he match it? [Dinny did not follow up on my offer.]

One [August] night [in Saratoga Springs] on [Nicholas F.] Brady's porch, we were watching horse-drawn carriages. Meanwhile, there were people who were picketing all around the horse auction in town. We got off the porch and walked across the street to see the horses [at the auction]. Those who were picketing carried signs suggesting . . . it was a crime to spend a million on a horse when there was so much hunger and homelessness. [I must have looked distraught]. When . . . asked what was wrong, I said, "I might know some people in that line."

I was in the middle for a long time. . . . I had to ask myself, "Did I want to stay in a Club, when all I did is attend social functions—go out to dinner and have lobster? If I can't contribute to the foundation, what can I contribute to?"

[At a meeting of the Jockey Club,] Jim Moseley [the Jockey Club Foundation Committee chairman] reported that "we're not giving 5 percent, we're giving 5.6 percent." [I felt as if his statement was] just a bunch of baloney. . . . I was very nervous. I felt I had to resign from a group that was so indifferent to the needs of people who take care of the horses that we race. . . .

I turned around at the meeting. I picked out a man. It was Paul Mellon—probably the richest man there. I said, "Everywhere you look, there's addiction. It's rampant. It's the quality of life we need to deal with." I thought I didn't have a vote here. I'm leaving as of this meeting. I walked out across the street . . . I felt so alone. Nobody had said anything. I cried in my car at the Reading Room parking lot.

Later, one fellow member said, "All my life I wanted to be in the Jockey Club. They gave me an invitation. I'm seated eight minutes in my first meeting, when someone stands up and resigns."

I think it's a wonderful legacy to leave my family. I'm the only one in its history to ever resign from the Jockey Club. I felt proud of it. I decided to sell my horses and I gave two and a quarter million dollars to the backstretch.

In fact, no one *had* ever before resigned from the Jockey Club for reasons of personal conscience and in so public a manner. True, some members had resigned when they became ambassadors. Even C. V. Whitney was said to have resigned when he sold all his horses. This was different. It was also unforgettable, at least to another Club member, whose recollection is remarkably similar to Ryan's. He characterized the Foundation Committee's decision not to distribute more than that required by law as "relative stupidity." Further, he admitted that when he witnessed Ryan's protest, he came close to "standing up with him." He described the group's response to Ryan's exit. "[Jim Ryan] left in tears. He believed strongly in what he was doing. [He] left, and everybody felt [bad]."

THE CHALLENGE OF THE 1990s

The challenge that Jim Ryan extended to the Jockey Club's chairman Dinny Phipps stands in contrast to a more recent challenge Paul Mellon posed to the Club itself. In 1993, Mellon's horse Sea Hero won the Kentucky Derby. Chrysler Corporation had established a $1 million bonus for that year's 1993 Triple Crown races. Another horse won the Preakness but died during the running of the Belmont, which was won by yet a third horse. It was because Mellon's horse was the only horse to win one Triple Crown race and to finish in all three that Mellon received Chrysler's bonus. Mellon donated the money to the Jockey Club's foundation for equine research and asked the Club to double match it.[56] The Club did. A million dollars for their horses, but no increase in help for track workers. The Club once again demonstrated the nature of its obligation to racing—that is, to the thoroughbred.

Today, the Club continues to allocate funds to horses as well as to indigent workers. Its foundation for horses, the Grayson-Jockey Club Research Foundation, was formed in 1984 through a merger with the Grayson Foundation. The available figures show that the amounts currently set aside and distributed for horses exceed that for track workers.

The corpus of the equine foundation in fiscal 1995–1996 was more than $11 million, with donations for horse research amounting to $665,000. The corpus of the foundation for indigent track workers for the same year was $7.5 million, with distributions totaling $613,000—due to rising medical costs, that figure was twice the amount distributed the previous year.[57] Though the differences between donations and distributions in the two foundations are not that great, we are, after all, talking about differences spent on the welfare of animals and humans.

CONCLUSION
The Winners' Circle

Jockey Club members still go to Saratoga Racecourse for the August racing season. The grandeur of that track exemplifies the way of life associated with early racing in the United States, as well as racing at Europe's Ascot and Epsom—which America's racing aristocracy has tried to emulate. The pomp and circumstance of today's Saratoga clubhouse is reminiscent of a hundred years ago, when elegantly dressed men and women gathered to watch horses race from a privileged vantage point far removed from the general public in the grandstands. Saratoga remains the realm of self-assured men in suits and women immaculately groomed and attired. There, Club members have made it their custom to be available during the afternoon races. Anyone who has paid the required fee and is properly dressed may ask attendants about particular members and be directed to the members' box seats. It is as if kings (and queens) are holding court. Journalists who cover the racing season have recently reported that "class" is no longer visible at the Saratoga track. They are mistaken. That's what Saratoga is about.

A QUICK TRIP THROUGH CLUB HISTORY

At the end of the nineteenth century, America's richest men were its "robber barons," who then controlled the nation's industries, financial markets, and lands. Because their fortunes were self-made and their backgrounds ordinary, they were often rejected by so-called proper society. In order to gain legitimacy, many joined the best men's clubs, became Episcopalian, married well, and sent their sons to the right schools. They also adopted a life-style they felt was unassailable—that of European aristocrats—and built lavish mansions, amassed vast art collections, and bought yachts and the finest thoroughbred horses.

A few of the robber barons who took up thoroughbred racing assumed its total control. In 1894, they founded the Jockey Club in New York City. The men of the Jockey Club became keepers of the registry of the thoroughbred horse in North America—the stud book. With responsibility for the integrity of the breed, the men would make the claim that the thoroughbred horse—actually of mixed pedigree—was a purebred. The thoroughbred was a horse Club members would come to idealize and identify with. Their concern over the horse's bloodlines may have reflected the preoc-cupation of some with their own backgrounds.

To cement their position in society, as well as from altruistic mo-tives, the men of the Jockey Club and their family members have be-come congressmen and presidential advisors on financial and military policies and left a legacy of public service that was beneficial to their interests. They have served in the military and have become great philanthropists, renowned for having founded the nation's ma-jor museums, libraries, and private schools. They have left a less aus-picious legacy of assistance to common laborers at their racetracks.

Many of the men of the Club came to cultivate the rules of so-cial etiquette, rules reinforced in the prep schools and Ivy League colleges that they attended. They also projected an image of open-ness to those not of their social set. Still, the Club has remained ex-clusive, as it has tended in later years to admit contributors to racing who are useful to the Club's interests. While the style of Jockey Club members has undergone some change, they have ap-parently held to the aim of their predecessors—to remain powerful.

THE JOCKEY CLUB'S INFLUENCE ON RACING

The Right Blood describes the influence on racing of the Jockey Club over time. If power in the United States has traditionally resided with a single ruling group, as C. Wright Mills claims, early members of the Club, as the nation's financial and industrial kings, comprised a "power elite."[1] It would appear, though, that contemporary Club members no longer occupy such a singular power position in industry, finance, or government. Yet the Jockey Club has survived a century of change—change in society and change in racing. Not only has it lasted; it has remained influential. Clues to that endurance and power seem to lie in U.S. society and contemporary beliefs as well as in the Club itself.

While the Club has lost some prerogatives in racing, it has maintained control of America's registry of thoroughbreds, *The American Stud Book*. Members' belief in ascription as opposed to achievement as a measure of value is a belief they continue to promulgate in racing. The belief, here referred to as the myth of pedigree, has become accepted as near fact in the sport. Its strength is tribute to the organization's continued influence, as well as its members' economic investments in racing, breeding, and syndication of major stallions.

The influence of the Club would also seem in step with the nation's longstanding beliefs in the superiority of certain bloodlines. One cannot help but wonder about the extent to which these beliefs are supported by movements in society that emphasize genetic factors in human development and performance. In an age in which many attribute illness, crime, poverty, personal characteristics, and any number of other factors to genetic deficiencies, we are increasingly attributing success in learning, achievement, and general performance to genetic advantage. It is not far-fetched, therefore—if we believe that one commits a crime, cannot learn, or becomes ill because of his ancestry—to say that a horse can win a race because of his forebears. The continued power of the belief in superior bloodlines in racing is evidenced by a public willing to pay increasingly high prices to buy as well as breed to horses with those bloodlines. Such trust in blood proves very lucrative for those who control the major thoroughbred syndicates.

The Jockey Club's claims that it has protected and improved the thoroughbred are not convincing, however. The breed seems neither more swift nor as strong as it was a century ago. The Club's premise of the importance of equine bloodlines seems increasingly shaky. One of the most successful horses of all time, John Henry, had been gelded early in his career because his blood was considered not worth passing on. Racing fans will also remember Seattle Slew, the non-Club, unimpressively bred yearling that sold for $17,500 at a Fasig-Tipton sale and went on to become the only undefeated Triple Crown winner in history. In 1998, there was tremendous public interest in Real Quiet, who nearly won the Triple Crown, a horse whose bloodlines were called blue collar. The horse surprised everyone when he won the 1998 Kentucky Derby. When he also won the Preakness, those who trust in bloodlines suggested it was because his competition was not that good. When Real Quiet then lost the Belmont, though only by a nose, they said it was because he was not bred for the distance. Although a loss by such a small fraction in a mile and a half race may be attributed to any number of factors, those who subscribe to the breeding premise tended to see it as largely a matter of blood.

Today's racing public may be less aware than were earlier racing aficionados of the Eastern establishment, and not even particularly knowledgeable about the Club's new-family, new-money members. Yet over and over it has been Jockey Club members who have bred, owned, and raced some of America's most famous horses. August Belmont II, of the New York banking family, bred the legendary and nearly unbeaten Man o' War. In the 1940s, Calumet baking powder baron Warren Wright bred two Triple Crown winners, Whirlaway (1941) and Citation (1948). Alfred G. Vanderbilt II's near Triple Crown winner, Native Dancer, thrilled the nation when his gray form streaked across the new black-and-white television screens of the 1950s. "Penny" Tweedy (now Helen Chenery) raced Secretariat, who won the Triple Crown in 1973. Canadian brewer E. P. Taylor bred an all-time leading sire, Northern Dancer. Allen Paulson, a mechanic who rose to the office of CEO of Gulfstream Aerospace, owned Cigar, the nearly undefeated Horse of the Year in 1996.

I have come to believe that these extremely wealthy and successful men and women gain vitality through association, even identification, with the thoroughbred. I had found earlier that grooms and riders at the track are inclined to identify with specific horses they have worked with or ridden.[2] Here, I found among the socially sophisticated and often well-educated men and women of postindustrial society a similar personal identification and involvement with their thoroughbreds.

KEEPING POWER

During the twentieth century, the nation's economy moved from an industrial to a technological one, and much·of the change occurred during the century's last two decades. Today's economy is dominated by high technology rather than railroads, mining, and manufacturing. There is thus less domination of the economy by that segment of society from which Jockey Club members have traditionally come. This change might partially explain why fewer contemporary members number among the nation's richest individuals, whose fortunes are primarily self-made rather than inherited.

Yet Club members remain influential because, as business moguls, they conform to American society, its commitment to capitalism, and its preoccupations with money and power and the superiority of some groups over others. In a capitalist economy, entrepreneurs flourish and often become heroes, though seldom without criticism. Contemporary America is both drawn to and ambivalent about its high-tech entrepreneurs, much as a nineteenth-century public related to its industrialists, who were reviled as unscrupulous and praised as self-made men.

America's aristocratic families, including those of the Jockey Club, are believed to have lost some of their national power and, with it, some of their social position as well.[3] This has been attributed to a public less willing to give exclusive privilege to upper-class white Anglo-Saxon Protestants. It has also been said that dynastic wealth seems to dissipate beyond the fifth generation, often because of divorce, high living, and marriages with outsiders.[4] Today, members of the Jockey Club do control a smaller portion of the nation's wealth than did the Club's founders. Indeed, in 1999, no members of the Club were among the country's top 150 billionaires.[5]

Still, we have seen indications that Club members remain nationally influential, in part through their substantial representation on major corporate boards, continued involvement in the financial sector, and close, even familial, ties to powerful, conservative groups. In the 1970s, members of the Club reportedly held "most of the key seats in the directorships of U.S. corporations, banks, foundations, museums, hospitals, and universities."[6] This coincides with the view that upper-class, white Anglo-Saxon Protestants have been able to sustain considerable influence through institutions, as well as through family and informal networks.[7] Indeed, this look at the Jockey Club suggests that its members continue to be influential at the national level, as well as in the racing industry.

INSIDE THE CLUB TODAY

Currently a tax-exempt organization with approximately one hundred members, the Jockey Club continues to operate out of its office in New York City. From its founding until 1999, 347 individuals have been members of the Club; most of them were kin or related by marriage, attended the same schools, and did business together (see the appendix).

The style of members of the Club has changed since the days of William K. Vanderbilt, and even those of William Woodward I in the first half of the twentieth century. Today's members defer to, wine and dine, host meetings for, and listen to the viewpoints of outsiders—and even invite some who would once have been outsiders to join them. They are masters and mistresses of the social graces, those valuable good manners learned in early childhood, refined in prep school, and perfected in Ivy League circles. Yet power in some form remains the objective—not unlike their forefathers, the "robber barons." Unlike them, however, today's Jockey Club members can wield influence and at the same time manage to look good in the public eye.

Their power has been effected through both personal and professional relations.[8] Members of the Club have intermarried and have had the informal benefit of old-school, men's clubs, and high-church ties. They have derived advantage from the positions they occupy in formal organizations, such as membership on corporate boards. They have also reaped benefit from the etiquette of their social set, as it has contributed to their considerable influence within the racing industry and among those with whom industry figures come in contact.

PROTECTING THE CLUB

The statement of one longtime member that "this business of the Jockey Club is all about power" seems to me an accurate assessment. The Club has maintained power in the sport, if sometimes from behind the scenes. For this to be true, over time, the Club must have become versatile in handling threats to its influence. This has been the case. We have seen that a small number of individuals at the very top of the racing industry have over the years held onto their influence in thoroughbred racing. They have been able to do so in large part through the Jockey Club with its continued control over certain aspects of the sport—the stud book, other major organizations in racing, and major tracks in America and Canada.

The Club has kept close ties with those charged with regulating the sport. It has organized to operate tracks in New York State. It became service oriented. It has lent financial support to projects that other groups proposed and could not afford, including DNA identification for thoroughbreds. As the nation's population has become more heterogeneous, the Club has opened its doors to a select few outside its social set. In the new high-tech economy, it has invested in technology, including around-the-clock televised racing and on-line betting. In the face of changing tax laws, it has turned to friends in political office. While the Club was founded in part to develop a sport that would serve its members' leisure interests and provide for a way of life they had come to embrace, it has organized the present industry in ways that protect those interests. The future of the Club may depend on how well it continues to adapt itself toward those ends.

Thoroughbred racing has itself proved resilient. This is amazing in light of the many other sports that command an increasingly large share of the public's attention, the proliferation of casino gambling, and the lack of a Triple Crown winner for more than two decades. A booming economy has certainly helped. Americans now have money to spend on any number of luxury items, including thoroughbreds, even though these horses are expensive to maintain and generally losing propositions.

It has been said that history repeats itself. As far as the history of the Jockey Club is concerned, that would seem to be the case.

Americans are again intrigued with entrepreneurs who on occasion exploit them. We believe again that some individuals are better than others—a belief that gives the advantage to those with "the right blood." Some of us are nostalgic for the Gilded Age, and the formality, luxury, and graciousness it symbolized. Buying a racehorse is one way to recapture those times.

Racing may also remain attractive for the same reason that it appealed to some of the robber barons a century ago—not so much because of its promise of legitimacy and social status, but because it carries with it associations with aristocracy. It is still "the sport of kings."

THE CLUB RECEIVING ITS PUBLIC

The August season at Saratoga Springs is where Jockey Club families have gathered for generations. Here they hold lavish invitation-only parties, some of which raise substantial funds for favorite causes. Here they are on parade.

Outside the box-seat entrance to the clubhouse, just before the first post of the day, the line of limousines extends for some distance. Drivers open the doors for well-dressed men and women as they arrive. Among them are well-known actors and famous jockeys. The women are striking and often younger than their escorts. One older woman drives herself in her black Rolls-Royce—perhaps so privileged that she is above bowing to custom.

Nearby a ragtime band plays—trombone, clarinet, banjo, and base violin. The band members sing the lyrics from a popular song of the Twenties. "You've got to e-liminate the negative, ac-centuate the positive, latch on to the affirmative, and don't mess with Mr. In-between."

Inside the clubhouse, the men all seem to have a commanding sense of themselves. They wear suits and ties, occasionally a sports jacket. While racing fans walk by and stare, the men appear to pay no attention. This is their turf.

The women are gorgeous. Their faces could have been sculpted by Michelangelo. There is nothing casual in their attire or grooming. The rule seems to be to wear black, though white or tastefully flowered dresses are also seen. The women walk with a natural grace that seems almost inbred and most assuredly was perfected in private school. They never hurry. The younger among them have long hair, invariably straight.

During races on the long August afternoons, Club members receive the public in the box-seat section of the clubhouse. Here, as at all tracks, the least expensive seats are in a grandstand area, the more costly in a clubhouse area and, within that, the even more expensive box seats. At Saratoga Racecourse, those who have box seats for the season enter the clubhouse area through a separate entrance. Club members occupy a large number of the center section box seats in the first two rows nearest the track. One may visit them there on request. Of course, when the races begin, all talking must cease. Attention must be focused on the race. Everyone knows it is improper to talk at such times. At least, everyone who is anyone.

Appendix:
Members of the Jockey Club,
1894–1999

The information on members of the Jockey Club includes primary professional affiliation; family background/wealth; marriages/associations with Club members; education; principal ownerships/directorships; political offices; philanthropy/foundations; military service; racing organizations; other sports/clubs; Jockey Club offices; political affiliation; religion; worth/estate; major horses; stable name; primary residence; and dates of Jockey Club membership.[1]

Less common abbreviations used in the Appendix: admin., administrator; assn., association; bldg., building; chmn., chairman; dir., director; fndtn., foundation; gen., general; mgr., manager; nongrad., nongraduate; NYRA, N.Y. Racing Association; NYSE, New York Stock Exchange; ptnr., partner; rep., member of the House of Representatives; sen., senator; TOBA, Thoroughbred Owners and Breeders Association; vp, vice president.

Abercrombie, Josephine E., only daughter of fndr. Abercrombie Minerals Co. and Cameron Iron Works; multimillionaire oil, gas, and real estate heiress; 4th husband was E. Barry Ryan; gen. ptnr. Pin Oaks Partners (building company); Abercrombie Fndtn.; TOBA; boxing promoter; Houston, Tex; 1994–1999.

Alexander, Helen, granddaughter of Robert J. Kleberg, Jr.; gen. mgr.

King Ranch (Tex.); pres. TOBA; Middlebrook Farm; Lexington, Ky.; 1986–1999.

Alexandre, J. Harry, from shipping-line family; close friend of August Belmont II; wife was a Jerome and relative of Winston Churchill; Coaching Club; Staten Island, N.Y.; 1902–1912.

Allbritton, Joseph Lewis, broadcasting and banking magnate; owns several ABC–affiliated TV stations; chmn. Riggs Bank; Reagan Presidential Fndtn.; navy WWII; Republican; Lazy Lane Farm; Washington, D.C.; 1991–1999.

Anthony, John Ed, 3d-generation timber and lumber baron; Loblolly Stable (racing partnerships/syndications); vp. TOBA; Hot Springs, Ark.; 1994–1999.

Asbury, Eslie, chief of staff, Good Samaritan Hospital, Cincinnati; introduced to Queen Elizabeth at Ascot by John Hay Whitney; friend of R. A. Fairbairn and John Clark; cofounder Keeneland; dir. Grayson Fndtn.; Cincinnati, Ohio; 1953–1988.

Baker, Charles, outdoor-advertising exec.; trustee Ontario Jockey Club; WWII; bred Norcliffe (sire of 1992 Kentucky Derby winner); Ontario, Can.; 1975–1999.

Bancroft, Thomas Moore, chmn. Mt. Vernon Mills (textiles); married daughter of William Woodward I; Princeton Univ.; member War Production Board WWII; Old Westbury, L.I., N.Y.; 1967–1970.

Bancroft, Thomas Moore, Jr., son of Thomas Moore Bancroft; 1st wife, Margaret Bedford of Standard Oil fortune; Princeton Univ.; chmn. NYRA; Harrow Hill; Muttontown, N.Y.; 1973–1996.

Bancroft, William Woodward, son of Thomas Moore Bancroft; Princeton Univ.; Old Brookville, N.Y.; 1976–1999.

Barklie, Archibald, N.Y. and Newark banker and broker; army remount WWI; Philadelphia, Pa.; 1917–1937.

Bassett, James Edward III, son of a leader in formation of Keeneland; Yale Univ. (Scroll and Key); chmn. Keeneland; pres. Breeders' Cup; marines WWII (Purple Heart); Jockey Club steward; Lexington, Ky.; 1985–1999.

Battson, Leigh M., dir. Union Oil Co.; with Charles H. Strub built Santa Anita; chmn. Santa Anita; member Pacific Union and California Clubs; resigned from Jockey Club in 1969; Beverly Hills, Calif.; 1959–1969.

Beard, Louie A., Harry Payne Whitney's stud farm overseer; John Hay

Whitney's farm manager; U.S. Military Academy; army WWI; champion polo player; Tex.; 1944–1954.

Bell, John A. III, from Pennsylvania dairy farm family; broke yearlings for trainer Max Hirsch in the 1940s; Cromwell Bloodstock Agency; Princeton Univ.; WWII; chmn./trustee TOBA; chmn./trustee American Horse Council; Jockey Club steward; stands Affirmed (Triple Crown, 1978); Jonabell Farm; Lexington, Ky.; 1980–1999.

Belmont, August II, son of August Belmont I, German, Rothschild agent, founder of August Belmont and Co., chmn Democratic Nat'l. Committee, minister to the Hague, consul general to Austria, financier of NYC subway system; member NYSE; co-owner Belmont Park and Monmouth Park; army WWI; controlled *New York Times* with J. P. Morgan; Jockey Club chmn.; Episcopalian; bred Man o' War; Nursery Stud; NYC.; founder–1924.

Belmont, August III, son of August Belmont II; Harvard Univ.; raced sailboats, not horses; resigned from Jockey Club in 1914 to serve in WWI; 1909–1914.

Belmont, August IV, son of August Belmont III; St. Mark's; Harvard Univ.; chmn. Dillon, Read, and Co.; navy WWII; chmn. American Kennel Club; pres. Nat'l. American Retriever Club; Jockey Club chmn.; Easton, Md.; 1977–1995.

Belmont, Oliver Hazard Perry (Harry), brother of August Belmont II; 2d wife, Alva (Smith), ex-wife of William K. Vanderbilt; St. Paul's; U.S. Naval Academy; U.S. rep. D/N.Y.; NYC; 1894–1908.

Belmont, Perry, brother of August Belmont II; Harvard Univ.; B.L.L. Columbia; minister to Spain; U.S. rep. D/N.Y.; Spanish-American War; army remount WWI; Rhode Island Society, Sons of the Revolution; Newport, R.I.; founder–1947.

Belmont, Raymond, son of August Belmont II; Harvard Univ.; 1st wife was actress; WWI; polo star; Leesburg, Va.; 1924–1934.

Billings, Cornelius Kingsley Garrison, son of Chicago public utilities magnate; chmn. family-owned Peoples Gas Light and Coke Co.; chmn. Union Carbide and Carbon; part owner Jamaica Racecourse; Republican; NYC property now Fort Tryon Park and Cloisters Museum; 1914–1937.

Binger, James H., CEO Honeywell; head NYC Jujamcyn theater chain; wife was daughter of William L. McKnight; Yale Univ.; McKnight

Fndtn.; steward Jockey Club; Republican; wife worth $620 million (*Forbes* 1999); Tartan Farms, Fla.; Minneapolis, Minn.; 1976–1999.

Bishop, Francis Cunningham, son of Heber R. Bishop, fndr. Bishop and Co. (banking house); St. Paul's; Harvard Univ.; Society of Colonial Lords of the Manor; Mt. Kisco, N.Y.; 1907–1927.

Bishop, Ogden Mills, brother of Francis Cunningham Bishop; St. Paul's; Columbia; resigned from Jockey Club in 1928; lived in Paris until death (1955); 1909–1928.

Bonnie, Edward S., attorney, Brown, Todd and Heyburn; Yale Univ.; counselor Horsemen's Benevolent and Protective Assn.; said to have done work for TOBA; Louisville, Ky.; 1985–1999.

Bonsal, Frank A., Jr., son of steeplechase rider; 2d cousin of A. J. (Sandy) Cassatt III; Glyndon, Md.; 1984–1999.

Bontecou, Frederick H., descendant of member NYSE; dir. Nat'l. Bank of Poughkeepsie; Brown Univ. (nongrad.); N.Y. state sen.; Dutchess County Republican chmn.; lieut. gov. nominee on Thomas E. Dewey slate; Republican; Millbrook, N.Y.; 1958–1959.

Bostwick, Albert Carlton, descendent of Jabez S. Bostwick (Standard Oil associate of John D. Rockefeller); nephew of F. Ambrose Clark; stepfather of Andrew G. C. Sage; St. Paul's; Albert C. Bostwick Fndtn.; army air corps WWI; sec./treas. Nat'l. Steeplechase and Hunt Assn; Episcopalian; Old Westbury, L.I., N.Y.; 1930–1980.

Bostwick, George Herbert (Pete), brother of A. C. Bostwick; married daughter of F. S. von Stade; sister married Ogden Phipps; St. Paul's; trustee NYRA; gentleman steeplechase rider and leading high-goal polo player; Episcopalian; 1942–1982.

Bowers, John Myer, ptnr. Bowers and Sands (law firm dealing with Supreme Court litigation); executor of J.G.K. Lawrence's will; dir. Coney Island Jockey Club; Presbyterian; Democrat; resigned from Jockey Club in 1896; NYC; 1894–1896.

Bradford, John H., associate of Leonard Jerome; educated in Boston; treas./presiding judge Coney Island Jockey Club; Jockey Club steward; NYC; 1895–1908.

Brady, James Cox II, grandson of public utilities magnate Anthony N. Brady I, member NYSE, business assoc. of W. C. Whitney and Thomas Fortune Ryan; fraternity brother of Paul Mellon; Yale Univ. (Scroll and Key); chmn. Purolator Products; pres. Brady Security and Realty Corp.; dir. Chrysler Corp.; chmn. NYRA; vice chmn. Jockey Club; Gladstone, N.J.; 1939–1971.

Brady, James Cox, Jr. (III), son of James Cox Brady II; St. Paul's; Yale Univ. (Scroll and Key); exec. family-owned real estate firm; Brady Fndtn.; sec./treas. Jockey Club; Far Hills, N.J.; 1973–1999.

Brady, Nicholas Frederick (II), son of James Cox Brady II; St. Mark's; Yale Univ.; MBA Harvard Univ.; chmn. Dillon, Read, and Co.; chmn. Purolator Courier Corp.; dir. Bessemer Securities Corp.; U.S. sen. R/N.J.; sec. of treas.; Darby Fndtn.; chmn. Jockey Club; Republican; among richest 100,000 in U.S., 1991; resigned from Jockey Club in 1988 to take cabinet appointment; Far Hills, N.J. and Gaston, Md.; 1966–1988, 1993–1999.

Brann, William L., father-in-law of Louis R. Rowan; bred Challedon (Horse of the Year, 1939, 1940); estate of over $2 million largest ever filed in Frederick, Md.; 1939–1951.

Brittingham, Baird C., owner NYSE-traded Lumber Industries, Inc.; Yale Univ.; Wilmington, Del.; 1968–1999.

Brown, Henry Carroll, stock broker; married daughter of Montana copper magnate; sued her estate after he owed her $1 million and resigned from Jockey Club in 1912; NYC; 1909–1912.

Brown, Jesse, likely the only son of Samuel S. Brown, predeceased his father; 1897–1904.

Brown, Samuel S., inheritor of coal and coke operation; Washington and Jefferson College (nongrad.); pres. Ohio RR; dir. Nat'l. Bank of Commerce; Civil War volunteer; 32d-degree Mason; Squirrel Hill (Pittsburgh), Pa.; founder–1905.

Bruce, Howard, chmn. Maryland Shipbuilding and Drydock; head Baltimore Nat'l. Bank; Virginia Military Institute; dir. Baltimore and Ohio RR, Md. Casualty Corp.; Business Advisory Council; Episcopalian; Baltimore, Md.; 1939–1961.

Bull, George Henry, son of financier and dir. Saratoga Assn. Robert M. Bull.; St. Mark's; track star at Columbia Univ.; member NYSE; pres. Saratoga Assn. and Empire City Racing Assn; dir. Belmont Park and Hialeah Park; steward Jockey Club; Episcopalian; Democrat; NYC; 1921–1943.

Bull, Henry Worthington, son of William L. Bull, pres. of NYSE; wife was a Livingston; ptnr. Bull, Holden and Co. (stock-brokerage house); Columbia; pres. Turf and Field Club and Nat'l. Steeplechase and Hunt Assn.; N.Y.; 1928–1958.

Burke, Charleton F., son of Los Angeles real estate pioneer; UC Berkeley; vp Santa Anita; dir. Union Bank of Los Angeles; army remount

WWI; chmn. California Horse Racing Board; Pacific Coast chmn. U.S. Polo Assn.; San Marino, Calif.; 1937–1962.

Butler, James (II), son of Irish immigrant grocery business fndr. and pres. Empire City Racing Assn.; killed at forty-nine when thrown from a horse; Catholic; Bedford Hills, N.Y.; 1937–1940.

Butler, James (III), son of James Butler (II); Yale Univ. (nongrad.); pres. Empire City Racing Assn.; army WWII; resigned from Jockey Club in 1956 due to pressure of business interests; Locust Valley, L.I., N.Y.; 1946–1956.

Camden, Johnson Newlon, Jr., son of U.S. sen. D/WV and brother-in-law of Standard Oil associate William Payne Thompson; U.S. sen. D/Ky.; Democrat; Ky.; 1924–1942.

Campbell, Alexander G., Jr., Lexington, Ky.; 1989–1999.

Carver, George William Douglas, ptnr. Carver Dodge Oil; married a Hitchcock; St. Paul's; Princeton Univ.; dir. Reading and Bates Off-shore Drilling; navy WWII; sec./treas. Jockey Club; b. Glen Cove, N.Y.; Denver, Colo.; 1975–1981.

Cassatt, Alexander J., son of financier; pres. Pennsylvania RR; educated in Europe; member NYSE; married Pres. Buchanan's niece; co-owner Monmouth Park; signed charter for Nat'l. Steeplechase Assn.; Chesterbrook Farm; Pittsburgh, Pa.; founder–1906.

Cassatt, Edward B., son of Alexander J. Cassatt; army WWI; Chester-brook Farm; Pittsburgh, Pa.; 1909–1921.

Cella, Charles Joshua, grandson of Oaklawn Park fndr., theatre and real estate magnate; 3d-generation racetrack owner; chmn. Oaklawn Jockey Club; pres. Southern Real Estate and Financial; breeds Labrador Retrievers; Independent; St. Louis, Mo; 1974–1999.

Chandler, Alice Headley, daughter of Hal Price Headley; Abercrombie Fndtn.; bred Sir Ivor (Epsom Derby, 1969); Mill Ridge Farm; Lexington, Ky.; 1989–1999.

Chanler, William Astor, son of John Winthrop Chanler, U.S. rep. D/N.Y.; mother was an Astor; Phillips Academy; Harvard Univ.; U.S. rep. D/N.Y.; Spanish-American War; organizer of WWI Lafayette Escadrille; fellow Royal Geographic Society of London; Democrat; Barrytown, N.Y.; died in France; 1895–1934.

Chenery, Christopher Tompkins, chmn. Southern Natural Gas; Washington and Lee Univ.; dir. Offshore Co.; trustee NYRA; fndr. Grayson Fndtn.; army WWI; bred Secretariat (Triple Crown, 1973); Pelham Manor, N.Y.; 1951–1973.

Chenery, Helen Bates, formerly Penny Tweedy, daughter of C. T. Chenery; Smith College; owner Secretariat (Triple Crown, 1973); Lexington, Ky.; 1983–1999.

Cheston, George Morris, attorney; married niece of General Motors heir Isabel Dodge Sloane, who bred Cavalcade (Kentucky Derby, 1934); Harvard Univ.; treas. Nat'l. Citizens for Eisenhower; Republican; Philadelphia, Pa.; 1965–1999.

Chillingworth, Sherwood C., attorney Richfield Oil; Harvard Univ.; L.L.B. Stanford Univ.; pres. Chillingworth Corp. (real estate); vp Oak Tree Racing Assn.; Oak Tree Charitable Fndtn.; steward Jockey Club; Calif.; 1995–1999.

Clark, Frederick Ambrose, grandson of Edward Clark, attorney for Singer Manufacturing who became its president; uncle of Albert Carlton Bostwick, George H. Bostwick, and Stephen C. Clark, Jr.; went on hunts with Prince of Wales; Coaching Club; pres. Meadow Brook Steeplechase Assn.; inherited one-fifth of $30 million; Episcopalian; Westbury, L.I., N.Y.; 1919–1964.

Clark, John C., owner radio and TV stations; dir. Marine-Midland Trust, Endicott Johnson Corp., Security Life Insurance, and Clark–Cleveland, Inc.; pres. Hialeah Park; dir. Belmont Park and Saratoga Racecourse; trustee NYRA; pres. Thoroughbred Racing Assn.; steward Jockey Club; Binghamton, N.Y.; 1943–1974.

Clark, Stephen C., Jr., nephew of Frederick Ambrose Clark; son of fndr. Nat'l. Baseball Hall of Fame; owner Albany *Knickerbocker Press;* dir. Singer Company; admin. Nat'l. Steeplechase and Hunt Assn; 1971–1992.

Clason, Augustus, descendent of family for which Clason's Point on L.I. Sound was named; proprietor Monmouth Park Stock Farm; gentleman rider; resigned from Jockey Club in 1903; NYC; founder–1903.

Clay, Robert N., pres. Top Yield Industries, Inc. (bloodstock agency); dir. PNC Bank; dir. Breeders' Cup; Blood-Horse Charitable Fndtn.; pres. TOBA; Three Chimneys Farm; Midway, Ky.; 1991–1999.

Clyde, B. F., said to be Cassatt's Philadelphia neighbor who had his own racetrack; Pa.; date not recorded–1905.

Cochran, Alexander Smith, maternal grandson of carpet mogul Alexander Smith; pres. Alexander Smith and Sons Carpet; St. Paul's; Yale Univ.; left $250,000 to St. Paul's; yachtsman; coinheritor of $50 million; raised on 600-acre Yonkers estate; 1913–1929.

Cochran, Gifford Alexander, brother of Alexander Smith Cochran; St. Paul's; Yale Univ.; coinheritor of $50 million; NYC; 1921–1930.

Combs, Leslie II, great-grandson of Lexington lawyer; developed syndication for thoroughbreds; friend of Warren Wright, Jr.; Spendthrift Farm (bankruptcy filed 1988); Lexington, Ky.; 1959–1990.

Corning, Parker, grandson of Erastus Corning, iron manufacturer and U.S. rep. D/N.Y., for whom Corning, N.Y., is named; steel and woolen manufacturer; St. Paul's; Yale Univ.; 7-term U.S. rep. D/N.Y.; Albany, N.Y.; 1935–1943.

Cowdin, John Elliott, head Johnson-Cowdin-Emmrich (silk merchants); Harvard Univ.; dir. Bank for Savings; dir. Westchester Racing Assn.; pres. Queens County Jockey Club; 10-goal rating in polo; sec./treas. Jockey Club; resided in Pierre Lorillard's Tuxedo Park, N.Y.; 1908–1941.

Daingerfield, Keene, grandson of Foxhall Daingerfield, who married sister of James R. Keene and managed Keene's stud farm; nephew of Algernon Daingerfield, sec. Jockey Club; U.Va. (nongrad); horse trainer; track steward; Lexington, Ky.; 1989–1993.

Davis, Joseph E., W. Va. coal mine operator; nephew of Henry Gassaway Davis, U.S. sen. D/W. Va.; Yale Univ.; dir. Island Creek Coal and Pond Creek Pocahontas, vp Blaine Coal Mining; army WWI; master Meadow Brook Hunt; Coaching Club; sec./treas. Jockey Club; Republican; Upper Brookville, L.I., N.Y.; 1920–1955.

Dean, J. Simpson, among founders of Delaware Park; family intermarried with du Ponts; master of foxhounds; steeplechase rider; Del.; 1948–1978.

de Roulet, Vincent, married sister of John Hay Whitney; ambassador to Jamaica; resigned from Jockey Club in 1965 to take position as N.Y. racing commissioner; N.Y. and Lane, Me.; 1963–1965, 1969–1975.

Dixon, Fitz Eugene, Jr., nephew of George D. Widener II; ptnr. NYSE-registered firm; Harvard Univ. (nongrad.); ltd. ptnr. Phila. Phillies; $400 million (*Forbes* 1995); Episcopalian; Lafayette Hill, Pa.; 1958–1999.

Dizney, Donald R., Double Diamond Farm; steward Jockey Club; 1997–1999.

Donner, John O., b. Hamburg, Ger.; fndr. De Castro and Donner (sugar refining); supt. American Sugar Refining Co.; appointed principal expert Sugar Trust; steward Jockey Club; NYC; founder–1899.

Dragone, Allan R., with Celanese Corp.; CEO Akzo America; MBA Harvard Univ.; dir. Arcadian Corp.; chmn. NYRA; steward Jockey Club; among richest 100,000 in U.S. (1991); NYC; 1988–1999.

Dreyfus, Jack Jones, Jr., fndr. Dreyfus Fund (mutual fund); fndr. Dreyfus Charitable Fndtn.; chmn. NYRA; Jewish; Hobeau Farms, Fla.; NYC; 1969–1999.

Duchossois, Richard Louis, CEO Duchossois Industries, ranked 303 of top 500 private companies (*Forbes* 1997); chmn. Arlington International Racecourse; Duchossois Fndtn.; WWI; exec. comm. Thoroughbred Racing Assn; steward Jockey Club; among richest 100,000 in U.S. (1991); Republican; Barrington, Ill.; 1987–1999.

du Pont, Helena Allaire Crozer, widow of Richard C. du Pont, who died in WWII glider crash; trustee NYRA; Woodstock Fndtn.; bred Kelso (1960s champion); Bohemia Stable; Chesapeake City, Md.; 1983–1999.

du Pont, William (Willie), Jr., son of principal stockholder E. I. Du Pont de Nemours and Co., a cousin of Pierre S. du pont II, great-great-grandson of founder of du Pont dynasty; chmn. Delaware Trust; dir. E. I. du Pont de Nemours; pres. Delaware Park; Wilmington, Del.; 1932–1965.

du Pont, William III, son of William du Pont, Jr; Pillar Stud; Orlando, Fla.; 1981–1999.

Duryea, Herman B. (Harmanus Barkulo), son of Brooklyn attorney and Republican assemblyman; raced sloops and horses with Harry Payne Whitney; pres. U.S. Field Trial Club; leased W. C. Whitney's stable at his death in 1904; N.Y.; 1905–1916.

Dwyer, Philip J., for whom Dwyer Handicap is named; butcher who amassed fortune in racing; pres. Brooklyn Jockey Club, pres. Queens County Jockey Club; N.Y.; founder–1917.

Ellis, Rudolph, dir. Pennsylvania RR, Fourth St. Nat'l. Bank, and AT&T; resigned from Jockey Club in 1896; Philadelphia, Pa.; founder–1896.

Engelhard, Charles William (II), son of founder of Englehard Corp.; chmn. Englehard Minerals and Chemicals Corp.; St. Paul's; Princeton Univ.; Foreign Policy Assn., Commission for Economic Development; Charles Engelhard Fndtn.; $300 million estate; owned

Nijinsky II (English Triple Crown); Democrat; Episcopalian; Crag-
wood Stable; Far Hills, N.J.; 1963–1971.

Eustis, George P., maternal grandson of banker and Lehman Brothers
associate William M. Corcoran; son of George Eustis, Jr., U.S. rep.
American Party/LA; nephew of James Biddle Eustis, U.S. sen. D/LA
and ambassador to France; sister married Thomas Hitchcock (II);
1912–1915.

Eustis, William Corcoran, brother of George P. Eustis; mgr. Corcoran
estate and dir. Corcoran Gallery in Wash., D.C.; wife was daughter
of U.S. vp Levi P. Morton; Cambridge Univ. and Harvard Law
School; sec. U.S. Embassy, London; army WWI; Washington, D.C.;
1896–1921.

Evans, Edward P., son of Thomas M. Evans; CEO Macmillan Publishing; Spring Hill Farm; Casanova, Va.; 1996–1999.

Evans, Robert Sheldon, son of Thomas M. Evans; MBA Columbia
Univ.; CEO Crane Co., vp Evans and Co.; steward Jockey Club;
Stamford, Conn.; 1991–1999.

Evans, Thomas Mellon, grandmother's first cousin was Andrew Mellon; employed with Gulf Oil; Yale Univ.; fndr. Evans and Co. (NYC
brokerage firm affiliated with Prudential Securities); chmn. Crane
Corp.; Pittsburgh, Pa.; 1978–1997.

Ewing, William, ptnr. J. P. Morgan and Co.; investment banker Clark,
Dodge and Company; St. Paul's; Yale Univ.; dir. American Can;
Links Club; Council on Foreign Relations; Republican; Episco-
palian; Mt. Kisco, N.Y.; 1951–1965.

Fairbairn, Robert A., broker NYSE; ptnr Fairbairn and Hilliard, exec.
Nat'l. Biscuit; Coaching Club; bred Clydesdales; owner with 1936
syndicate of Blenheim; Westfield, N.J.; 1926–1951.

Fanshawe, William S., ptnr. Harvey Fisk and Sons (bankers), head
W. F. Fanshawe and Co. (investment securities); Columbia Univ.;
NYC; 1904–1926.

Farish, William Stamps (II), pres. Humble Oil and Refining, chmn.
Standard Oil of N.J.; married daughter of Bayard Sharp; sister married Edward Harriman Gerry; member Petroleum Industry War
Council; Episcopalian; Houston, Tex., and Millbrook, N.Y.; 1941–
1942.

Farish, William Stamps III, son of William Stamps Farish (II); married
daughter of Ogden Phipps; chmn. Churchill Downs; William
Stamps Farish Fndtn.; vice chmn. Jockey Club; Farish family

worth $400 million (1992); Lane's End Farm; Versailles, Ky.; 1970–1999.

Farish, William Stamps, Jr. (IV), son of William Stamps Farish III; raced in partnership with Bayard Sharp; business mgr./sales dir. Lane's End Farm; Versailles, Ky.; 1996–1999.

Fellowes, Cornelius, pres. Nat'l. Horse Show of America; NYC; 1896–1900.

Field, Marshall III, grandson of Marshall Field I, Chicago dept. store magnate and principal stockholder Pullman Co.; married ex-wife of Ogden Phipps; educated privately; fndr. Field Enterprises (private media corp.); publisher *World Book Encyclopedia, Chicago Daily News;* WWI (Silver Star); Republican-turned-Democrat; Catholic; Lloyd Harbor, L.I., N.Y.; 1922–1956.

Firestone, Russell A., son of Harvey S. Firestone, fndr. Firestone Tire and Rubber; Phillips Exeter; Princeton Univ.; vp Firestone Bank, dir./gen. mgr. Firestone Tire and Rubber; dir. Metropolitan Jockey Club and Hialeah Park; Akron, Ohio; 1948–1951.

Fischer, Charles T., fndr. Fisher Body Co., General Motors Corp.; vp General Motors, dir. Nat'l. Bank of Detroit, Detroit Edison, Michigan Bell Telephone; Dixiana Stables; Lexington, Ky.; 1952–1963.

Fitzsimons, Hugh A., Jr., chmn. Texas Racing Commission; pres. Texas Thoroughbred Assn.; San Antonio, Tex.; 1992–1999.

Fletcher, Walter D., chmn. Torsion Balance; married daughter of William C. Langley; Columbia Univ.; dir. Union Pacific RR, Oregon Short Line RR, Los Angeles and Salt Lake RR; trustee NYRA; N.Y. deputy attorney general; steward Jockey Club; N.Y.; 1949–1972.

Follansbee, John Gilbert, nephew of James R. Keene; Harvard Univ.; Mexican ranching and mining interests; close friend of Mexico's president Diaz; NYC; 1898–1914.

Forbes, William H., son of fndr. J. M. Forbes and Co. and assoc. of J. P. Morgan and Co.; Forbes family owns Naushon Island near Martha's Vineyard; Boston, Mass.; founder–1897.

Fowler, Anderson, family in coal and iron business; married sister of James Cox Brady (II); St. Paul's classmate of Alfred G. Vanderbilt II; Princeton Univ.; New Jersey legislator; WWII (Bronze Star); master of foxhounds; Gladstone, N.J.; 1957–1997.

Frostad, George, dir. Ontario Jockey Club; chief steward Jockey Club of Canada; Bo-Teek Farms; Ontario, Can.; 1981–1999.

Galbreath, Daniel Mauck, son of John W. Galbreath; pres. family-owned Pittsburgh Pirates; steward Jockey Club; Republican; among richest 100,000 in U.S. (1991); Columbus, Ohio; 1968–1995.

Galbreath, John W., chmn. Galbreath Co. (real estate); daughter married James W. Phillips; trustee NYRA; steward Jockey Club; owned Swaps (Kentucky Derby, 1955); Darby Dan Farm; Columbus, Ohio; 1933–1988.

Galway, James, b. Ireland; relative of Robert Galway, member NYSE; NYC fire commissioner; raced trotting horses; steward Jockey Club; NYC; founder–1910.

Garrett, George Angus, vp Dupont Nat'l. Bank; Cornell (nongrad) and Univ. of Chicago; gen. ptnr. Merrill Lynch, Pierce, Fenner and Smith; ambassador to Ireland; army WWI; Washington, D.C.; 1953–1971.

Gebhard, Frederic, inheritance was $80,000 annually; related to Vanderbilts by marriage; Catholic; Garden City, L.I., N.Y.; 1894–1910.

Gelb, Richard Lee, son of Lawrence M. Gelb, fndr. Clairol; Phillips Academy; Yale Univ.; MBA with dist. Harvard Univ.; pres. Clairol, purchased by Bristol-Meyers, CEO Bristol Meyers Squibb; trustee NYRA; Lawrence M. Gelb Fndtn.; NYC; 1978–1999.

Gerry, Edward Harriman, son of Robert L. Gerry; married sister of William Stamps Farish (II); St. Paul's; Harvard Univ.; Gerry Brothers and Co., NYC; 1956–1999.

Gerry, Henry Averell, son of Robert L. Gerry; St. Paul's; Harvard Univ.; Gerry Brothers and Co., NYC; 1956–1999.

Gerry, Martha F., wife of Edward Harriman Gerry; sister of William Farish (II); dir. Cold Spring Harbor Laboratory; William Stamps Farish Fndtn.; Mill Neck, L.I., N.Y.; 1983–1999.

Gerry, Robert Livingston, great-grandson of Elbridge Gerry, Declaration of Independence signer and U.S. vp under James Madison; brother of Peter Goelet Gerry, U.S. sen. D/RI; owner *Providence News-Tribune;* brother-in-law of W. A. Harriman; Harvard Univ.; head Gerry Offices/Estates; dir. Cruikshank Co., Oregon RR and Navigation, Oregon Short Line RR; trustee Farmers Loan and Trust and Central Hanover Bank and Trust; Episcopalian; Delhi, N.Y.; 1903–1957.

Gilpin, M. Tyson, grandson of thoroughbred breeding-stock importer; St. Paul's; Princeton Univ.; pres. Fasig-Tipton (horse auctioneers); army intelligence; dir. Virginia Thoroughbred Assn.; Boyce, Va.; 1955–1999.

Goodman, John K., son of banker and cattle rancher; Yale Univ.; air force WWII; chmn. Arizona Racing Commission; head Nat'l. Assn. of Racing Commissioners; steward Jockey Club; among richest 100,000 in U.S. (1991); Tucson, Ariz.; 1978–1999.

Grayson, Cary Travers, for whom Grayson Fndtn. was named; descendent of William R. Travers; personal physician to Woodrow Wilson; chmn. American Nat'l. Red Cross; WWII (Navy Cross); dir. Nat'l. Capital Horse Show; Episcopalian; Blue Ridge Farm; Washington, D.C.; 1922–1938.

Grayson, James Gordon, son of C. T. Grayson; employed with Investment Finance Corp. of World Bank; Yale Univ. (Skull and Bones); navy WWII; Blue Ridge Farm; Upperville, Va.; 1971–1997.

Greene, James O., son of pres. Western Union Telegraph; married daughter of mayor of NYC; studied medicine, but went into telegraph business; cofounder Meadow Brook Hunt Club; NYC; 1894–1924.

Griswold, Frank Gray, N.Y. maritime family that intermarried with Lorillards; in original Four Hundred; educated in Germany and France; Republican; Episcopalian; NYC; 1902–1937.

Guest, Raymond R., son of Henry Phipps's daughter Amy and Capt. Frederick Edward Guest, 1st cousin of Winston Churchill; 2d wife an Astor; 3d wife Princess Caroline Murat; Phillips Academy; Yale Univ.; Va. state sen.; U.S. ambassador to Ireland; WWI (Bronze Star); famous polo player; King George, Va.; 1954–1991.

Guest, Winston Frederick Churchill, brother of Raymond R. Guest; St. Paul's; 1st wife was granddaughter of fndr. Woolworth's; 2d wife a blueblood who had a brief escapade as Ziegfield Follies showgirl; 10-goal polo player; 1962–1982.

Guggenheim, Harry Frank, grandson of mining/smelting mogul Meyer Guggenheim; Yale Univ. (nongrad); B.A., M.A. Cambridge Univ.; senior ptnr. Guggenheim Bros.; trustee NYRA; ambassador to Cuba; pres. Daniel and Florence Guggenheim Fndtn., Solomon Guggenheim Fndtn., and Harry Frank Guggenheim Fndtn.; navy WWI; owned Dark Star (Kentucky Derby, 1953); Jewish; Sands Point, L.I., N.Y.; 1951–1971.

Haggin, James Ben Ali, mining ptnr. of George Hearst, U.S. sen. D/Calif.; gold and silver investor; holdings in Anaconda Copper and Wells Fargo; stables on San Francisco's Nob Hill; Episcopalian; Democrat; $15 million estate; Elmendorf Farm, Ky.; San Francisco, Calif.; founder–1914.

Haggin, Louis Lee II, great-grandson of James B. Haggin; son-in-law of Hal Price Headley; Princeton Univ.; chmn. Keeneland Assn.; army WWII; pres. Thoroughbred Racing Assn.; sec./treas. Jockey Club; Lexington, Ky.; 1951–1980.

Haggin, Louis Lee III; son of Louis Lee Haggin II; 1997–1999.

Hancock, A. B. (Bull), Jr., son of Arthur Boyd Hancock, livestock breeder and owner Claiborne Farm; Princeton Univ.; pres. TOBA; Claiborne Farm; Paris, Ky.; 1955–1972.

Hancock, Arthur B. III, son of Bull Hancock; bred Gato del Sol (Kentucky Derby, 1982); Stone Farm; Ky.; 1981–1999.

Hancock, Dell, daughter of Bull Hancock; photographer; trustee TOBA; pres. Kentucky Thoroughbred Assn.; Ky.; 1995–1999.

Hancock, Seth W., son of Bull Hancock; Claiborne Farm; Paris, Ky.; 1978–1999.

Hanes, John W., N.C. textile heir; Yale Univ.; ptnr. Charles D. Barney; dir. Internat'l Mercantile Marine, Pan-Am Airways, and Aviation Corp.; chmn. NYRA; undersecretary of treasury; member Securities and Exchange Commission; steward Jockey Club; Westchester County, N.Y.; 1952–1987.

Hanger, William Arnold, son of ptnr of Mason and Hanger–Silas Mason Co., Lincoln Tunnel contractor; attended Univ. of Pennsylvania and U.S. Naval Academy; dir. Churchill Downs, Hialeah, and Keeneland; Richmond, Ky.; 1939–1976.

Harper, Joseph W., maternal grandson of movie producer Cecil B. DeMille; CEO Del Mar Thoroughbred Club; exec. vp Oak Tree Racing Assn.; Cecil B. DeMille Fndtn.; steward Jockey Club; Calif.; 1983–1999.

Harriman, William Averell, son of RR baron and member NYSE E. H. Harriman; sister married Robert Livingston Gerry; with George Herbert Walker bought August Belmont II's stable; 2d wife, ex-wife of C. V. Whitney; 3d wife, Pamela Digby Churchill Hayward; Yale Univ. (Skull and Bones); chmn. Union Pacific RR; ambassador to USSR, ambassador to Great Britain, sec. of commerce, governor of N.Y.; resigned from Jockey Club in 1943 to become ambassador; Republican-turned-Democrat; N.Y.; 1923–1943.

Harris, John C., from ranching family; chmn. Bay Meadows Operating Co.; board member Tan Foran Racing Assn; pres. Calif. Thoroughbred Breeders Assn.; steward Jockey Club; Harris Farms, Coalinga, Calif.; 1988–1999.

Haskell, Amory Lawrence, vp General Motors Corp. export division; sold Triplex Safety Glass to Libbey-Owens-Ford Glass; Pomfret School; Princeton Univ.; navy WWI; chmn. Monmouth Park Jockey Club; Episcopalian; Woodland Farm; Red Bank, N.J.; 1953–1966.

Headley, Hal Price (II), fndr. Keeneland; daughter married son of Louis Lee Haggin II; a Headley married C. V. Whitney's sister; Princeton Univ. (nongrad); Beaumont Farm; Lexington, Ky.; 1958–1962.

Heckscher, John Gerard, from German immigrant family in the coal, iron, and zinc business; engaged in duel at NYC's Union Club; dir. Saratoga Racing Assn.; L.I., N.Y.; 1896–1908.

Hendrie, George Muir, family in Hendrie Cartage transportation business; 3d-generation chmn. Ontario Jockey Club; Ontario, Can.; 1994–1999.

Henry, Leonard D., dir. Continental Airlines, American Shipbuilding, and General Tire; U.S. Military Academy; trustee NYRA; WWI; pres. Jockey Club Research Fndtn.; Episcopalian; 1976–1985.

Hettinger, John A., dir. Fasig-Tipton (horse auctioneers); Yale Univ.; trustee NYRA; Grayson Fndtn., Hettinger Fndtn, Jockey Club Fndtn.; chmn. Nat'l. Museum of Racing; steward Jockey Club; Akindale Farm, N.Y.; 1983–1999.

Hirsch, Clement L., son of fndr. Army/Navy store; fndr. Kal Kan Food (dog food) and fndr. Stagg Foods; fndr. Oak Tree Racing Assn.; vp Del Mar Thoroughbred Club; Oak Tree Charitable Fndtn.; marines WWII; Newport Beach, Calif.; 1994–1999.

Hitchcock, Francis R., brother of Thomas Hitchcock (II); Columbia Univ.; pres. Saratoga Racing Assn.; master Meadow Brook Hunt; steward Jockey Club; raced in France in later years; Park Avenue, NYC; 1895–1926.

Hitchcock, Thomas Hitchcock (II), son of Thomas Hitchcock (I), principal stockholder in *New York Sun;* married granddaughter of William Corcoran, Wall Street associate of Lehman Brothers; brother-in-law of George P. Eustis and William Corcoran Eustis; bought Long Island farmland with E. D. Morgan; Oxford Univ.; among principal backers of Belmont Park; master Meadow Brook Hunt; Westbury, L.I., N.Y.; 1895–1941.

Hitt, William F., son of U.S. rep. Robert R. Hitt R/Ill. and asst. secretary of state; brother of Robert Stockwell Reynolds Hitt, minister to Guatemala; 1st wife was daughter of U.S. sen. Stephen B. Elkins R/W. Va.; 2d wife was a Woodward; St. Paul's; Yale Univ.; resigned from Jockey Club in 1951; NYC; 1937–1951.

Hooper, Fred W., one of 12 children of Georgia farmer and cattleman; fndr. Hooper Construction Co. (South's largest construction co.); bred Hoop, Jr. (Kentucky Derby, 1945); 1975–1999.

Hooper, Robert Chamblet, of one of Boston's oldest families; St. Paul's; winner Grand Nat'l. Steeplechase; Boston, Mass.; 1900–1908.

Houghton, E. Edward, married niece of James Cox Brady II; Buckingham Farm; Chestertown, Md.; 1976–1999.

Howe, Richard Flint, ptnr. International Harvester; business associate of Florence Clark, wife of F. Ambrose Clark; Harvard Univ.; vp 1st Nat'l. Bank, Kenosha, Wis.; dir. Simmons Mfg.; Wilson appointment to Aircraft Board; Unitarian; Republican; Kenosha, Wis., and Jericho, L.I., N.Y..; 1930–1943.

Howe, William Deering, son of Richard Flint Howe; Groton; Harvard Univ.; pres. Transair, Inc.; member Shearman, Sterling, and Wright (lawyers, NYC); 1st mayor, Brookville, L.I., N.Y.; 1935–1948.

Howland, Samuel Shaw, descendent of Mayflower Puritan leader John Howland; son of banker for Hudson River RR; 1st wife was daughter of August Belmont I; gen. mgr. Westchester Racing Assn.; Washington, D.C.; 1894–1925.

Humphrey, George Macoffin, chmn. Pittsburgh Consolidation Coal; CEC Nat'l. Steel Corp.; pres. M. A. Hanna (iron ore shipping); CEC Industrial Rayon Corp.; L.L.B. Michigan Law School; dir. Phelps Dodge and Nat'l. City Bank of Cleveland; trustee NYRA; sec. of treasury; Committee for Economic Development; Links Club; Republican; Cleveland, Ohio; 1950–1970.

Humphrey, G. Watts, Jr., grandson of George Macoffin Humphrey; Yale Univ.; pres. GWH Holdings (private holding company); Blood–Horse Charitable Fndtn.; part owner St. Louis Cardinals; steward Jockey Club; Shawnee Farm; Harrodsburg, Ky.; Pittsburgh, Pa.; 1976–1999.

Hunter, John, founding co-investor Saratoga Racecourse; chmn. Jockey Club; resigned from Jockey Club in 1896; N.Y.; founder–1896.

Iselin, Charles Oliver, grandson of early 1800s Swiss banker Adrian Iselin; member NYSE; part of yacht syndicate with W. K. Vanderbilt and Edwin Morgan; L.L.B. Columbia Law School; 2d wife, Hope Goddard, 1st woman to crew in America's Cup; Glen Head, L.I., N.Y.; 1895–1932.

Iselin, Philip H., fndr. Kay Dunhill Corp. and Korell Corp. (women's apparel); pres. Monmouth Park; CEO N.Y. Jets; Port Washington, N.Y., and Oceanport, N.J.; 1974–1976.

Jackson, Howell Edmunds, descendent of Howell E. Jackson, U.S. sen. D/Tenn. and U.S. Supreme Court associate justice; grandnephew of General Motors mogul William Harding, whose racing silks, registered in 1825 with Nashville Jockey Club, are nation's oldest; trustee NYRA; Belle Meade; Nashville, Tenn.; 1949–1973.

Jackson, William Harding, relative of Howell E. Jackson, U.S. sen. D/Tenn. and U.S. Supreme Court associate justice; ptnr. J. H. Whitney and Co. (investment firm); ptnr. Carter, Ledyard and Milburn, dir. Spencer Chem. Co. and Thomas Industries; resigned from Jockey Club in 1950 to become deputy director CIA; 1947–1950.

Janney, Stuart Symington, Jr. (II), married Barbara Phipps, daughter of Henry C. Phipps; leading amateur rider of 1930s and 1940s; steward Jockey Club; bred Ruffian (Kentucky Derby, 1974); Locust Hill Farm; Md.; 1954–1988.

Janney, Stuart Symington III, son of S. S. Janney II; head Brown Asset Mgmt. (investment banking); chmn. Bessemer Trust, N.A.; legislative asst. U.S. sen. R/Md. Charles Mathias; foreign policy asst. U.S. sen. R/Tenn. Howard Baker; special asst. sec. of state; John S. Phipps Family Fndtn.; steward Jockey Club; Baltimore, Md.; 1992–1999.

Jeffords, Walter M., married niece of Samuel D. Riddle; contested Riddle's will that excluded him; Yale Univ.; member Nat'l. Steeplechase and Hunt Assn.; steward Jockey Club; Faraway Farm, Lexington, Ky.; Glen Riddle, Pa.; 1925–1960.

Jeffords, Walter M., Jr., son of Walter M. Jeffords; Yale Univ.; pres. Brooklyn Borough Gas; chmn. Northern Utilities; Dobson Fndtn.; army WWII; vp Nat'l. Museum of Racing; South Padre Island, Tex.; 1968–1990.

Jenkins, Spalding Lowe, pres. Md. State Fair, Laurel operators, and pres. Maryland Jockey Club, Pimlico operators; army remount WWI; 1915–1926.

Jones, Richard I. G., married daughter of Jane du Pont and pres. Delaware Park; Yale Univ.; senior ptnr. Prickett, Jones, Elliott,

Kristol and Schnee (law firm); ptnr. Walnut Green (bloodstock agency); steward Jockey Club; Wilmington, Del.; 1975–1999.

Jones, Russell B., Jr., brother of Richard I. G. Jones; married into Manhattan real estate Mortimer family; ptnr. Walnut Green (bloodstock agency); Pa. racing commissioner; Pittsburgh, Pa.; 1989–1999.

Jones, W. Alton, board chmn. Cities Service Co.; W. Alton Jones Fndtn.; Charlottesville, Va.; 1958–1962.

Jones, Warner L., descendant of fndr. Frankfort Distilleries, producer of Four Roses; great-nephew of Churchill Downs's 1st president; cousin of Thruston B. Morton; chmn. Churchill Downs; army WWII; owned Raja Baba (world's leading sire, 1980); Episcopalian; Jockey Club steward; Hermitage Farm; Ky.; 1971–1994.

Keck, Howard Brighton, son of William M. Keck, fndr. Superior Oil Company and chief supporter of Pres. Nixon; chmn. Superior Oil, bought by Mobil (1984); CEO Falconridge Nickel Mines Ltd; W. M. Keck Fndtn.; steward Jockey Club; worth $400 million (*Forbes* 1995); bred Ferdinand (Kentucky Derby, 1986); resigned from Jockey Club in 1996 in ill health; Tex.; 1963–1996.

Keene, Foxhall P., son of James R. Keene; Harvard Univ.; golfer, racing car driver, and leading steeplechase rider; Old Westbury, L.I., N.Y.; 1894–1935.

Keene, James Robert, b. London; made fortune as stock manipulator on San Francisco exchange; member NYSE; among financiers of Belmont Park; bred Foxhall (Grand Prix, 1918); steward Jockey Club; Castleton Stud; Cedarhurst, L.I., N.Y.; founder–1913.

Kelly, Edward J., son of N.Y. banker; commodore New Rochelle Yacht Club; Catholic; New Rochelle, N.Y.; founder–1901.

Kernan, Francis A., descendent of Francis Kernan, U.S. rep. D/N.Y. and U.S. sen. D/N.Y.; ptnr. White, Weld and Co. (transcontinental oil pipeline financiers); trustee NYRA; fndr. Lincoln Center for the Performing Arts; steward Jockey Club; NYC; 1960–1986.

Kerr, James R., CEO Avco Corp. (defense contractor), chmn. Avco Broadcasting Corp., vp/dir. marketing European American Bank, dir. Avco Delta, Lehman Corp.; member Defense Advisory Council; air force (1942–1954); La Jolla, Calif.; 1978–1995.

Kilroe, Frank Eugene (Jimmy), son of Edward P. Kilroe, pres. Metropolitan Jockey Club and M.D. whose clients included Pierre Lorillard; 1st wife was daughter of Jockey Club exec. sec. Marshall

Cassidy; 2d wife was ex-wife of E. Barry Ryan; Columbia Univ.; vp Santa Anita; army WWII; steward Jockey Club; Pasadena, Calif.; 1981–1996.

Kissel, Peter F. F., bred Pass Catcher (Belmont, 1971); Gladstone, N.J.; 1968–1987.

Kleberg, Robert Justus, Jr. (IV), maternal grandmother was daughter of fndr. King Ranch, Tex.; pres. King Ranch, Tex.; dir. King Ranch (Australia, Argentina, Brazil, Morocco, Spain); Robert J. Kleberg, Jr. and Helen C. Kleberg Fndtn.; trustee NYRA; bred Assault (Triple Crown, 1946); Tex.; 1939–1974.

Kline, C. Mahlon, son of fndr. Smith, Kline Beckman; chmn. Smith Kline, and French, Inc.; Philadelphia, Pa.; 1949–1967.

Knapp, Edward Spring, relative of Gideon Lee Knapp (II); Episcopalian; Bay Shore, L.I., N.Y.; house subsequently owned by August Belmont II; founder–1895.

Knapp, Gideon Lee (II), practiced medicine until father died, then devoted himself to sports; steward Jockey Club; Presbyterian; NYC; founder–1895.

Knapp, Harry Kearsage, brother of Gideon Lee Knapp; Columbia Univ. (Phi Beta Kappa.); dir. Corn Exchange Bank and Kings Country Trust; dir. Saratoga Racing Assn.; pres. Racquet and Tennis Club; vice chmn. Jockey Club; Islip, L.I., N.Y., and NYC; 1894–1926.

Knapp, Theodore J., son of Harry K. Knapp; member NYSE representing same firm as George H. Bull; 1928–1947.

Knight, John Shively (Jack), son of fndr. Knight Newspapers, Inc.; chmn. Knight Newspapers; Knight-Ridder Inc. was 1974 merger with (Bernard G.) Ridder Publications; married aunt of Daniel G. Van Clief; Cornell Univ.; John S. and James L. Knight Fndtn.; Akron, Ohio; 1961–1981.

La Boyteaux, William Harvell, pres. Johnson and Higgins (insurance brokers); dir. Grace Nat'l. Bank of N.Y.; purchased Fasig-Tipton (horse auctioneers); Holmdel, N.J.; 1943–1947.

LaMontague, Harry, b. France; turf patron and sculptor; owned Conniver (winning filly, 1945); 1948–1959.

Landry, John T., senior vp/dir. marketing Phillip Morris; creator of the Marlboro Man; senior vp Lotus Development; trustee NYRA; Saratoga Springs, N.Y.; 1985–1997.

Langley, William Clark, ptnr. W. C. Langley and Co. (NYSE banking investment firm); daughter married Walter D. Fletcher; St. Paul's;

Yale Univ.; dir. American Chicle; Republican; Episcopalian; West-bury, L.I., N.Y.; 1959–1962.

Lavin, A. Gary, doctor of veterinary medicine; secretary Gray-son–Jockey Club Research Fndtn.; steward Jockey Club; Longfield Farm; Goshen, Ky.; 1994–1999.

Lawrence, James G. K., pres. Coney Island Jockey Club; John M. Bow-ers was executor of will; from Groton, Mass.; founder–1895.

Lawrence, Prescott, son of J. G. K. Lawrence; Harvard Univ.; horse show exhibitor and judge; Coaching Club; founder–1921.

Leeds, William B., married relative of supt. of Pennsylvania RR; pres. Rock Island RR and American Tin Plate; left $35 million estate; Oyster Bay, L.I., N.Y.; 1904–1908.

Lewis, Robert B., owner Foothill Beverage (beer distributor); chmn. Thoroughbred Owners of California; bred Silver Charm (Kentucky Derby and Preakness, 1997); Calif.; 1997–1999.

Liebau, F. Jack, with N.J. Financial Corp.; co-owns horses with Sher-wood C. Chillingworth; CEO Bay Meadows Operating Co.; pres. California Thoroughbred Breeders Assn.; Irvine, Calif.; 1991–1999.

Loew, William Goadby, married daughter of George F. Baker, chmn. 1st Nat'l. Bank of N.Y.; son of member NYSE; Coaching Club; 1949–1955.

Long, Arthur F., pres. D. F. King and Co., specialist in pricing of ten-der offers in corporate mergers and takeovers; Columbia Univ.; trustee NYRA; L.I., N.Y.; 1981–1988.

Lorillard, Pierre (II), grandson of tobacco magnate Peter Lorillard and son of Pierre Lorillard I, fndr. Tuxedo Park; head P. Lorillard and Co.; cofndr. Monmouth Park; resigned from Jockey Club in 1938; N.Y.; 1904–1938.

Mabee, John C., fndr. Big Bear Grocery chain; fndr./chmn. Golden Eagle Insurance Co.; chmn. Del Mar Thoroughbred Club; San Diego, Calif.; 1985–1999.

McBean, Peter, head McBean Properties (family investments and trusts); San Francisco, Calif.; 1965–1996.

Mackay, Clarence H., son of John W. Mackay, Comstock Lode mining and telegraph magnate; member NYSE; held ball for Prince of Wales; Harbor Point, L.I., N.Y.; 1901–1938.

McKellar, Donald McCallum (II), vp internat'l. operations Field En-terprises; friend, business associate, and racing ptnr. of Marshall

Field III; WWII; Illinois Racing Board; steward Jockey Club; Episcopalian; Garden City, L.I., N.Y.; 1977–1997.

McKinney, Price, with Corrigan-McKinney Co.; chief trustee of estate of James W. Corrigan, heir of Cleveland steel fortune; committed suicide in Cleveland mansion; Cleveland, Ohio; 1913–1926.

McKnight, William Lester, CEO Minnesota Mining and Mfg. Co.; daughter married James H. Binger; McKnight Fndtn.; St. Paul, Minn.; 1968–1978.

McManus, James K. (Jim McKay), CBS and ABC sports commentator; host of ABC *Wide World of Sports*; regular commentator on the Triple Crown races; Loyola Univ.; Bellefield Farm; Monkton, Md.; 1987–1999.

MacMillen, William Charles, Jr., pres. William C. MacMillen and Co. (investment banking); L.L.B. Albany Law School; dir. Republic Nat'l. Bank N.Y., Republic N.Y. Corp., Manhattan Savings Bank; air force WWII (Legion of Merit); resigned from Jockey Club in 1988; Lawrence, N.Y.; 1988–1988, 1993–1999.

Macomber, A. Kingsley, with oil fortune bought William K. Vanderbilt's French racing empire of horses and farm for $2.5 million and raced abroad; top money winner in 1917; Calif.; 1917–1955.

Maddy, Kenneth L., Calif. state sen. and GOP majority leader; supporter of horse industry in state legislature; Republican; Calif.; 1994–1999.

Mangurian, Harry T., Jr., co-owner New England Patriots; 6th leading breeder in 1997; Mockingbird Farm; Ocala, Fla.; 1997–1999.

Manley, William H., manufacturer of cigars; owned Cuban plantation; Jamaica, L.I., N.Y.; 1909–1914.

Mansell, Frank L., Wall Street investment banker; Republican Nat'l. Finance Committee; Links Club; Pacific Union Club; Hobe Sound, Fla., and NYC; 1995–1999.

Markey, Gene, novelist, screenwriter, movie producer; married 3 actresses; 4th wife, widow of Warren Wright of Calumet Farm; Dartmouth; WWI, WWII (Bronze Star); Catholic; Lexington, Ky.; 1962–1980.

Martin, John William Y., Jr., grandson of Samuel K. Martin, Chicago real estate magnate, who owned real estate in the Loop; son of Md. sportsman; Worthington Farms; Glyndon, Md.; 1992–1999.

Martin, Townsend Bradley, grandson of Henry Phipps; descendent of F. Townsend Martin of original Four Hundred; officer Bessemer

Securities; co-investor in Monmouth Park; owner N.Y. Jets; Republican; Episcopalian; 1955–1982.

Mather, Charles E. II, steel fortune heir; had horses with Leslie
Combs II; pres. Saratoga Reading Room; chmn. Nat'l. Museum of
Racing; 1957–1982.

Maxwell, Howard W., vp Atlas Portland Cement Co.; vp 1st Nat'l. Bank
of Glen Cove, L.I.; sister married a Whitney; Princeton Univ.; dir. N.Y.
Trust Co. and Central RR of N.J.; Glen Cove, L.I., N.Y.; 1922–1947.

Mellon, Paul, son of Andrew W. Mellon, fndr. Mellon Nat'l. Bank,
ambassador to Great Britain, sec. of treasury; fraternity brother of
James Cox Brady II; Choate; Yale Univ. (Scroll and Key); 2d wife
"Bunny" Lambert was heir to Listerine fortune; chmn. NYRA;
trustee Nat'l. Gallery; Andrew W. Mellon Fndtn.; member English
Jockey Club; vice chmn. Jockey Club; $1.4 billion (*Forbes* 1998);
bred Mill Reef (English Derby, 1971) and Sea Hero (Kentucky
Derby, 1993); 4,200-acre estate, Upperville, Va.; 1947–1999.

Meyerhoff, Robert E., pres. family-owned Henderson-Webb, Inc.
(townhouse construction and mgt.); Robert and Jane Meyerhoff
Fndtn.; Fitzhugh Farm; Baltimore, Md.; 1994–1999.

Miller, Andrew, sec./treas. Life Publishing Co.; b. Ontario, Can.; Harvard Univ. classmate of Theodore Roosevelt; sec./treas. Saratoga
Racing Assn.; steward Jockey Club; Park Avenue, NYC; 1895–1919.

Miller, MacKenzie, Hall of Fame trainer; trained for Paul Mellon;
chmn. Nat'l. Museum of Racing; 1997–1999.

Mills, James P., great-grandson of Anthony J. Drexel, partner of J. P.
Morgan in Drexel, Morgan and Co.; married granddaughter of
Francis G. du Pont; St. Paul's; 1965–1987.

Mills, Ogden Livingston, grandson of gold mogul, pres. Bank of Calif.
Darius Ogden Mills and political Livingston family; 1st wife, Margaret Stuyvesand Rutherford, daughter of Mrs. W. K. Vanderbilt;
sister Gladys married Henry Carnegie Phipps; Harvard Univ.; N.Y.
state sen.; U.S. rep. R/N.Y.; sec. of treasury; army WWI; Republican; Woodbury, L.I., N.Y., and Newport, R.I.; 1928–1937.

Moore, Edward S., vp St. Louis and San Francisco RR, American Brake
Shoe and Foundry, Finance and Trading Corp, and Beech-Nut
Packing; St. Paul's; Yale Univ. (nongrad.); dir. American Can;
Chicago, Ill., and Old Westbury, L.I., N.Y.; 1944–1948.

Morgan, Edwin Denison (III), grandson of Edwin Denison Morgan,
U.S. sen. R/N.Y., chmn. Republican Nat'l. Committee, N.Y. gover-

nor, and distant relative of J. P. Morgan; member NYSE; member of yacht syndicate with W. K. Vanderbilt and Oliver Iselin; son was brokerage ptnr. of Richard Whitney; Harvard Univ.; commodore N.Y. Yacht Club; Westbury, L.I., N.Y.; 1895–1933.

Morgan, John Pierpont, son of fndr. international banking house J. S. Morgan and Co., London, and George Peabody's ptnr.; chmn. J. P. Morgan and Co. (leading private U.S. banker); member NYSE; educated overseas; pres. Metropolitan Museum of Art; Episcopalian; $69.5 million estate; NYC; 1894–1913.

Morris, Alfred Hennen, grandson of English steamship mogul Francis Morris, ptnr. of F. B. Morse in initial telegraph line, importer of Eclipse from England, and cofounder of Jerome Park; Harvard Univ.; co-owner of Morris Park; N.Y. State assemblyman; vice chmn. Jockey Club; Democrat; Presbyterian; NYC; founder–1959.

Morris, John Albert (II), son of Alfred Hennen Morris; Harvard Univ.; chmn. Cue Publishing, part owner *New Orleans Times Picayune*; assoc. Stone and Webster and Chas. D. Barney and Co.; ptnr. Gude, Winmill and Co.; Pomfret School; Harvard; owner Jamaica Racecourse; trustee NYRA; army WWI; pres. Union Club, N.Y.C.; Mason; steward Jockey Club; Episcopalian; Cedarhurst, L.I., N.Y.; 1928–1985.

Morris, John Albert, Jr. (III), son of John A. Morris (II); Trinity College; U. of Ky. Medical School; associate professor, surgical sciences, Vanderbilt Univ.; resigned from Jockey Club in 1996; Nashville, Tenn.; 1981–1996.

Morton, Thruston Ballard, chmn. Ballard and Ballard; vice chmn. Liberty Nat'l. Bank and Trust; brother of Rogers Clark Ballard Morton, U.S. rep. R/Md., chmn. Republican Nat'l. Committee, sec. of interior, sec. of commerce; cousin of Warner L. Jones; chmn. Churchill Downs; U.S. rep. and U.S. sen. R/Ky.; chmn. Republican Nat'l. Committee; Republican; Episcopalian; Louisville, Ky.; 1974–1982.

Moseley, James Brady, nephew of James Cox Brady II; Harvard Univ.; chmn. Suffolk Downs; Jockey Club Fndtn.; John G. Cavanagh Trust; steward Jockey Club; among richest 100,000 in U.S. (1991); raised in Far Hills, N.J.; Hamilton, Mass.; 1970–1998.

Nuckols, Charles, Jr., 9th leading breeder in 1997; pres. Thoroughbred Club of America; Midway, Ky.; 1997–1999.

O'Connell, Walter Francis, wife was member of Daughters of the American Revolution; Hilton Head Island, S.C.; 1981–1996.

Oglebay, Crispin, chmn. Oglebay, Norton and Co. (largest Great Lakes shippers); St. Paul's; Yale Univ. (Scroll and Key); chmn. Ferro Machine and Foundry, pres. Atwater Dock Co. and Brule Smokeless Coal, vp Castile Mining Co. and Montreal Mining; Republican; Episcopalian; Cleveland, Ohio; 1943–1949.

Olin, John Merrill, son of fndr. Olin Corp. (electrochemical and metals company); chmn. Olin Chemical Corp.; Cornell Univ.; John M. Olin Fndtn.; St. Louis, Mo.; 1969–1982.

Oxnard, Henry Thomas, for whom Oxnard, Calif. is named; son of Brooklyn sugar refinery owner; pres. American Beet Sugar Co.; Harvard Univ.; Blue Ridge Stud; Upperville, Va.; 1904–1922.

Parr, Henry A. III, descendent of Henry A. Parr, merchant, bank director, controller of Richmond, Va., electric railways, and developer of Isthmus of Panama manganese mines; 1943–1977.

Parr, Ral, relative of Henry A. Parr III; 1912–1939.

Parsons, Schuyler Livingston, mother was direct descendent of explorer Robert Livingston, father was head of Parsons and Petit (chemical dealers); raced with H. K. Knapp; steward Jockey Club; NYC; 1906–1917.

Paulson, Allen Eugene, airline mechanic, became fndr./chmn. Gulfstream Aerospace Co., which sold out to Chrysler; CEO Full House Resorts; owner of Cigar (Horse of the Year, 1996); he and his sons worth $300 million (1985); Republican; San Diego, Calif.; 1996– 1999.

Payne, Oliver Hazard, son of Standard Oil magnate Henry B. Payne, U.S. rep. and U.S. sen. D/Ohio; treas. Standard Oil; sister married W. C. Whitney; Phillips Academy; Yale Univ. (nongrad.); Civil War; exec. American Tobacco and Tenn. Coal and Iron; resigned from Jockey Club in 1903; Cleveland, Ohio; founder–1903.

Peace, John H., chmn. William Esty Co. (advertising), that developed slogan "Winston Tastes Good Like a Cigarette Should" for maiden account with RJR Reynolds Tobacco; trustee NYRA; Arnold P. Gold Fndtn.; Scarsdale, N.Y.; 1991–1999.

Pease, Perry R., friend and Harvard Univ. classmate of Alexander Cassatt (II); introduced to racing by John A. Morris; raced with Francis A. Kernan at Cambridge Stable; Harvard Univ.; trustee NYRA; N.Y.; 1960–1982.

Perry, William Haggin, great-grandson of James Ben Ali Haggin; ptnr A. R. Hancock; married daughter of F. S. von Stade; steward Jockey Club; Middleburg, Va.; 1956–1993.

Phillips, James W., son-in-law of John Galbreath; atty. Galbreath Co.; Columbus, Ohio; 1981–1996.

Phipps, Henry Carnegie, son of Henry Phipps, Pittsburgh ptnr. of steel magnate Andrew Carnegie; married Ogden Livingston Mills's sister, who started family stable Wheatley and bred Bold Ruler (Horse of the Year, 1957); St. Paul's; Pittsburgh, Pa.; 1930–1953.

Phipps, Michael Grace, cousin of Ogden Phipps; St. Paul's; Yale Univ. (Scroll and Key); pres. Bessemer Properties, Palm Beach; dir. W. R. Grace and Co. (chemicals); 10-goal polo player; 1959–1973.

Phipps, Ogden, son of Henry Carnegie Phipps; 1st wife later married Marshall Field III; son by 1st wife married daughter of Czechoslovakian count; 2d wife was sister of George H. Bostwick; St. Paul's; Harvard Univ.; trustee NYRA; 9 times champion of court tennis; chmn. Jockey Club; bred Buckpasser (Horse of the Year, 1966); Republican; Old Westbury, L.I., N.Y.; 1939–1999.

Phipps, Ogden Mills, son of Ogden Phipps by 2d wife; brother-in-law of William Stamps Farish III; Yale Univ.; head Bessemer Trust; chmn. NYRA; chmn. Jockey Club; NYC; 1965–1999.

Pope, George A., Jr., grandson of 14,000-acre ranch owner in California; son of fndr. Pope-Talbot Steamship; dir. Calif. Thoroughbred Breeders Assn.; 5-goal rating in polo; Calif.; 1962–1979.

Pratt, Herbert Lee, descendant of Standard Oil ptnr. of John D. Rockefeller, also fndr. Pratt Institute, Brooklyn; a Pratt married a daughter of William Woodward; Amherst College; dir. Charles Pratt and Co., Bankers Trust, and American Can; NYC and Glen Cove, L.I., N.Y.; 1922–1945.

Preston, Ralph J., atty.; Princeton Univ.; deputy commissioner Red Cross—Europe, WWI; Park Ave., NYC and Jericho, L.I., N.Y.; 1896–1919.

Purdey, William A., grandson of William H. La Boyteaux; son of London manufacturer of shotguns; bred Dance Floor (3d in Kentucky Derby, 1992) then owned by rap star "Hammer"; Colts Neck, N.J.; 1979–1999.

Reynolds, David Parham, son of fndr. Reynolds Aluminum; Princeton Univ. (nongrad.); chmn. Reynolds Metals and Eskimo Pie; Richard S. Reynolds Fndtn.; among richest 100,000 in U.S. (1991); Richmond, Va.; 1976–1999.

Reynolds, Richard S., Jr., son of fndr. Reynolds Aluminum; chmn. Reynolds Metals; ptnr Reynolds and Co. (banking, NYC); Richard S. Reynolds Fndtn.; Presbyterian; Richmond, Va.; 1976–1980.

Richards, Reuben F., married daughter of James Cox Brady II; Harvard Univ.; CEO Inspiration Resources (agribusiness and mining) and Minoroco (USA), NYC; chmn. Terra Industrial Inc., NYC, and Engelhard Corp.; vp Citibank; among richest 100,000 in U.S. (1991); Republican; Far Hills, N.J., and NYC; 1976–1999.

Ridder, Bernard J., chmn. Ridder Publications, board member (John S.) Knight-Ridder, Inc.; publisher *New York Journal of Commerce, Pasadena Star News*; officer Oak Tree Racing Assn.; pres. Calif. Thoroughbred Breeders Assn.; Pasadena, Calif.; 1979–1983.

Riddle, Samuel D., descendent of Scottish immigrant textile magnate for whom Glen Riddle, Pa., is named; raced with his nephew Walter M. Jeffords; owned Man o' War; bred War Admiral (Triple Crown, 1937); Philadelphia, Pa.; 1920–1951.

Robbins, Jack K., veterinarian to the leading money winner John Henry; founding dir. Oak Tree Racing Assn.; Oak Tree Charitable Fndtn.; pres. American Assn. of Equine Practitioners; Calif.; 1995–1999.

Robbins, S. Howland, son of banker; pres. NYC Fire Commission; Civil War volunteer; NYC; 1896–1901.

Robinson, Jesse Mack, owner auto loan co. chain; chmn. Atlantic American Corp. (investment banking); pres./CEO Gray Communications; dir. 1st Nat'l. Bank of Atlanta; J. Mack Robinson Fndtn.; worth $750 million (*Forbes* 1999); Atlanta, Ga.; 1995–1999.

Roebling, Joseph M., great-grandson of John A. Roebling, patent owner and supplier of cable for suspension bridges, including the Brooklyn and the Golden Gate; Princeton Univ.; chmn. Roebling Div. of the Colorado Fuel and Iron Corp.; co-investor in Monmouth Park; steward Jockey Club; Trenton, N.J.; 1956–1980.

Rogers, William P., exec. Rogers and Wells, NYC; Colgate; Cornell Law School; bd. Dreyfus Fund; trustee NYRA; U.S. attorney general, sec. of state; navy WWII; 1975–1999.

Ross, Donald Peabody, married Wilhelmina du Pont; Yale Univ. (Scroll and Key); fndr. Delaware Park; Ross Fndtn.; steward Jockey Club; Brandywine Stable; Wilmington, Del.; 1941–1973.

Ross, Donald Peabody, Jr., son of Donald Peabody Ross; Yale Univ.; with Border Co. (family organization); Ross Fndtn.; chmn. Del. Racing Assn.; steward Jockey Club; Wilmington, Del.; 1972–1999.

Ross, Samuel, chmn. Barber and Ross, Inc. (hardware and building material); charter member Washington Board of Trade; Washington, D.C.; 1906–1930.

Rowan, Louis R., chmn. Louis Rowan and Co. (equine insurance specialists); co-owned horses with Wheelock Whitney; married daughter of William L. Brann; chmn. R. A. Rowan and Co. (real estate and property mgt.); original stockholder Santa Anita; fndr. Oak Tree Racing Assn.; pres. Calif. Thoroughbred Breeders Assn.; Republican; Pasadena, Calif.; 1967–1988.

Ruppert, Jacob, Jr., son of fndr. Jacob Ruppert Brewery, pres. Astoria Silk Works; U.S. rep. D/N.Y.; on N.Y. governor's staff; pres. N.Y. Yankees; Democrat; Catholic; 135-acre estate Garrison, N.Y.; 1894–1939.

Ryan, E. Barry, grandson of Thomas Fortune Ryan; 2d wife married F. E. Kilroe; professional horse trainer; 1957–1993.

Ryan, James P., fndr. Ryland Homes; built homes on Israel's West Bank; fndr. Ryan Family Fndtn.; resigned from Jockey Club in 1989 due to disagreement over monies Jockey Club reserves for indigent racetrack workers; Ryehill Farm; Mt. Airy, Md.; 1981–1989.

Ryan, John Barry, Jr. (II), grandson of Thomas Fortune Ryan; married daughter of Otto Kahn, multimillionaire ptnr. with Jacob Schiff in Kuhn, Loeb and Co.; reporter; resigned from Jockey Club in 1965; 1950–1965.

Ryan, Thomas Fortune, of Irish descent; transit associate of W. C. Whitney and P.A.B. Widener (I); member NYSE; controlling dir. in over 30 corps.; contributed $20 million to Catholic Church; $200 million estate; Democrat; Catholic; NYC; 1922–1928.

Sage, Andrew G. C., brother of Henry Williams Sage; gen ptnr. Lehman Brothers; stepson of Albert C. Bostwick; Westminster School; Yale Univ.; breeder of champion pointers; Park Ave., NYC; 1928–1952.

Sage, Henry Williams, maternal grandson of Civil War governor of Pa., and paternal grandson of lumber mogul Henry Williams Sage, fndr. Cornell Univ.; son of William Henry Sage, Yale Univ. (Scroll and Key), sec./treas. Sage Land and Development, trustee Cornell Univ.; vp Sage Land and Development Co.; Westminster School; Yale Univ.; army WWI; Republican; Episcopalian; Old Brookline, L.I., N.Y.; 1926–1938.

Sams, Timothy H., member Ind. Thoroughbred Development Advisory Committee; Carmel, Ind.; 1989–1999.

Samuel, Ernest L., assoc. of Samuel and Sons (steel and aluminum distribution); owns Eclipse Award–winning horses; Sam-Son Farm; Ontario, Can.; 1989–1999.

Sanford, John, grandson of John Sanford, carpet mogul and U.S. rep. D/N.Y.; son of Stephen Sanford, U.S. rep. R/N.Y.; Yale Univ.; pres. Stephen Sanford and Sons, chmn. Bigelow-Sanford Carpet Co. and Amsterdam City Nat'l. Bank; U.S. rep. R/N.Y.; steward Jockey Club; Amsterdam, N.Y.; 1895–1939.

Schiff, John M., grandson of Jacob Henry Schiff, developer of Kuhn, Loeb and Co., member NYSE, and fndr. American Jewish Committee; Yale Univ.; married daughter of George F. Baker, Jr., chmn. 1st Nat'l. Bank of N.Y.; senior ptnr. Kuhn, Loeb and Co.; honorary chmn. Lehman Brothers after merger with Kuhn, Loeb and Co.; trustee NYRA; Schiff Fndtn.; pres. Boy Scouts of America; steward Jockey Club; L.I., N.Y.; 1953–1987.

Schiff, Peter G., son of John M. Schiff; trustee NYRA; Schiff Fndtn.; Oyster Bay, L.I., N.Y.; 1994–1999.

Schiffer, Kenneth M., Yale Univ.; army remount WWII; pres. Calif. Thoroughbred Breeders Assn.; steward Jockey Club; Hat Ranch; Temecula, Calif.; 1978–1990.

Schley, Reeve, vp Chase Nat'l. Bank; best friend of James Cox Brady II; St. Paul's; Yale Univ.; L.L.B. Columbia Univ.; chmn. Sundstrand Corp. and Underwood Corp., pres. Somerset Trust; vice chmn. Monmouth Park; pres. American-Russian Chamber of Commerce; head Lend-Lease to Russia, WWII; Republican; Episcopalian; Raritan Stable; Far Hills, N.J.; 1953–1960.

Schley, Reeve, Jr., son of Reeve Schley; St. Paul's; Yale Univ.; chmn. Monmouth Park; Far Hills, N.J.; 1960–1993.

Sharp, Bayard, son of sister of Pierre Samuel du Pont, head Du Pont and General Motors; daughter married William S. Farish II; dir. Delaware Park; prominent in steeplechase racing; steward Jockey Club; worth $335 million (*Forbes* 1995); Greenville, Del.; 1952–1999.

Shields, Joseph V., Jr., trustee NYRA; trustee TOBA; made $9,000 contribution to N.Y. governor Pataki's 1997 reelection campaign; 1997–1999.

Shouse, Jouett, son of Disciples of Christ minister; Kans. state sen.; U.S. rep. D/Kans.; asst. sec. of treasury; endorsed legislation that legalized pari-mutuel betting at Ky. tracks; Democrat-turned-Republican; Lexington, Ky.; 1956–1968.

Smith, Gerard S., investment banker; trustee NYRA; perennial head of the Belmont Ball; 1920s Nat'l. Open polo star; steward Jockey Club; Catholic; Brooklyn, N.Y.; 1956–1974.

Sommer, Viola, widow of N.Y. hotel, shopping mall, luxury apt. bldg. magnate Sigmund Sommer; co-owner of Las Vegas Aladdin Hotel and Casino; trustee NYRA; worth $440 million (*Forbes* 1995); Park Ave, NYC, and Great Neck, L.I., N.Y.; 1988–1999.

Stevens, Robert L., said to be a member of the Stevens family that catered all the N.Y. racetracks and ball parks; St. Paul's; 1897–1907.

Steward, John, died suddenly in Wyoming; interred in Santa Barbara, Calif.; 1895–1923.

Stewart, W. Plunkett, son-in-law of Alexander Cassatt; member NYSE; Coaching Club; 1932–1948.

Stone, Whitney, chmn. Stone and Webster, Inc. (engineering); cousin of John Hay Whitney; St. Paul's; attended Harvard Univ.; dir. American Express, Chase Manhattan Bank; trustee NYRA; steward Jockey Club; NYC; 1939–1979.

Strauss, Robert Schwarz, sen. ptnr. Akin, Gump, Strauss, Haver and Feld (law firm); special agent FBI; dir. Columbia Univ. Pictures, Xerox Corp., Braniff Airways, Archer-Daniels-Midland Co.; treas. Democratic Nat'l. Committee; ambassador to Russia; Strauss Fndtn.; Jewish; Democrat; Wash., D.C.; 1988–1999.

Strawbridge, George, Jr., heir to fortunes of John T. Dorrance Campbell Soup and Philadelphia's Strawbridge department store (started in 1868 and bought by May Dept. Store in 1996); dir. Core States Financial Corp.; exec. committee Buffalo Sabres, Nat'l. Hockey League; Steeplechase Fndtn., Margaret Dorrance Strawbridge Fndtn. of Pa.; $825 million (*Forbes* 1999); Augustin Stable; Wilmington, Del.; 1976–1999.

Strub, Robert P., son of Charles Strub, DDS, pres. San Francisco Seals Baseball Club and head of group that founded Santa Anita; Stanford; chmn. Santa Anita Operating Co; vice chmn. Santa Anita Realty Enterprises, Inc.; army WWII; Catholic; Calif.; 1983–1993.

Sturgis, Frank Knight, member Strong, Sturgis and Co. (brokers); pres. Madison Square Garden Co.; pres. NYSE; in original Four Hundred; steward Jockey Club; NYC; founder–1932.

Sutherland, Dwight G., head Sutherland Lumber Co.; D.D.S. Fndtn.; Kansas City, Mo.; 1997–1999.

Talbott, Harold Elstner, vp family-owned H. E. Talbott Co. (construction); attended Yale Univ.; chmn. North American Aviation; head Dayton Wright Aeroplane Co.; chmn. Standard Cap and Seal Corp.; dir. Chrysler Corp., Mead Corp., Electric Autolite, Madison

Square Garden Co.; trustee NYRA; sec. of air force; Republican; NYC; 1952–1957.

Taylor, Charles Plunkett Bourchier, son of E. P. Taylor; trustee Ontario Jockey Club; founding dir. Breeders' Cup; free-lance journalist who covered the Vietnam and Arab-Israeli wars; Windfields Farm; Ontario, Can.; 1983–1997.

Taylor, Edward Plunkett, grandson of Canadian brewery entrepreneur; head Canadian Breweries, selling 1/2 of beer consumed in Canada; head Argus Corp., controlling Massey-Ferguson; bred Northern Dancer (Kentucky Derby and Preakness, 1964) and Nijinsky (syndicated $5 million+, 1970); chmn. Ontario Jockey Club; 700-acre Windfields Farm; Ontario, Can.; 1953–1989.

Taylor, Shirley H., pres. TOBA; races primarily in England; Busby, Mont.; 1989–1999.

Thieriot, Charles H., son of member NYSE; Harvard Univ.; trustee NYRA; vp Nat'l. Museum of Racing; Locust Valley, N.Y.; 1978–1999.

Thomas, Joseph A., ptnr. Lehman Bros. (investment bankers); Yale Univ. (Scroll and Key); dir. Litton Industries, Getty Oil, Black and Decker Mfg.; Links Club; Pacific Union Club; Old Brookville, N.Y.; 1965–1977.

Thompson, Lewis Steenrod, son of William P. Thompson; with his brother W. P. Thompson, Jr., owned large game preserve and stock farm on Red Bank, N.J., estate; owner of Brookdale Farm, where Regret (Kentucky Derby winning filly, 1912) was foaled; Sunny Hill Plantation; Thomasville, Ga., and Red Bank, N.J.; 1895–1936.

Thompson, William Payne, relative of member NYSE; pres. Nat'l. Lead Co.; brother-in-law of U.S. sen. Johnson N. Camden; vp Standard Oil; dir. U.S. Nat'l. Bank, Southern Nat'l. Bank, Ohio River RR; Confederate army; steward Jockey Club; NYC; founder–1896.

Thompson, William Payne, Jr., son of William P. Thompson; Lawrenceville School; Harvard Univ. (nongrad.); Knickerbocker, Union, Brook, Racquet, and Tennis clubs; Westbury, L.I.; 1896–1922.

Thorne, Oakleigh Blakeman, great-grandson of banker and Commerce Clearing House purchaser; Harvard Univ.; chmn. Commerce Clearing House; Millbrook Tribute Garden, Inc. (fndtn.), Oakleigh L. Thorne Fndtn.; worth $800 million (*Forbes* 1999); 900-acre Thorndale Estate; Millbrook, N.Y.; 1981–1999.

Tracy, Benjamin F., N.Y. appellate judge; organized N. Y. Republican Party; sec. of navy; resigned from Jockey Club to head commission to develop charter of Greater N.Y.; NYC; 1894–1896.

Tuckerman, Bayard, Jr., direct descendent of George Walton, Declaration of Independence signer; married Phyllis Sears; St. George's School; Harvard Univ.; ptnr. O'Brien, Russell, and Co. (insurance); dir. Rockland Atlas Nat'l. Bank, Ritz Carlton Hotel; pres. Suffolk Downs; WWI; Republican; Westport, Mass.; 1953–1974.

Valpredo, Donald J., Calif. racing commissioner; Valpredo Farms; Bakersfield, Calif.; 1991–1999.

Van Clief, Daniel G., son of owner of Erie Canal barge company and fox-hunting enthusiast who married Woolworth heiress; nephew of wife of John S. Knight; Choate School; dir. Fasig-Tipton (horse auctioneers); dir. Laurel Racecourse; Va. state rep.; WWII; Democrat; Va.; 1955–1987.

Van Clief, Daniel G., Jr., son of Daniel G. Van Clief; chmn. Fasig-Tipton (horse auctioneers); pres. Breeders' Cup, Ltd.; CEO National Thoroughbred Racing Assn.; Nydrie Stud (bloodstock agent); Jockey Club Fndtn.; among richest 100,000 in U.S. (1991); 3,000-acre Nydrie Stud; Esmont, Va.; 1991–1999.

Vanderbilt, Alfred Gwynne (II), great-great-grandson of Cornelius Vanderbilt; son of Alfred Gwynne Vanderbilt I and Bromo Seltzer heiress; St. Paul's; Yale Univ. (nongrad.); vice pres. Pimlico, pres. Belmont Park; chmn. NYRA; steward Jockey Club; bred Native Dancer (Horse of the Year, 1952); Mill Neck, N.Y.; 1937–1999.

Vanderbilt, William Kissam, grandson of steamship and railroad magnate Cornelius Vanderbilt; member NYSE; vp N.Y. Central and Hudson River RR; chmn. N.Y., Chicago and St. Louis RR; 1st wife, Alva (Smith), married O.H.P. Belmont; 2d wife was daughter of E. H. Harriman; son Harold Stirling invented contract bridge; son "Willie K." sponsored 1st official race for motorcars; sister married William Seward Webb; in later years raced in France; NYC; founder–1920.

von Stade, F. S. (Francis Skiddy), family founded F. S. von Stade Co. (bristle importers); married daughter of J. P. Morgan ptnr. Charles Steele; one daughter married George H. Bostwick and another married W. Haggin Perry; St. Paul's; Harvard Univ.; trustee NYRA; pres. Saratoga Assn.; cofndr. Nat'l. Museum of Racing; Coaching Club; champion polo player; steward Jockey Club; Old Westbury, L.I., N.Y.; 1935–1967.

Wadsworth, Craig Wharton, Harvard Univ. (nongrad.); served in secretarial capacities in American embassies in London, Teheran, Bucharest, Montevideo, Buenos Aires, Rio de Janeiro, Brussels; Spanish-American War; Republican; Episcopalian; resigned from position in London embassy and Jockey Club in 1909; Geneseo, N.Y.; 1900–1909.

Walcott, A. F., pres. Monmouth Park Assn.; NYC; founder–1906.

Walker, George Herbert, fndr. H. Walker and Co. (banking and investments); member NYSE; raced horses with W. Averell Harriman; pres. W. A. Harriman and Co.; underwriter of Madison Square Garden; member N.Y. racing commission; pres. U.S. Golf Assn.; St. Louis, Mo.; 1926–1953.

Walker, Joseph, Jr., trustee NYRA; steward Jockey Club; Unionville, Pa.; 1956–1999.

Webb, William Seward, pres. Wagner Sleeping Car Co.; married sister of William Kissam Vanderbilt; in original Four Hundred; resigned from Jockey Club in 1900; NYC; founder–1900.

Weber, Charlotte Colket, member Campbell Soup John T. Dorrance family; Sorbonne/Ecole du Louvre; Live Oak Fndtn.; Republican; worth $1.5 billion (*Forbes* 1999); Live Oak Plantation; Ocala, Fla.; 1997–1999.

Webster, Reginald Nathaniel, b. Dublin; chmn. Standard-Thomson Corp.; dir. Reynolds Metals Co.; Palm Beach, Fla.; 1966–1983.

Wetherill, Cortright (Corty), married daughter of P.A.B. Widener II, who raced steeplechase horses; Happy Hill Farm; White Horse, Pa.; 1955–1988.

Wetmore, George Peabody, son of China-trade mogul; Yale Univ. (Skull and Bones); co-owner Monmouth Park; governor of R.I.; U.S. sen. R/R.I.; in original Four Hundred; Republican; Newport, R.I.; founder–1921.

Whitney, Betsey Cushing Roosevelt, widow of John Hay Whitney; 1st husband was FDR's son; Greentree Fndtn.; worth $600 million (*Forbes* 1995); resigned from Jockey Club in 1996 due to ill health; West 51st, NYC; 1986–1996.

Whitney, Cornelius Vanderbilt, son of Harry Payne Whitney; 1st wife later married W. A. Harriman; Groton; Yale Univ.; chmn. Bay Mining and Smelting Co.; bd. chmn. Pan American World Airways; Democrat; Episcopalian; resigned from Jockey Club temporarily in 1958 when he was getting his 3d divorce and sold his horses;

MEMBERS OF THE JOCKEY CLUB

Wheatley Hills, L.I., mansion now N.Y. Institute of Technology; 1930–1958, 1962–1992.

Whitney, Edward Farley, ptnr/vp J. P. Morgan and Co.; Harvard Univ.; Park Place, NYC, and Oyster Bay, L.I., N.Y.; 1916–1928.

Whitney, Harry Payne, son of W. C. Whitney; married Cornelius Vanderbilt's great-granddaughter Gertrude; Yale Univ. (Skull and Bones); dir. Guggenheim Exploration Co.; 10-goal rating in polo; steward Jockey Club; bred Regret (Kentucky Derby, 1915); NYC; 1900–1930.

Whitney, John Hay (Jock), son of Payne Whitney; Groton; Yale Univ. (Scroll and Key); 1st wife was Philadelphia horsewoman; 2d wife was ex-wife of son of FDR; publisher *New York Herald Tribune;* trustee NYRA; ambassador to Great Britain; army WWII; steward Jockey Club; bred Tom Fool (Horse of the Decade, 1960); N.Y.; 1928–1982.

Whitney, Payne, son of W. C. Whitney; Yale Univ.; married Sec. of State John Hay's daughter Helen, who founded family stable, Greentree; dir. Great Northern Paper Co., 1st Nat'l. Bank, NYC; vp Whitney Realty Co.; steward Jockey Club; largest individual estate ever appraised ($186 million); Manhasset, L.I., N.Y.; 1920–1927.

Whitney, Richard, pres. NYSE; brother of George Whitney, ptnr. J. P. Morgan and Co.; Groton; Harvard Univ.; senior ptnr. Richard Whitney and Co.; resigned from Jockey Club following conviction for grand larceny; master of foxhounds; Far Hills, N.J.; 1931–1938.

Whitney, Wheelock, head Whitney Management Co.; owned horses with Louis R. Rowan; Yale Univ.; Whitney Fndtn.; steward Jockey Club; Republican; Minneapolis, Minn.; 1974–1999.

Whitney, William Collins, married sister of Oliver Payne; Yale Univ. (Skull and Bones); Harvard Law School; member NYSE; associate of Thomas Fortune Ryan and P.A.B. Widener I in NYC street railways; ptnr. of Rockefellers, Harknesses, and Pratts in original Standard Oil trust; owner Saratoga Racecourse; sec. of navy; in original Four Hundred; Democrat; NYC; founder–1904.

Whittingham, Charles, Hall of Fame trainer; trained Ferdinand (Kentucky Derby, 1986); 1997–1999.

Widener, George D. (II), nephew of J. E. Widener; educated privately; married Jessie Sloane of Dodge-Sloane General Motors family; dir. Electric Storage Battery Co., Provident Nat'l. Bank; pres. Belmont Park; trustee NYRA; chmn. Jockey Club; Republican; Episcopalian; Philadelphia, Pa.; 1916–1971.

Widener, Joseph Early, son of P.A.B. Widener I, member NYSE and utilities magnate associate of W. C. Whitney; educated privately; Harvard Univ. (nongrad.); owner/pres. Belmont Park, pres. Hialeah; vice chmn. Jockey Club; Elmendorf Farm; Philadelphia, Pa., and Palm Beach, Fla.; 1901–1943.

Widener, Peter A. B. II, son of J. E. Widener; married Gertrude Peabody; pres. Hialeah; WWI; Elmendorf Farm; 1930–1948.

Widener, Peter A. B. III, son of P.A.B. Widener II; Widener Memorial Fndtn.; Saratoga, Wyo.; 1955–1999.

Willmot, David S., son of Donald G. Willmot; CEO Ontario Jockey Club; said to be among most influential persons in Canadian sports; Ontario, Can.; 1996–1999.

Willmot, Donald Gilpin, chmn. Molson Companies Ltd., vp Bank of Nova Scotia, dir. Crown Life Insurance Co.; Anglican; Kinghaven Farm; King, Ontario, Can.; 1983–1994.

Wilson, Richard Thornton, Jr., son of Confederate cotton broker R. T. Wilson, whose children married into Goelet, Vanderbilt, and Astor families; member NYSE; in original Four Hundred; steward Jockey Club; NYC; 1896–1929.

Wimpfheimer, Jacques D., 3d generation in American Velvet Co. textiles; Princeton Univ.; A. Wimpfheimer and Bros.; chmn. TOBA; member Internat'l. Breeders Assn; Wimpfheimer Fndtn.; WWII; Jewish; Stonington, Conn.; 1985–1999.

Wing, S. Bryce, from family that owned Wing and Evans Chemical Co.; close friend of F. Ambrose Clark; pres. Nat'l. Steeplechase Assn.; chmn. Maryland Hunt Cup; Md.; 1953–1975.

Woodward, William I, chmn. Central Hanover Bank and Trust Co.; nephew of member NYSE; one daughter married Thomas Bancroft and another married John Pratt; Groton; Harvard Univ.; sec. U.S. embassy, London; member 1st Federal Reserve Board; chmn. Jockey Club; bred Gallant Fox (Triple Crown, 1930), Omaha (Triple Crown, 1935), Nashua (all-time leading money winner in 1950s); Belair Stud; Md.; 1917–1953.

Woodward, William II, son of William Woodward I; Groton; Harvard Univ.; trustee Hanover Bank; trustee NYRA; navy WWII; Belair Stud; NYC; 1954–1955.

Wright, Warren, son of inventor of Calumet baking powder; investor in Arlington Park; bred Whirlaway (Triple Crown, 1941), Citation

(Triple Crown, 1948); Presbyterian; Republican; Calumet Farm, Lexington, Ky.; Chicago, Ill.; 1937–1950.

Wygod, Martin J., head Medco Containment (U.S. pharmacy benefits management and mail-order company) bought by Merck ($6.6 billion in 1993); head of Merck's prescription drug business; Rose Fndtn.; River Edge Farm; Buellton, Calif.; 1996–1999.

Young, William T., developed Big Top Peanut Butter that became Proctor and Gamble's Jiff; chmn. Royal Crown Cola; board Humana, Inc., Reynolds Metals, and 1st Security Nat'l. Bank and Trust; steward Jockey Club; bred Grindstone (Kentucky Derby, 1996) and Cat Thief (Breeders Cup Classic, 1999); Overbrook Farm; Lexington, Ky.; 1989–1999.

Zeigler, William, Jr., heir to $16 million estate of his uncle William Zeigler, Sr., Royal Baking Powder magnate; Columbia Univ. and Harvard Univ. (nongrad.); founded Standard Brands, Inc.; owned El Chico (best two-year-old, 1938); 1938–1958.

Notes

INTRODUCTION

1. Garland E. Allen, "Science Misapplied: The Eugenics Age Revisited," *Technology Review* 99 (1996): 22–31; Wray Herbert, "Politics of Biology," *U.S. News and World Report*, April 12, 1997, 72–74, 77–80; Erica Goode, "Linking Drop in Crime to Rise in Abortion," *New York Times*, August 20, 1999, A14.

1. JOCKEYING FOR POWER

1. Roger Longrigg, *The History of Horse Racing* (New York: Stein and Day, 1972), 19–20; the quotation is from the book's jacket.
2. Ibid., 60–96.
3. William C. Ewing, *Sports of Colonial Williamsburg* (Richmond: Diety Press, 1937), 2.
4. W. S. Vosburgh, *Racing in America, 1866–1921* (New York: Scribner, 1922); John Hervey, *Racing in America, 1665–1865* (New York: Scribner, 1944), 17; Bernard Livingston, *Their Turf: America's Horsey Set and Its Princely Dynasties* (New York: Arbor House, 1973), 23; the quotation is from John Dizikes, *Sportsmen and Gamesmen* (Boston: Houghton Mifflin, 1981), 137.
5. Livingston, *Their Turf*; Kent Hollingsworth, *The Kentucky Thoroughbred* (Lexington: University of Kentucky Press, 1976).
6. Details of early racing at Saratoga Springs and the life of John Morrissey rely on Dixon Wecter, *The Saga of American Society: A Record of Social Aspirations, 1607–1937* (New York: Scribner, 1937), 434; Mel Heimer, *Fabulous Bawd: The Story of Saratoga* (New York: Holt, 1952), 67–131; George Waller, *Saratoga: Saga of an Impious Era* (Englewood Cliffs, N.J.: Prentice-Hall, 1966), 119–132; Longrigg, *History of Horse Racing*, 222; Richard Sasuly, *Bookies and Bettors: Two Hundred Years of Gambling* (New York: Holt, Rinehart and Winston, 1982), 60–61.
7. Tammany Hall from the 1860s through the 1890s has come to stand for urban corruption and the mutual dependence of politics and crime, and Boss Tweed for the evils of patronage and bribery in city government. They were the pawns of the elite, as well as of organized criminals. Though Tweed was convicted in 1871, Tammany

remained the tool of the industrial and financial elite into the twentieth century. See Seymour J. Mandelbaum, *Boss Tweed's New York* (New York: Wiley, 1965).

8. E. Digby Baltzell, *Philadelphia Gentlemen: The Making of a National Upper Class* (Glencoe, Ill.: Free Press, 1958); Frederic Cople Jaher, *The Urban Establishment: Upper Strata in Boston, New York, Charleston, Chicago, and Los Angeles* (Urbana: University of Illinois Press, 1983).

9. According to Thomas B. Brewer (*The Robber Barons: Saints or Sinners* [New York: Holt, Rinehart and Winston, 1970], 1,101), the term "robber baron" originated in the 1860s with E. L. Godkin, editor of *The Nation*, and was used by Senator Scharz of Missouri in the 1870s and by the Populists and writers and reformers of the Progressive Era shortly thereafter. See also Gustavus Myers, *History of the Great American Fortunes* (1907; rpt. ed. New York: Random House, 1936); Matthew Josephson, *The Robber Barons: The Great American Capitalists, 1861–1901* (New York: Harcourt Brace, 1934); Ferdinand Lundberg, *America's 60 Families* (New York: Lyle Stuart, 1937), 50–53; Stewart H. Holbrook, *The Age of the Moguls* (Garden City, N.Y.: Doubleday, 1953); Baltzell, *Philadelphia Gentlemen*; Ferdinand Lundberg, *The Rich and the Super-Rich: A Study in the Power of Money Today* (New York: Lyle Stuart, 1968), 551–552; Frederic Cople Jaher, "Style and Status: High Society in Late Nineteenth-Century New York," in *The Rich, the Well-Born, and the Powerful: Elites and Upper Classes in History*, ed. Frederic Cople Jaher (Chicago: University of Illinois Press, 1973), 265.

10. See Irvin G. Wyllie, *The Self-Made Man in America* (New York: Free Press, 1954), for the "poor boys make good" view. The robber barons have also been viewed as entrepreneurial, ingenious, and creative, as well as unscrupulous and criminal. The views vary by writer (historian, revisionist, or journalist), the writer's objectives (to eulogize, justify, understand, or discredit), and the sentiment of the time.

11. Materials on Thomas Fortune Ryan are drawn from *Who Was Who*; *Dictionary of American Biography*; Jaher, *The Urban Establishment*; Cleveland Amory, *Who Killed Society?* (New York: Harper, 1960), 352–356.

12. Baltzell, *Philadelphia Gentlemen*, 116.

13. The specifics on the founding of the Jockey Club in America are taken from a book commissioned by the Club (Vosburgh, *Racing in America*, 44–47); J.K.M. Ross, *Boots and Saddles: The Story of the Fabulous Ross Stable in the Golden Days of Racing* (New York: Dutton, 1956); Hollingsworth, *The Kentucky Thoroughbred*; the Club's official membership list.

14. The personal history of Cornelius Vanderbilt is drawn largely from Burton J. Hendrick, *The Age of Big Business: A Chronicle of the Captains of Industry* (New Haven: Yale University Press, 1921); Josephson, *The Robber Barons*, 15; Wecter, *Saga of American Society*, 130–134; Wayne Andrews, *The Vanderbilt Legend: The Story of the Vanderbilt Family, 1794–1940* (New York: Harcourt Brace, 1941), 171–172; Wheaton Joshua Lane, *Commodore Vanderbilt: An Epic of the Steam Age* (New York: Knopf, 1942), 164; Moses Yale Beach, *The Wealthy Citizens of New York* (1845/1855; rpt. ed. New York: Arno, 1973), 30; Heimer, *Fabulous Bawd*, 78; Holbrook, *Age of the Moguls*, 11, 16, 325; Lucius Morris Beebe, *The Big Spenders* (Garden City, N.Y.: Doubleday, 1966), 10, 170; Waller, *Saratoga*, 140; Allen Churchill, *The Splendor Seekers: An Informal Glimpse of America's Multimillionaire Spenders—Members of the $50,000,000 Club* (New York: Grosset and Dunlap, 1974), 1–17; Clifford Browder, *The Money Game in Old New York* (Lexington: University Press of Kentucky, 1986), 36; John Steele Gordon, *The Scarlet Woman of Wall Street* (New York: Weidenfeld and Nicholson, 1988), 64. Details on his business practices are drawn largely from Myers, *History of the Great American Fortunes*, 273–327; Josephson, *The Robber Barons*, 14, 67; Holbrook, *Age of the Moguls*, 11–28; Browder, *The Money Game*, 34–38, 84–85, 97–205.

15. As cited in Yale Magrass, *Thus Spoke the Moguls: The New Deal and Other Transformations of Upper Class Ideology* (Cambridge, Mass.: Schenkman, 1981), 26.

16. Lane, *Commodore Vanderbilt*, 162–163.

17. Material on William Henry Vanderbilt is drawn from John Moody, *The Masters of Capital: A Chronicle of Wall Street* (New Haven: Yale University Press, 1919), 21–23; Andrews, *The Vanderbilt Legend*, 236; Holbrook, *Age of the Moguls*, 324–325; Churchill, *The Splendor Seekers*, 36–53; Clarice Stasz, *The Vanderbilt Women: Dynasty of Wealth, Glamour, and Tragedy* (New York: St. Martin's, 1991), 91.

18. As cited in Myers, *History of the Great American Fortunes*, 344; Josephson, *The Robber Barons*, 187.

19. William Kissam Vanderbilt's history relies on Myers, *History of the Great American Fortunes*, 378; Andrews, *The Vanderbilt Legend*, 275–277, 281–284; Holbrook, *Age of the Moguls*, 326–327; Amory, *Who Killed Society?* 488, 491; Jerome Zerbe, *The Art of Social Climbing* (Garden City, N.Y.: Doubleday, 1965), 123–135; Beebe, *The Big Spenders*, xxi; Churchill, *The Splendor Seekers*, 54–75; Leonard Silk and Mark Silk, *The American Establishment* (New York: Basic Books, 1980), 238; Florence Adele Sloane, *Maverick in Mauve: The Diary of a Romantic Age* (Garden City, N.Y.: Doubleday, 1983), 58–59; Jerry E. Patterson and Diane Guernsey, "Who Created Society?" *Town and Country* (December 1992):162; Louis Auchincloss, *The Vanderbilt Era: Profiles of a Gilded Age* (New York: Scribner's, 1989), 45–52.
20. Sloane, *Maverick in Mauve*, 58–59.
21. The history of William Collins Whitney and his descendants is taken largely from Lincoln Steffens, *The Shame of the Cities*, vol. 2 (1904; rpt. ed. New York: Hill and Wang, 1957), 147–156, 195–214; Myers, *History of the Great American Fortunes*, 380–383; Josephson, *The Robber Barons*, 296, 335–336, 341, 352, 383, 385–400; Lundberg, *America's 60 Families*, 56; Wecter, *Saga of American Society*, 127, 439; Amory, *Who Killed Society?* 501–503; Beebe, *The Big Spenders*, ix, xiii,171; Mark D. Hirsch, *William C. Whitney, Modern Warwick* (1948; rpt. ed. New York: Archon, 1969); Livingston, *Their Turf*, 45–58; Churchill, *The Splendor Seekers*, 134–154; W. A. Swanberg, *Whitney Father, Whitney Heir* (New York: Scribner, 1980), 198–221; E. J. Kahn, Jr., *Jock: The Life and Times of John Hay Whitney* (Garden City, N.Y.: Doubleday, 1981). Of the biographies of W. C. Whitney, that by Swanberg is less adulatory than that by Hirsch.
22. Albert H. Walker, *The Payne Bribery Case and the United States Senate* (Hartford: Clark and Smith, 1886).
23. Churchill, *The Splendor Seekers*, 139.
24. Such new stock may be totally worthless or so inflated or watered that it is without any actual value.
25. Churchill, *The Splendor Seekers*, 139.
26. The writer Henry Adams is credited with the statement.
27. Ibid.
28. Myers, *History of the Great American Fortunes*, 3.
29. According to Churchill (*The Splendor Seekers*, 142), muckraker Burton J. Hendrick, Whitney's contemporary, gave him this name.
30. Swanberg, *Whitney Father, Whitney Heir*, 218–219.
31. Edwin G. Burrows and Mike Wallace, *Gotham: A History of New York City to 1898* (New York: Oxford University Press, 1999), 953–954.
32. There has been much controversy surrounding the birth of August Belmont I. It has generally been held that he was born in Alzey, Germany, on December 8, 1816, the son of Simon and Frederika (Elsass) Belmont (*Dictionary of American Biography* and others who rely on this source, including Amory, *Who Killed Society?* 446). The Belmont family was among the town's most prominent, with considerable lands and vineyards (J. H. Richard Gottheil, *The Belmont-Belmonte Family: A Record of 400 Years* [New York: Privately printed, 1917], 163–173). According to the birth records in Alzey, Simon and Frederika Belmont had three children. The son born on December 8, 1813, was named Aaron, later changed to August (Alzey *Registry of Births*). Perhaps because this son was born three years prior to what has been regarded as the birth date of August Belmont I, it has been said that "the American financier August Belmont, although born in Alzey, is not necessarily related to . . . [this] family" (Dan Rottenberg, *Finding Our Fathers: A Guidebook to Jewish Genealogy* [New York: Random House, 1977], 171; *The Universal Jewish Encyclopedia: Reading Guide and Index* [New York: 1939–1948]). Other stories are that he was born August Schönberg, the son of Simon Schönberg, a poor merchant in Alzey, or that he was an illegitimate Rothschild (Stephen Birmingham, *"Our Crowd": The Great Jewish Families of New York* [New York: Harper and Row, 1967], 24, 32).
33. Materials on August Belmont I are drawn largely from Beach, *The Wealthy Citizens of New York*, 6, 10; *Dictionary of American Biography* (1928):169–170; Josephson, *The Robber Barons*, 55, 242, 291, 302; Wecter, *Saga of American Society*, 154; Sidney Ratner, ed., *New Light on the History of Great American Fortunes: American Millionaires of 1892 and 1902* (New York: Kelley, 1953); Amory, *Who Killed Society?* 447; William H. P. Robertson, *The History of Thoroughbred Racing in America* (New York: Bonanza, 1964), 104;

Beebe, *The Big Spenders*, 370–372; Livingston, *Their Turf*, 30–31; Jaher, *The Urban Establishment*, 260; Birmingham, *"Our Crowd,"* ch. 16; Irving Katz, *August Belmont: A Political Biography* (New York: Columbia University Press, 1968); Stephen Birmingham, *America's Secret Aristocracy* (Boston: Little, Brown, 1987), 213–217; Maureen E. Montgomery, *"Gilded Prostitution": Status, Money, and Trans-Atlantic Marriages, 1870–1914* (New York: Routledge, 1989), 36; *American National Biography* (1991).

34. As cited in Birmingham, *America's Secret Aristocracy*, 216.
35. Amory, *Who Killed Society?* 447.
36. Wecter, *Saga of American Society*, 154.
37. Katz, *August Belmont*.
38. Stasz, *The Vanderbilt Women*, 37.
39. Birmingham, *"Our Crowd,"* 129.
40. Birmingham, *America's Secret Aristocracy*, 215–216.
41. Information on August Belmont II and his brothers came from Josephson, *The Robber Barons*, 339; Wecter, *Saga of American Society*. 154; Amory, *Who Killed Society?* 448; John Tebbel, *The Inheritors: A Study of America's Great Fortunes and What Happened to Them* (New York: Putnam, 1962), 147–152; Beebe, *The Big Spenders*, 171; Livingston, *Their Turf*, 31. The dealings of August Belmont and Company, sometimes in association with J. P. Morgan and Company, are drawn from Myers, *History of the Great American Fortunes*, 535–537, 569, 579–581; Josephson, *The Robber Barons*, 414–415; Anna Rochester, *Rulers of America: A Study of Finance Capital* (New York: International, 1936); Lundberg, *America's 60 Families*, 56–57, 74; Gustavus Myers, *The Ending of Hereditary American Fortunes* (1939; rpt. ed. New York: Kelley, 1969), 136–137; Amory, *Who Killed Society?* 84; Beebe, *The Big Spenders*, 283; Sasuly, *Bookies and Bettors*, 76; *American National Biography* (1991); Clifton Hood, *722 Miles: The Building of the Subways and How They Transformed New York* (Baltimore: Johns Hopkins University Press, 1993).
42. Jaher, *The Urban Establishment*, 251; Patterson and Guernsey, "Who Created Society?" 162.
43. Vosburgh, *Racing in America*, 44.
44. Details on the establishment of a racing commission in New York are drawn from the *New York Times* coverage from February 1895 to February 1896; Hollingsworth, *The Kentucky Thoroughbred*, 17.
45. *New York Times* obituary on Philip Dwyer (June 10, 1917). Materials on gambling on the New York tracks in these early years come from Sasuly, *Bookies and Bettors*, 55–122.
46. Vosburgh, *Racing in America*, 44; quotation is from Heimer, *Fabulous Bawd*, 169–170.
47. Heimer, *Fabulous Bawd*, 200.
48. Materials on James R. Keene are drawn from Vosburgh, *Racing in America*, 44; Hollingsworth, *The Kentucky Thoroughbred*, 64; Dizikes, *Sportsmen and Gamesmen*, 155.
49. Bernard Baruch's entry in the *Dictionary of American Biography*.
50. Sasuly, *Bookies and Bettors*, 82.

2. THE MYTH OF PEDIGREE

1. Mark Twain, *The Adventures of Huckleberry Finn* (New York: Airmont, 1962), 120.
2. Birmingham, *America's Secret Aristocracy*, 308.
3. The materials on social Darwinism and eugenics are drawn from Richard Hofstadter, "The Pervasive Influence of Social Darwinism," in *The Robber Barons, Saints or Sinners*, ed. Thomas B. Brewer (New York: Holt, Rinehart and Winston, 1970); Nicolas F. Hahn, "Too Dumb to Know Better: Cacogenic Family Studies and the Criminology of Women," *Criminology* 18 (1980):3–25; Mark Haller, *Eugenics: Hereditarian Attitudes in American Thought* (New Brunswick, N.J.: Rutgers University Press, 1984); Daniel J. Kevles, *In the Name of Eugenics: Genetics and the Uses of Human Heredity* (New York: Knopf, 1985); Nicole Hahn Rafter, *Partial Justice: Women in State Prisons, 1800–1935* (Boston: Northeastern University Press, 1985), 69–74; Allen, "Science Misapplied"; Herbert, "Politics of Biology."
4. Materials on E. H. Harriman are drawn from Myers, *Ending of Hereditary American Fortunes*, 192–193; Birmingham, *America's Secret Aristocracy*, 194; those on Mary Williamson Averell Harriman are drawn from Haller, *Eugenics*, 65, 125.
5. The materials on Cold Spring Harbor Laboratory are drawn from the laboratory's flyer

by David Micklos, *The First Hundred Years: Cold Spring Harbor Laboratory* (Long Island, N.Y.: Cold Spring Harbor Laboratory, 1988).

6. Hofstadter, "The Pervasive Influence of Social Darwinism," 37, 38; Peter Collier and David Horowitz, *The Rockefellers: An American Dynasty* (New York: Holt, Rinehart and Winston, 1976), 105–107; Hahn, "Too Dumb to Know Better," 19–20; Kevles, *In the Name of Eugenics*, 54–56; Rafter, *Partial Justice*.

7. E. Digby Baltzell, *The Protestant Establishment Revisited* (New Brunswick, N.J.: Transaction, 1991), 134–142; Stephen Birmingham, *The Right People* (Boston: Little, Brown, 1968), 264–267.

8. Baltzell, *The Protestant Establishment Revisited*, 136.

9. As cited in Birmingham, *The Right People*, 266.

10. Ibid., 61.

11. Burrows and Wallace, *Gotham*, 1088.

12. See David M. Schneider and Raymond T. Smith, *Class Differences and Sex Roles in American Kinship and Family Structure* (Englewood Cliffs, N.J.: Prentice-Hall, 1973), 15.

13. John Dollard, *Caste and Class in a Southern Town* (Garden City, N.Y.: Doubleday, 1957), 79–80; the quote appears on p. 80.

14. Birmingham, *The Right People*, 12.

15. "W. B. Leeds Dies in a Paris Hotel," *New York Times*, June 24, 1908, 7.

16. Montgomery, *"Gilded Prostitution,"* 249–257.

17. The details of the social war between Alva Vanderbilt and Mrs. Astor are drawn from Amory, *Who Killed Society?* 234; Jaher, *The Urban Establishment*, 279; Sloane, *Maverick in Mauve*, 190; Stasz, *The Vanderbilt Women*, 83–86; Patterson and Guernsey, "Who Created Society?" 130–138, 159–162.

18. *New York Times* coverage includes "The Vanderbilt Wedding" (November 3, 1895, 16); "Miss Vanderbilt's Wedding" (November 6, 1895, 6); "She Is Now a Duchess" (November 7, 1895, 1). Other works drawn upon include Sloane, *Maverick in Mauve*; Patterson and Guernsey, "Who Created Society?" 130–138, 159–162; Auchincloss, *The Vanderbilt Era*, 48.

19. Birmingham, *America's Secret Aristocracy*, 160.

20. "Alfred Gwynne Vanderbilt Marries Jeanne Murray in Air Elopement," *New York Times*, December 13, 1945, 31; Livingston, *Their Turf*, 185.

21. Jim Yardley, "Heir to a Fortune, and to Tragedy," *New York Times*, May 8, 1999, B1.

22. Birmingham, *America's Secret Aristocracy*, 118.

23. "Woodward Case Marking Time," *New York Times*, November 5, 1955, 40.

24. The details of the Woodward shooting are taken from the *New York Times* coverage beginning on the front page on October 31, 1955, through to the grand jury decision on November 26, 1955.

25. Milton Bracker, "Wife Kills Woodward, Owner of Nashua; Says She Shot Thinking He Was a Prowler," *New York Times*, October 31, 1955, I1; "Couple Popular in Sporting Set," *New York Times*, October 31, 1955, 19; Charles Grutzner, "Prowler Admits Visit to Woodward Home," *New York Times*, November 2, 1955, I1.

26. "Woodward Case Is Marking Time," *New York Times*, November 5, 1955, 40; "Police Question Mrs. Woodward," *New York Times*, November 22, 1955; Milton Bracker, "Woodward Jury Finds No Crime after Widow Testifies in Shooting," *New York Times*, November 26, 1955, I3.

27. Milton Bracker, "Woodward Prowler Now Admits Being on Estate at Time of Killing," *New York Times*, November 8, 1955, I1; Homer Bugart, "Woodward Left Trusts to 2 Sons," *New York Times*, November 19, 1955, 36; "Prowler Discusses Woodward Case Aid," *New York Times*, November 9, 1995.

28. Details of the continuing tragedy are in Yardley, "Heir to a Fortune, and to Tragedy," B1; Eric Pace, "William Woodward 3d, 54, Ex-Reporter and Candidate," *New York Times*, May 5, 1999, B14.

29. Livingston, *Their Turf*, 75; "Business Mogul Whitney Dies at 93," *Las Vegas Review Journal*, December 12, 1992, 6A.

30. Longrigg, *History of Horse Racing*, 30–31, 57; Bill Barich, *Laughing in the Hills* (New York: Viking, 1980), 189.

31. Sanders Bruce, *The Thoroughbred Horse: His Origin, How to Breed and How to Select Him* (New York: Turf, Field and Farm, 1892), 307–317, on teazers, 4; Longrigg, *History of Horse Racing*, 58–62; Barich, *Laughing in the Hills*, 189–191.

32. Dizikes, *Sportsmen and Gamesmen,* 19.
33. For the taking over of the *The American Stud Book,* see the Jockey Club–authorized Vos-burg, *Racing in America* (pp. 43–47), and Jockey Club, *1993 Fact Book: A Guide to the Thoroughbred Industry in North America* (New York: Jockey Club, 1993).
34. When the Club took over *The American Stud Book,* there were only about 3,000 foals registered annually. Now, there are more than 51,000 registered a year. The total num-ber of horses registered with the Jockey Club as thoroughbreds from 1896 to 1993 is about 1.4 million (Jockey Club, *1993 Fact Book*).
35. Jockey Club, *Principal Rules and Requirements of the American Stud Book* (New York: Jockey Club, 1993), 6.
36. Marvin B. Scott, *The Racing Game* (Chicago: Aldine, 1968), 14.
37. Discussion of the identification techniques over time is drawn from the Jockey Club's annual Round Table discussions of August 14, 1960, 26; August 13, 1972, 7–10; Au-gust 15, 1976, 8–18; August 14, 1977, 8; August 13, 1978, 8; August 12, 1979, 8–12.
38. The three quotations in this sentence are taken from the First Round Table Discussion on Matters Pertaining to Racing (July 1, 1953, 6–7).
39. Eighth Annual Round Table Discussion on Matters Pertaining to Racing (August 14, 1960, 26).
40. Jockey Club, *Principal Rules and Requirements,* 6.
41. Livingston, *Their Turf,* 209; Hollingsworth, *The Kentucky Thoroughbred.*
42. The idea of the myth of pedigree has been recognized by a number of other writers on racing. See Livingston, *Their Turf,* for a chapter devoted to the issue.
43. David Schmitz, "Charming Results," *The Blood-Horse,* May 10, 1997, 2683–2685.
44. Donald N. Baker, "Sound Warnings," *The Blood-Horse* 16 (1996): 6018.
45. Jay Privman, "Green at Derby Gate: Fewer Starts for the Starters," *New York Times,* May 1, 1998, C2.
46. Baker, "Sound Warnings."
47. Edwin Anthony, "Great Sires of the Century," *The Blood-Horse,* February 7, 1998, 852–854.
48. Baker, "Sound Warnings."
49. Jay T. Keaney, "Training the Olympic Athlete," *Scientific American* (June 1996):63.
50. Kristin Ingwell, "Secretariat: All in the Genes?" *The Blood-Horse,* July 6, 1996, 3310.
51. Joseph Berger, "All-Time Also-Ran," *New York Times,* October 22, 1998, B1.
52. Kent Hollingsworth, "John Henry," *The Blood-Horse,* March 24, 1984, 2280.
53. Coverage of the 1998 Triple Crown races and Real Quiet are taken from Jay Privman, "Bob's World," *Kentucky Derby Souvenir Magazine,* a supplement to *The Blood-Horse,* May 2, 1998, 34–36; Jay Hovdey, "Fishing Trip," *The Blood-Horse,* May 9, 1998, 2716–2722; Ray Paulick, "The Rowdy Derby," *The Blood-Horse,* May 9, 1998, 2715; David Schmitz, "Real Speed," *The Blood-Horse,* May 9, 1998, 2740–2743; Jay Privman, "Derby Victory Doesn't Insure Respect," *New York Times,* May 15, 1998, C5; Jay Privman, "Blue-Collar Horse Reaches the Verge of Greatness," *New York Times,* May 17, 1998, SP4; Joseph Durso, "Real Quiet Has 2 Legs Up on Triple Crown," *New York Times,* May 17, 1998, SP1, 4; Jay Hovdey, "Loud and Clear," *The Blood-Horse,* May 23, 1998, 2974–2981; Joseph Durso, "The Breeder of Real Quiet Is Enjoying the Golden Ride," *New York Times,* June 3, 1998, C1, 4; Ray Paulick, "Quiet Credit," *The Blood-Horse,* June 6, 1998, 3198; David Schmitz, "Final Exam," *The Blood-Horse,* June 6, 1998, 3192–3193; Ray Paulick, "A Victory for the Sport," *The Blood-Horse,* June 13, 1998, 3295; John Veitch, "Uneasy Lies the Crown," *New York Times,* May 31, 1998, SP11.
54. Hovdey, "Fishing Trip," 2718.
55. Privman, "Blue-Collar Horse."
56. Veitch, "Uneasy Lies the Crown."
57. Schmitz, "Final Exam," 3192.
58. Paulick, "A Victory for the Sport."

3. OFF-TRACK EXPECTATIONS

1. Nelson W. Aldrich, Jr., *Old Money: The Mythology of America's Upper Class* (New York: Knopf, 1988), 141–190.
2. William Howells, *The Heathens: Primitive Man and His Religions* (Garden City, N.Y.: Doubleday, 1962), 178–195.

3. A. R. Radcliffe-Brown, "The Sociological Theory of Totemism," in *Structure and Function in Primitive Society* (1929; rpt. ed. New York: Free Press, 1952), 123; John Borneman, "Race, Ethnicity, Species, Breed: Totemism and Horse-Breed Classifications in America," *Comparative Studies in Society and History* 30 (1988):35.

4. Harmanus Barkulo Duryea's entry in the *Dictionary of American Biography*.

5. "Frederic Gebhard Dies in Garden City," *New York Times*, September 9, 1910, 9.

6. "Wm Payne Thompson, Sportsman, Dies at 50," *New York Times*, September 21, 1922, 17.

7. "Prescott Lawrence Dies," *New York Times*, November 14, 1921, 15.

8. Birmingham, *The Right People*, 107.

9. Sophy Burnham, *The Landed Gentry* (New York: Putnam, 1978), 57–61; Birmingham, *America's Secret Aristocracy*, 170–171.

10. J. Blan van Urk, *The Story of Rolling Rock* (New York: Scribner, 1950), author's note.

11. Robert Coles, *Privileged Ones: The Well-Off and Rich in America*, vol. 5 of *Children of Crisis* (Boston: Little, Brown, 1977), 12.

12. Peter Winants, unpublished manuscript on steeplechase racing, 1996 (used by permission).

13. Aldrich, *Old Money*, 181–182.

14. Winants manuscript.

15. Aldrich, *Old Money*, 181–182.

16. Kahn, *Jock*, 88.

17. Steve Cady, "Gerard S. Smith Is Dead at 70; Leading Polo Player 10 Years," *New York Times*, March 9, 1974.

18. "A. G. Vanderbilt Jr. Returns," *New York Times*, March 29, 1934, 7.

19. Discussion of the Spanish-American War is drawn largely from Alan Brinkley, *The Unfinished Nation: A Concise History of the American People* (New York: McGraw-Hill, 1993), 541–548; Burrows and Wallace, *Gotham*, 1207–1218.

20. Rochester, *Rulers of America*, 139; John E. Findlay, *Dictionary of American Diplomatic History*, 2d ed., rev. (Westport, Conn.: Greenwood, 1989).

21. Materials on the New York Stock Exchange of the early twentieth century and the Pujo Committee are drawn from Rochester, *Rulers of America*, 37; Lundberg, *America's 60 Families*, 104–105; archival materials from the Museum of American Financial History.

22. Michael Klepper and Robert Gunther, *The Wealthy 100* (New York: Citadel, 1996); Floyd Norris, "From Princes of Capitalism to the Bread Lines, How Fortunes Fared," *New York Times*, December 20, 1999, C27.

23. Tebbel, *The Inheritors*, 189–209; Michael Patrick Allen, *The Founding Fortunes: A New Anatomy of the Super-Rich in America* (New York: Dutton, 1987), 42–48.

24. "Mrs. Emerson, 75, of the '400' Dead," *New York Times*, January 30, 1960, 88.

25. Bernard Baruch, *Baruch: The Public Years* (New York: Holt, Rinehart and Winston, 1960), 126–129, 140–144.

26. Materials on Harding's administration and the Teapot Dome scandal are drawn from Collier and Horowitz, *The Rockefellers*, 165–166; Brinkley, *The Unfinished Nation*, 649–650; Sanford J. Mock, "Tempest beyond the Teapot," *Friends of Financial History*, 1995, 12–19.

27. Materials on Andrew W. Mellon are drawn from Myers, *History of the Great American Fortunes*, 707–709; Lundberg, *America's 60 Families*, 31, 42, 190–193, 292; Amory, *Who Killed Society?* 360–363; Tebbel, *The Inheritors*, 20; Paul Mellon, *Reflections on a Silver Spoon: A Memoir* (New York: Morrow, 1992), 431; Andrew Mellon's entry in the *Dictionary of American Biography*.

28. Myers, *Ending of Hereditary American Fortunes*, 276.

29. Materials on Jouett Shouse are taken from his entry in the *Dictionary of American Biography*.

30. Philip H. Burch, *Elites in American History*, vol. 3 (New York: Holmes and Meier, 1980), 57.

31. Materials on W. Averell Harriman are taken largely from Rochester, *Rulers of America*, 80; Bertram D. Hulen, "Harriman Named Envoy to Russia after Admiral Standley Resigns," *New York Times*, October 2, 1943, 1, 6; Alan S. Oser, "Ex-Gov. Averell Harriman, Adviser to 4 Presidents, Dies," *New York Times*, July 27, 1986, I1, 23.

32. Tom Durkin, "From So Old to So Valuable," *New York Times*, July 25, 1999, SP13.

33. Materials on Reeve Schley are drawn from David Shavit, *United States Relations with Russia and the Soviet Union* (Westport, Conn.: Greenwood, 1993); Patricia Beard, *Growing Up Republican: Christie Whitman, The Politics of Character* (New York: HarperCollins, 1996); and some who knew the family.

34. David Frier, *Conflict of Interest in the Eisenhower Administration* (Ames: Iowa State Universtity Press, 1969), 14, 210–211; Kahn, *Jock*, 316–317.

35. Information on George Macoffin Humphrey comes largely from his entry in the *Dictionary of American Biography*; Frier, *Conflict of Interest*, 14.

36. Information on Harold Elstner Talbott comes largely from his entry in the *Dictionary of American Biography*; Frier, *Conflict of Interest*, 78–90.

37. "America's Four Hundred Richest People," *Forbes*, October 15, 1995; G. William Domhoff, *The Bohemian Grove and Other Retreats* (New York: Harper and Row, 1974), 146–147.

38. Materials on the Bush family are drawn from Prescott Sheldon Bush's entry in the *National Cyclopedia of American Biography* 57:110; Lisa Napoli, "From Oil to Fish to the Internet: Zapata Tries Another Incarnation," *New York Times*, May 18, 1998, D5.

39. Materials on William Stamps Farish II are taken largely from his entry in the *Dictionary of American Biography*.

40. Materials on Anthony Nicholas Brady I are drawn largely from his entry in the *Dictionary of American Biography* and *Who's Who in America*.

41. Oser, "Ex-Gov. Averell Harriman," I1.

42. Francie Ostrower, *Why the Wealthy Give: The Culture of Elite Philanthropy* (Princeton, N.J.: Princeton University Press, 1995); Alex Kuczynski, "The Very Rich Pay to Learn How to Give Money Away," *New York Times*, May 3, 1998, I1, 48. For a look at the patterns of philanthropy in the twentieth century, see Allen, *The Founding Fortunes*; Thomas J. Billiteri, "Donors Big and Small Propelled Philanthropy in the 20th Century," *Chronicle of Philanthropy*, January 13, 2000, 29–32. The philanthropic activities discussed in this chapter do not exhaust the giving of Club members but are typical of their involvement.

43. Jaher, "Style and Status," 271–275.

44. On the bidding, see Josephson, *The Robber Barons*, 341. On the Sotheby auction, see Carol Vogel, "A Cezanne Leads in a $28 Million Auction of the Whitney Art Collection," *New York Times*, April 25, 1999, I45.

45. E. Digby Baltzell, *Puritan Boston and Quaker Philadelphia: Two Protestant Ethics and the Spirit of Class Authority and Leadership* (Boston: Beacon, 1979), 244–245.

46. Christopher Gray, "Namesake Precursors of Central Park West's Towers," *New York Times*, September 14, 1997, R7.

47. The specifics on Charles William Englehard are drawn from *Who Was Who*; Silk and Silk, *The American Establishment*, 22–27; Ann Hagedorn Auerbach, *Wild Ride: The Rise and Tragic Fall of Calumet Farms, Inc., America's Premier Racing Dynasty* (New York: Holt, 1994), 113; "America's 400 Richest People," 252.

48. Details on the role of Cornelius Vanderbilt in the founding of Vanderbilt University are from an article by Gaynell Doll ("Tales of the Commodore," *Vanderbilt Magazine* 77 [Summer 1994]: 6–11) in honor of Vanderbilt's two-hundredth birthday.

49. Beebe, *The Big Spenders*, 171.

50. On how the wealthy channel their giving, see Allen, *The Founding Fathers*, 185–214. In the text that follows, the discussion of the contemporary foundations associated with members of the Jockey Club is limited to those among the one thousand largest in the nation (Francine Jones, ed., *The Foundation 1000: In-Depth Profiles of 1000 Largest U.S. Foundations, 1998–1999* [New York: Foundation Center, 1998]).

51. For the quote, David Cay Johnston, "Foundations Can Give More, and Protect Assets, Study Says," *New York Times*, October 5, 1999, A18. On the Olin Foundation, see Allen, *The Founding Fathers*, 293–295.

52. Materials on the Field family are drawn from the entries of Marshall Field I and Marshall Field III in the *Dictionary of American Biography*; Lundberg, *America's 60 Families*, 430–431; John William Tebbel, *The Marshall Fields: A Study in Wealth* (New York: Dutton, 1947), 102–111; Amory, *Who Killed Society?* 397–403; Stephen D. Becker, *Marshall Field III* (New York: Simon and Schuster, 1964), 55–61; Beebe, *The Big Spenders*, 252; Lawrence Bergreen, *Capone: The Man and the Era* (New York: Simon and Schuster, 1994), 76.

53. Jim Romeo, "On the Road to West Egg," *Financial History*, Spring 1998, 18, 19, 35.
54. Discussion of Wiltwyck School is drawn largely from a book by one of the school's graduates (Claude Brown, *Manchild in the Promised Land* [New York: Macmillan, 1965]), as well as from William McCord and J. Sanchez, "Curing Criminal Negligence," *Psychology Today* (April 1982); Fox Butterfield, *All God's Children: The Bosket Family and the American Tradition of Violence* (New York: Knopf, 1995), 93.
55. The exploits of Tommy Hitchcock rely chiefly on Aldrich, *Old Money*, 173–183.
56. Materials on Alexander Smith Cochran are taken from his entry in the *Dictionary of American Biography*.
57. The commemorative painting of Saratoga Racecourse in 1917 was done by H. Dowling and was used subsequently to publicize the August season there.
58. Livingston, *Their Turf*, 68–69; Kahn, *Jock*, 145.
59. Joe H. Palmer, "The Riddle of Alfred Vanderbilt," *Saturday Evening Post*, February 21, 1953, 32–33, 78, 80, 83, 85; "Seeks Navy Commission," *New York Times*, April 4, 1942, 11:6; "Alfred G. Vanderbilt Is Divorced in Nevada," *New York Times*, June 14, 1942, 30:5; "Alfred G. Vanderbilt, 30, Inherits $5,000,000 More," *New York Times*, September 23, 1942, 27:7.
60. Kahn, *Jock*, 142.
61. As cited in ch. 10 of the unpublished manuscript on steeplechase racing by Peter Winants.
62. "Dr. Charles H. 'Doc' Strub," in *The Story of Santa Anita* (Santa Anita, Calif.: Santa Anita, n.d.); M. David Ermann and Richard J. Lundman, eds. *Corporate and Governmental Deviance* (New York: Oxford University Press, 1992), 12–16.

4. THE BUSINESS OF RACING

1. Information on the wrongdoings of these entrepreneurs draws on Walker, *The Payne Bribery Case*; O. H. Payne's entry in the *Dictionary of American Biography*; Lincoln Steffens, *The Autobiography of Lincoln Steffens* (New York: Harcourt, Brace, 1931), 2:447–448; Rochester, *Rulers of America*, 37, 71; Lundberg, *America's 60 Families*, 59, 204–240; Tebbel, *The Inheritors*, 20, 42-44.
2. Information on the Morris family is drawn from Nicholas Di Brino, *The History of Morris Park Racecourse and the Morris Family* (Bronx, N.Y.: Bronx County Historical Society, 1977); Alfred Hennen Morris's entry in *National Cyclopaedia of American Biography*; and John Albert Morris's entry in *Who's Who in America*.
3. The details of the challenge of the handling of the Brady estate are drawn from the *New York Times*: "Bradys under Fire on Handling Estate," March 14, 1923, 1; "Brady Let Estate Lose on B.R.T. Stock: Sold Own Holdings," March 15, 1923, 1, 2; "Says Brady Risked $2,500,000 of Trust," May 2, 1923, 1, 8; "Two Brady Heirs Seek Inquiry's End," May 3, 1923, 8; "Daughters to Fight Brady Accounting," May 5, 1923, 4; "Broker Got Seat with Bradys' Gift," January 25, 1924, 8; "Brady Heirs Make $8,429,314 Demand," June 26, 1923.
4. Materials on Cassatt are drawn from his entry in the *Dictionary of American Biography*.
5. Bessemer's full-page advertisement in *The Blood-Horse*, April 8, 1995. Information on the Phipps family firms is drawn from Burnham, *The Landed Gentry*, 88; Allen, *The Founding Fathers*, 110–111, 177–178, 371; David L. Heckerman, "Stuart Janney," *The Blood-Horse*, February 28, 1998, 1268–1270.
6. Richard Austin Smith, "The Heir Who Turned on the House of Phipps," parts 1 and 2, *Fortune*, October–November 1960.
7. Materials on John Mabee and problems with his insurance company are drawn from the coverage in *The Blood-Horse*: "Golden Eagle Insurance Seized," February 8, 1997; Ron Mitchell, "No Changes Planned in Mabee's Operation," February 15, 1997, 909; Jay Hovdey, "Mabee Turns to Horses in Insurance Battle," June 14, 1997, 3201.
8. Coverage of the Richard Whitney securities fraud case is drawn from the *New York Times* coverage beginning March 11, 1938, and continuing through November 2, 1938. Much of the coverage was front page; the article dealing with Whitney's sentencing, "Whitney Receives 5 to 10 Year Term" (April 12, 1938, 1, 21), summarizes the case.
9. "Whitney Indicted for Theft of $105,000 in Securities in Surprise Move by Dewey," *New York Times*, March 11, 1938, 1, 5.

10. Ibid. and "Whitney Arrested on Second Charge," March 12, 1938, 1, 18 (quote is on p. 18); "Whitney Pleads Guilty of Theft," March 15, 1938, 1, 12; "Whitney Hearings on Bankruptcy End," April 7, 1938, 16.

11. "Whitney's Brother Questioned by SEC," *New York Times,* March 26, 1938, 1,3.

12. "Whitney Examined Again by Doctors," *New York Times,* March 25, 1938, 43; "Whitney Receives 5 to 10 Year Term." The quote is from "Crash in 1929 Cost Whitney $2,000,000," *New York Times,* April 12, 1938, 21.

13. "Sing Sing Inmates in Awe of Whitney," *New York Times,* April 15, 1938, 10.

14. Tebbel, *The Inheritors,* 179-180.

15. "Whitney Hearing Bares More Deals," March 11, 1938, 4; "Whitney's Brother Lent Him $1,082,000," March 22, 1938, 1, 22; "Whitney's Brother Questioned by SEC," March 26, 1938, 1, 3; "Whitney to Appear before SEC Today," April 8, 1938, 3; "Whitney Tells SEC of Rise and Fall," April 9, 1938, 1, 27; Hugh O'Connor, "Whitney's Distress Known 2 Years Ago," April 13, 1938, 1, 18; "Lamont Cash Aided Whitney Last Fall," April 20, 1938, 33, 39; Hugh O'Connor, "Whitney Methods of Borrowing Told," April 22, 1938, 27, 33; "Punitive Sentence Asked for Whitney in Dewey Report," April 19, 1938, 1, 36.

16. Hugh O'Connor, "Simmons Admits Error on Whitney," *New York Times,* April 15, 1938, 10, and "Exchange Admits Firms Fix Funds," *New York Times,* May 13, 1938, 29.

17. "Punitive Sentence Asked for Whitney in Dewey Report," *New York Times,* April 10, 1938, 1; Hugh O'Connor, "Morgan Approves Loan to Whitney," *New York Times,* May 4, 1938, 1, 24.

18. "Whitney Receives Five- to Ten-Year Term; Court Berates Him," *New York Times,* April 12, 1938: 1, 21 (quote appears on p. 21).

19. "Whitney on Sing Sing Ball Team," *New York Times,* June 20, 1938, 7. On visitors see, Birmingham, *America's Secret Aristocracy,* 240.

20. Materials on John Pierpont Morgan are drawn from the *Dictionary of American Biography; Who Was Who;* Myers, *History of the Great American Fortunes,* 362-369; Lundberg, *America's 60 Families,* 34-35; Holbrook, *Age of the Moguls,* 153; and Amory, *Who Killed Society?* 82-85. For discussion of the Zodiac, see Birmingham, *America's Secret Aristocracy,* 208-209.

21. Birmingham, *The Right People,* 99.

22. The members of the Yale University fraternities Skull and Bones and Scroll and Key were obtained from Manuscripts and Archives, Yale University Library, Yale University, New Haven, Connecticut.

23. Birmingham, *The Right People,* 145.

24. Details on William Woodward I are taken from his entry in the *Dictionary of the American Biography* as well as from interviews of some who knew him well.

25. Materials on Peter Arnell Brown Widener I and his descendents are from Steffens, *The Shame of the Cities,* 156; Josephson, *The Robber Barons,* 341, 386; Wecter, *Saga of American Society,* 139; Holbrook, *Age of the Moguls,* 289; Tebbel, *The Inheritors,* 152-158; Livingston, *Their Turf,* 93-99; Baltzell, *Puritan Boston and Quaker Philadelphia,* 241-244.

26. Josephson, *The Robber Barons,* 386.

27. "Widener to Provide Cemetery for Horses," *New York Times,* June 18, 1929, 36.

28. Livingston, *Their Turf,* 40.

29. Lundberg, *America's 60 Families,* 41.

30. "Widener Will Urge Totalisator Here," *New York Times,* September 18, 1932, III1.

31. *Minutes of the New York State Racing Commission,* Book 1: 111 (September 30, 1935) (Albany, N.Y.: New York State, May 1934-June 1973).

32. Materials on Herbert Bayard Swope are drawn from the *Dictionary of American Biography;* Rochester, *Rulers of America,* 124; Sasuly, *Bookies and Bettors,* 92; and the recollections of a friend of Swope.

33. See Swope's entry in the *Dictionary of American Biography.*

34. The gambling activities of Rothstein are drawn largely from Heimer, *Fabulous Bawd,* 209; Ross, *Boots and Saddles,* 195-199; Robert Lacey, *Little Man: Meyer Lansky and the Gangster Life* (New York: Little, Brown, 1991), 48-50; Edward Hotaling, *They're Off: Horse Racing at Saratoga* (Syracuse, N.Y.: Syracuse University Press, 1995), 216-235.

35. Lacey, *Little Man,* 48.

36. *Minutes of the New York State Racing Commission,* Book 1:2. My descriptions of the meetings of the New York State Racing Commission are taken from hand-signed,

typed, official minutes. There were five large, leather-bound books of minutes of the Racing Commission that were housed with the current state regulatory organization, the New York State Racing and Wagering Board. The minutes contain summary statements rather than verbatim quotes and include budgets. Records of all meetings were kept, even those that took place over the telephone.

37. Ibid., Book 1:28 (July 26, 1934).
38. Ibid., Book 1:101 (1934).
39. Ibid., Book 1:31 (1934), 1:42 (August 23, 1934).
40. Ibid., Book 1:68 (January 12, 1935).
41. Ibid., Book 1:n.p. The page is headed "Proceedings of a Special Meeting of the New York State Racing Commission, held Tuesday, August 24, 1937, at the Saratoga Racetrack, Saratoga Springs, N.Y."
42. Ibid., Book 3:35–C, 35–D (March 4, 1944).
43. Livingston, *Their Turf*, 33; Carol Flake, "Old Club, New Rules," *Spur*, March–April 1990, 101.
44. Discussion of Arcaro's suspension and appearance before the Jockey Club is taken from my interview with him and from his obituary in *The Blood-Horse* (David Schmitz, "The Master," November 22, 1997).
45. *Merritt v. Swope*, 443 N.Y.S. 2d 902.
46. *Minutes of the New York State Racing Commission*, Book 3 (January 1943–December 1944):13.
47. Ibid., Book 3 (October 31, 1944; December 31, 1944).
48. Ibid., Book 4 (January 1947).
49. Jockey Club, *First Round Table Discussion on Matters Pertaining to Racing* (July 1, 1953):1.
50. Ibid., *Second Round Table Discussion on Matters Pertaining to Racing* (August 22, 1954): 18.
51. Materials on Henry Phipps and his descendents are drawn from Amory, *Who Killed Society?* 364–365; Lundberg, *The Rich and the Super-Rich*, 189–190; Hollingsworth, *The Kentucky Thoroughbred*, 139; Flake, "Old Club, New Rules," 103.
52. Jockey Club, *Seventeenth Annual Round Table Discussion on Matters Pertaining to Racing* (August 10, 1969):28.
53. Ibid., *Eighteenth Annual Round Table Discussion on Matters Pertaining to Racing* (August 16, 1970):13.
54. Ibid., *Twenty-fourth Annual Round Table Discussion on Matters Pertaining to Racing* (August 18, 1976):27.
55. Ibid., *Thirty-third Annual Round Table Discussion on Matters Pertaining to Racing* (August 11, 1985):37.
56. "Annual Report of the New York State Racing Commission to the Secretary of State for the Year 1954,"18–20; "Racing Group Is Named," *New York Times*, May 13, 1955, 29.
57. Much of the material on Marshall Cassidy relies on information contained in his personal notes and from an individual who knew him well.
58. The personal notes of Marshall Cassidy.
59. Ibid.
60. Jockey Club, *The Jockey Club 1999 Fact Book* (New York: Jockey Club, 1999), 26–27.
61. Ibid., 26.

5. QUALIFYING FOR THE CLUB

1. Brian Field, "Vanderbilt Will Become Youngest Member of the Jockey Club at Election Next Week," *New York Times*, March 28, 1937, V1.
2. These percentages total more than 50 percent because some of those who are married to Club members are also related by blood.
3. Rick Davis, "Run!" *Digest: Investment Ideas from the Best Minds on Wall Street*, September 27, 1999, 7.
4. Birmingham, *The Right People*, 12.
5. Discussion of William Astor Chanler and his family are drawn from Birmingham, *America's Secret Aristocracy*, 269–273.
6. Ibid., 272.
7. Paul Grondahl, *Mayor Erastus Corning: Albany Icon, Albany Enigma* (Albany: Washington Park Press, 1997), 50–54.

8. William Nack, "Blood Brothers and Bluegrass," *Sports Illustrated*, October 31, 1989, 76–80.
9. Jaher, "Style and Status," 278.
10. Information on the Fink case draws on the court records; the "Annual Report of the New York State Racing Commission to the Secretary of State for the Year 1949," including the official opinion of the Joint Board as Exhibit "B"; Livingston, *Their Turf,* 148.
11. "Annual Report of the NYSRC, Exhibit "B," 60.
12. *Fink v. Cole* 1951, 302 N.Y. 216; 97 N.E. 2d 873.
13. "Court Ends Jockey Club's Control of State Racing as Unconstitutional," *New York Times*, March 9, 1951, 1, 33 (quotation is from p. 1).
14. *Fink v. Cole*, 286 A.D. 73; 140 N.Y.S. 2d 708; *Fink v. Cole*, N.Y. 2d 48; 133 N.E. 2d 691; 150 N.Y.S. 2d 175.
15. *Fink v. Cole* 286 A.D. 87.
16. The information on Saratoga Springs casinos and the involvement of organized crime is drawn from Estes Kefauver, *Crime in America* (Garden City, N.Y.: Doubleday, 1951), 274–282; Heimer, *Fabulous Bawd*, 217–218, 225–243; Fred Cook, *The Secret Rulers: Criminal Syndicates and How They Control the U.S. Underworld* (New York: Duell, Sloan and Pierce, 1966), 160–165; Rufus King, *Gambling and Organized Crime* (Washington, D.C.: Public Affairs Press, 1969), 25–28.
17. Kefauver, *Crime in America*, 277–278; *Special Committee to Investigate Organized Crime in Interstate Commerce*, Pt. 7: *New York–New Jersey* (Washington, D.C.: U.S. Government Printing Office, 1951); Cook, *The Secret Rulers*, 161–165.
18. "9 Named to Study Sports Gambling," *New York Times*, September 2, 1951, 21.
19. "Vanderbilt Lauds Status of Racing," *New York Times*, December 6, 1951, 48.
20. "Interim Report of the New York State Joint Legislative Committee to Study All Laws, Rules and Regulations Relative to Horse Racing in New York State" (Albany: Williams Press, Inc., 1952), Legislative Document No. 49:62–63.
21. This is according to a 1937 listing (Lundberg, *America's 60 Families*, 26–27) of America's sixty most wealthy families.
22. Materials on the Guggenheims are drawn from Myers, *Ending of Hereditary American Fortunes*, 212–213; Holbrook, *Age of the Moguls*, 277–302; Tebbel, *The Inheritors*, 259–274.
23. Rochester, *Rulers of America*, 260.
24. "Amory L. Haskell, Turf Figure, Dies," *New York Times*, April 13, 1966, 43.
25. Materials on the Schiffs, beginning with Jacob H. Schiff, are drawn from Lundberg, *America's 60 Families*, 74; the *Dictionary of American Biography*; Birmingham, *The Right People*, 61; *The Blood-Horse* obituary on John M. Schiff (May 16, 1987).
26. Materials on Bernard Baruch are drawn from Lundberg, *America's 60 Families*, 26–27,190–193; his biography by Carter Field, *Bernard Baruch: Park Bench Statesman* (New York: McGraw-Hill, 1944), 30; Sasuly, *Bookies and Bettors*, 86–87.
27. Ann Hagedorn Auerbach, *Wild Ride: The Rise and Tragic Fall of Calumet Farms, Inc., America's Premier Racing Dynasty* (New York: Henry Holt, 1994), 110.
28. Discussion of these early years of Vanderbilt derive from the author's interview with him, as well as Paul Moran, "The Man Who Changed Racing," *Newsday*, October 27, 1985; Edward L. Bowen, "Alfred G. Vanderbilt," *Thoroughbred Times*, November 26, 1993, 2a, 4a, 38, 39; David Patrick Columbia, "Alfred Vanderbilt: Silver Spoons and Fast Horses," *Quest* (May 1993):36–39, 54.
29. Gene Markey's entry in *Who Was Who*.
30. "America's 400 Richest People," *Forbes*, 1999, 266.
31. John Edwards, "Racehorse Owner Bids for Casinos," *Las Vegas Review Journal*, May 17, 1997, 1D.
32. Materials on James Kerr and Avco Corporation are drawn from Claire Makin, "AVCO Rides the M-1 Tanks Back to the 500," *Fortune*, April 30, 1984, 325; Theresa M. Foley, "Smart Weapons Tested against Soviet Tanks," *Aviation Week and Space Technology*, August 22, 1988, 98–103.
33. Materials on the Olin family and Olin Corporation are drawn from Susan Q. Stranaham, "The Town That Ate Poison," *National Wildlife* (June–July 1984):16–19; Allen, *Founding Fortunes*, 366–367.
34. Auerbach, *Wild Ride*, 108.

35. For a discussion of the allegations of fraud and corruption surrounding the fall of Spendthrift, as well as Calumet, see Auerbach, *Wild Ride.*
36. Sasuly, *Bookies and Bettors*, 97; Edward L. Bowen, *The Jockey Club's Illustrated History of Throughbred Racing in America* (New York: Little, Brown and Company, 1994), 107.
37. Dave Palermo, "Gaming Companies May Be Short in Missouri Campaign," *Las Vegas Review Journal*, March 27, 1994, 15E, 16E.
38. Milton Bracker, "Move Afoot to Aid the Belair String," *New York Times*, November 11, 1955, I1.
39. David Schmitz, "The Cowboy Way," *The Blood-Horse*, September 6, 1997, 4737.
40. Ron Mitchell, "Eleven for History," *The Blood-Horse*, June 7, 1997, 3121–3124.

6. PHILANTHROPY AT THE TRACK

1. Beebe, *The Big Spenders*, 10.
2. The discussion of track workers is drawn primarily from the author's fieldwork (Carole Case, "Argot Roles in Horse Racing," *Urban Life* 13 [1984]:271–288; "Deviance as Rational Response," *Deviant Behavior* 8 [1987]:329–342; "Paddock Rites," *Sociological Inquiry* 58 [1988]:279–290), with attention to Marvin B. Scott, *The Racing Game* (Chicago: Aldine, 1968); John Rosecrance, "The Invisible Horsemen: The Social World of the Backstretch," *Qualitative Sociology* 8 (1985):248–265; Anthony J. Schefstad and Stuart Tiegel, "An Invisible Population and Its Visible Problem: Alcohol and Substance Abuse among Horsecare Workers," *Alcoholism Treatment Quarterly* 15 (1997): 1–16.
3. Norman Mauskopf, *Dark Horses* (Altadena, Calif.: Twin Palms, 1988), with photos by Mauskopf and text by Bill Barich. The pages are unnumbered.
4. Barich, *Laughing in the Hills*, 220.
5. Carole Case, *Down the Backstretch: Racing and the American Dream* (Philadelphia: Temple University Press, 1991).
6. Workers' compensation laws and the Fair Labor Standards Act are discussed in depth in Robert B. Stevens, ed., *Statutory History of the United States Income Security* (New York: McGraw-Hill, 1970), 38–43; Jack B. Hood, Benjamin A. Hardy, Jr., and Harold S. Lewis, Jr., *Workers' Compensation and Employee Protection Laws in a Nutshell*, 2d ed. (St. Paul: West, 1990), 7–27; Robert D. Lipman, Allison Plesur, and Joel Katz, "A Call for Bright-Lines to Fix the Fair Labor Standards Act," *Hofstra Labor Law Journal* 11 (1994):357–365.
7. Discussion of Vanderbilt's role in track management at Pimlico and Belmont Park is taken from Gerald Pidge, "Vanderbilt Enthusiastic over Winter Racing Here," *Time*, July 18, 1934; "Alfred Vanderbilt's Belmont Makes Racing Popular," *Life*, July 8, 1940; G.F.T. Ryall, "Profiles: All in Fun," *New Yorker*, September 28, 1940, 26–33; Palmer, "Riddle of Alfred Vanderbilt"; as well as Vanderbilt's discussion with the author.
8. Heimer, *Fabulous Bawd*, 221.
9. Grayson-Jockey Club Research Foundation, "Happy Holidays," a supplement to *The Blood-Horse*, October 19, 1996; *The Grayson-Jockey Club Research Foundation 1996 Annual Report.*
10. Grayson-Jockey Club Research Foundation, "Happy Holidays"; *The Jockey Club 1996 Annual Report and Summary of Activities.*
11. Carter Field, "Dora Dear Takes Victory Handicap," *New York Times*, November 16, 1944; "War Relief Benefit Day," *New York Times*, May 29, 1945, 19.
12. Information on the 1946 strike is taken from the *New York Times,* including: "Belmont Picketed in Labor Dispute," May 23, 1946, 25; James Roach, "Coincidence Victor over Richmond JAC," May 24, 1946, 24; "Belmont Park Fans in No Rush to Leave as Strike Draws Near," May 24, 1946, 2; "Fans at Belmont Have Tedious Wait," May 25, 1946, 6; James Roach, "Gallorette First in Numba Handicap," May 25, 1946, 21; "Track Union Selected," August 4, 1946, 32.
13. The one-day strike is covered in the *New York Times*, specifically: James Roach, "Medal, Hired Man Score at Jamaica," April 18, 1946, 32; "Exercise Riders, Grooms Strike at Jamaica Today," May 2, 1946, 25; Joseph C. Nichols, "Cole Hopes to End Strike Today," May 3, 1946, 17; William D. Richardson, "Grooms End Strike with Demands Met," May 4, 1946, 20.
14. Materials on the 1947 strike are from the *New York Times:* "Race Track Boys Pick AFL,"

September 11, 1947, 20; "Mayor Obtains Delay in Race Track Strike," October 9, 1947, 1; Lawrence Resner, "Grooms at Jamaica Strike; 20 to 70 Horses Scratched," October 16, 1947, 1; Lawrence Resner, "Mayor, Angered by Turfmen, Seen Set to End Racing Here," October 17, 1947, 1, 3; Lawrence Resner, "Strike at Jamaica Halts Races Today; State Intervenes," October 18, 1947, 1, 19; Lawrence Resner, "Strike at Jamaica Settled; Racing Reopens Tomorrow," October 19, 1947, 1, 5; "More Owners Sign Race Strike Pact," October 29, 1947, 15.

15. Resner, "Strike at Jamaica Halts Races Today," 1, 19.
16. Resner, "Mayor, Angered by Turfmen," 1, 3.
17. "Turfman Home Planned," *New York Times*, November 8, 1952, II8.
18. Fourth Annual Round Table Discussion, August 19, 1956, 12–15, 58–60.
19. Ibid., 13.
20. Sixth Annual Round Table Discussion, August 17, 1958, 12.
21. Fourteenth Annual Round Table Discussion, August 14, 1966, 21.
22. Sixth Annual Round Table Discussion, 41.
23. *Minutes of the New York State Racing Commission*, October 8, 1964.
24. Steve Cady, "No Break Seen in Boycott of Aqueduct Racing," *New York Times*, April 27, 1969, L1, 6; Steve Cady, "State Racing Head Rails at Boycott," *New York Times*, April 29, 1969, L50.
25. Cady, "No Break Seen," L1, 6.
26. Kent Holllingsworth, "Á Partnership for Life," *Thoroughbred Times*, August 14, 1992, 12, 14, 15.
27. In allowance races, horses are assigned weights according to prior performance. In handicap races, the track handicapper assigns weights to equalize every horse's chance to win. Stakes races carry the most prestige and purses that include nominating, entrance, and starting fees, plus money added by the track.
28. Materials on Buddy Jacobson's life and boycott of New York tracks are drawn primarily from the *New York Times* coverage: Cady, "No Break Seen," L1, 6; Cady, "State Racing Head Rails," L50; "Maryland Suspends Jacobson, Leader in Boycott at Aqueduct," May 17, 1969, L21; Robert Lipsyte, "Buddy Rides Again," November 13, 1969, 58; Glenn Fowler, "Buddy Jacobson, Horse Trainer and Convicted Slayer, Dies at 58," May 17, 1989, B5.
29. Lipsyte, "Buddy Rides Again," 58.
30. Fowler, "Buddy Jacobson, Horse Trainer," B5.
31. Carey Winfrey, "Light and Dark in a Picture of Jacobson," *New York Times*, April 15, 1980, II3.
32. Lipsyte, "Buddy Rides Again," 58.
33. Ibid.
34. Ibid.
35. Winfrey, "Light and Dark," II3.
36. "Maryland Suspends Jacobson, Leader in Boycott at Aqueduct," *New York Times*, May 17, 1969, L21; Joe Nichols, "New York State Racing Commission Suspends Jacobson for 45 Days," *New York Times*, February 18, 1970, 55; "Appeal Weighed in Jacobson Case," *New York Times*, February 12, 1972, L20.
37. "Appeal Weighed in Jacobson Case," L20.
38. Steve Cady, "An Exiled Horseman Is Spending Another Winter of Discontent," *New York Times*, February 12, 1972, L9.
39. "Jury Picked for Suit Against N.Y.R.A.," *New York Times*, June 8, 1974, L26.
40. Steve Cady, "Jacobson Gains a Hollow Court Victory," *New York Times*, March 9, 1973, 34.
41. "Jacobson Is Granted Right for Lawsuit," *New York Times*, November 22, 1973, 60.
42. "Vanderbilt Tells of Board Vote to Refuse Stalls to Jacobson," *New York Times*, June 12, 1974, L56; "Dreyfus Testifies in Jackson Case," *New York Times*, June 13, 1974, L59.
43. Michael Strauss, "A Jury of Six Decides Against Jacobson on Denial of Stall Space by N.Y.R.A.," *New York Times*, June 19, 1974, L56.
44. *McKinney's Unconsolidated Laws of New York. Thoroughbred Racing*, 1985, Section 221, Pension plans for backstretch employees, #1 and #2, Racing, Wagering, Breeding. Section 221, Pension plans for backstretch employees, #2.
45. Information on the murder case is drawn from the *New York Times* coverage, beginning with Buddy Jacobson's arrest on August 8, 1978 (Robert D. McFadden, "Noted

Racehorse Trainer Charged with the Murder of an East Side Man," August 8, 1978, II6) to his conviction on April 13, 1980.

46. "Tape Is Heard at Jacobson Trial," *New York Times*, February 1, 1980, II3.

47. McFadden, "Noted Racehorse Trainer Charged," II6; Paul L. Montgomery, "Prosecution Continues Its Case as Jacobson Trial Enters Fifth Week," *New York Times*, February 24, 1980, 28.

48. Selwyn Raab, "Victim's Alleged Role in Drug Case Called Boon to Jacobson's Defense," *New York Times*, October 11, 1979, II9.

49. Joseph B. Treaster, "Witness Sought in Bronx Killing Seized in South," *New York Times*, August 25, 1982, B1.

50. Montgomery, "Prosecution Continues Its Case," 28; Fred Ferretti, "Judge to Hear Motion of Misconduct in Jacobson Case," *New York Times*, October 24, 1979, II3; "Deadlock Reported at Jacobson's Trial," *New York Times*, April 11, 1980, B7; Lee A. Daniels, "Jacobson Guilty of Slaying Rival for Model's Affections," *New York Times*, April 13, 1980, L37.

51. Les Ledbetter, "Merola Says He Warned Officials 3 Weeks Ago of a Jacobson Escape," *New York Times*, June 2, 1980, I1; Wolfgang Saxon, "Jacobson Flees a Jail in Brooklyn While Awaiting Murder Sentence," *New York Times*, June 1, 1980, I1, 40; Joseph P. Fried, "Police Searching for Jacobson Issue a List of Aliases and Search for Auto," *New York Times,* July 3, 1980, B3.

52. Joseph P. Fried, "Jacobson's 'Friends and Relatives' Said to Have Helped in Recapture," *New York Times*, July 11, 1980, B4.

53. Lee A. Daniels, "Buddy Jacobson Seized in Suburb of Los Angeles," *New York Times*, July 10, 1980, I1.

54. Fowler, "Buddy Jacobson, Horse Trainer."

55. Winfrey, "Light and Dark," II3.

56. *The Grayson-Jockey Club Research Foundation 1996 Annual Report*, 16.

57. Jockey Club, *The Jockey Club 1996 Annual Report; The Grayson-Jockey Club Research Foundation 1996 Annual Report.*

CONCLUSION

1. C. Wright Mills, *The Power Elite* (New York: Oxford University Press, 1956).

2. See Case, *Down the Backstretch.*

3. Those who contend that the power and prestige of the nineteenth-century industrial elites have declined include Amory, *Who Killed Society?*; Baltzell, *Philadelphia Gentlemen* and *The Protestant Establishment Revisited* (New Brunswick, N.J.: Transaction Press, 1991); Jaher, *The Urban Establishment*, 280–281; Robert C. Christopher, *Crashing the Gates: The De-WASPing of America's Power Elite* (New York: Simon and Schuster, 1989); Richard Brookhiser, *The Way of the WASP: How It Made America, and How It Can Save It, So to Speak* (New York: Free Press, 1991).

4. Baltzell, *Philadelphia Gentlemen*; Jaher, "Style and Status," 265.

5. Lundberg, *America's 60 Families*, 26–27; "America's 400 Richest People," *Forbes*, October 11, 1999.

6. Livingston, *Their Turf*, 30.

7. Some conclude that the power and influence of these elites remain quite strong. See especially these works by G. William Domhoff: *Who Rules America?* (Englewood Cliffs, N.J.: Prentice-Hall, 1967); *The Higher Circles: The Governing Class in America* (New York: Random House, 1970); *The Bohemian Grove and Other Retreats;* "Social Clubs, Policy-Planning Groups, and Corporations," *Insurgent Sociologist* 75 (1975):173–184; *The Powers That Be: Processes of Ruling-Class Domination in America* (New York: Random House, 1978); and *Who Rules America Now? A View for the Eighties* (Englewood Cliffs, N.J.: Prentice-Hall, 1983).

8. High-church and private-school ties are considered bases of power: see, by E. Digby Baltzell, *Philadelphia Gentlemen; The Protestant Establishment: Aristocracy and Caste in America* (New York: Random House, 1964); and *The Protestant Establishment Revisited.* Positions in the corporate structure are viewed as power bases: see Robert Perrucci and Marc Pilisuk, "Leaders and Ruling Elites: The Interorganizational Bases of Community Power," *American Sociological Review* 35 (1970):1040–1057; Michael Patrick Allen, "The Structure of Interorganizational Elite Cooptation: Interlocking Corporate Director-

ships," *American Sociological Review* 39 (1974):395–406; Andrew Hacker, "What Rules America?" *New York Review of Books* 22 (1975):9–13. Family, networks, and corporations are viewed as operating bases of influence: see Domhoff, *The Bohemian* Grove, "Social Clubs," and *Who Rules America Now?* (chap. 3); Maurice Zeitlin, "Corporate Ownership and Control: The Large Corporation and the Capitalist Class," *American Journal of Sociology* 79 (1974):1073–1119.

APPENDIX

1. The sources of information for this list are numerous, but in addition to interview materials, they include *American National Biography, Dictionary of American Biography, National Cyclopaedia of American Biography, Who's Who in America, Who Was Who, International Who's Who, Canadian Who's Who, Biographical Directory of the United States Congress 1774–1989 Bicentennial Edition, Reference Book of Corporate Managements, Directory of Corporate Affiliations, Dictionary of American Diplomatic History, Who's Wealthy in America, Forbes* "America's 400 Richest People" (1995 and 1999), *The Foundation 1000: In-Depth Profiles of the 1000 Largest U.S. Foundations 1998/1999, Notable Names in American History*, and regular use of *The Blood-Horse* and the *New York Times*.

Index

Note: A "*t*" following a page number refers to data within a table. **Boldfaced** numbers refer to pages in the Appendix on which biographical information can be found.

About the Author

Carole Case holds a doctorate in sociology. She has written previously on thoroughbred racing in New York in *Down the Backstretch: Racing and the American Dream* (1991). She is also coauthor of *The Black Book and the Mob* (1995), which describes those blacklisted by Nevada's regulators from entering casinos in the state.